The Car Owner's
HANDBOOK

RAY STAPLEY is Canada's best-known auto mechanic and car columnist. For years his popular advice in the Toronto *Telegram* has answered readers' questions on cars with humor, down-to-earth horse sense, and above all, real understanding—because he's heard all the questions many times before, from his own devoted customers.

The Car Owner's
HANDBOOK

by Ray Stapley

illustrations by Blair Drawson

DOUBLEDAY CANADA LIMITED, TORONTO, ONTARIO

DOUBLEDAY & COMPANY, INC., GARDEN CITY, NEW YORK

Contents

INTRODUCTION 9

THE ENGINE 21

THE FUEL SYSTEM 39

THE ELECTRICAL SYSTEM 66

THE COOLING SYSTEM 89

THE EXHAUST SYSTEM 117

THE DRIVE TRAIN 132

THE SUSPENSION SYSTEM 159

THE TIRES 181

THE BRAKES 199

THE LUBRICATION SYSTEM 221

THE BODY 238

ACCESSORIES 256

HOW TO BUY A CAR 273

TROUBLE-SHOOTING GUIDE 288

INDEX 307

LIST OF ILLUSTRATIONS

Diagram

1. Cutaway side view of engine — 22
2. The four cycles of internal combustion — 23
3. Piston, piston rings, piston pin, and connecting-rod assembly — 25
4. Connecting-rod bearing inserts — 28
5. Front crankshaft pulley — 30
6. The engine camshaft — 31
7. The valve train — 32
8. Exploded view of hydraulic valve lifter — 33
9. The fuel system — 42
10. The gasoline tank — 43
11. Badly twisted flexible gasoline hose — 48
12. Typical single-action fuel pump — 48
13. Cutaway view of single-barrel carburetor — 51
14. Dry-cartridge-type air cleaner — 59
15. Compressing the fuel/air mixture — 63
16. Effect of correct and incorrect fuel-burning process — 64
17. Cutaway view of battery — 68
18. Typical fuse panel — 75
19. Typical V-8 engine — 83
20. Arrangement of starting system, ignition system, and charging system — 84
21. Side view of engine cooling system — 90
22. Exploded view of water pump — 98
23. Typical cooling-system thermostat — 105
24. Automatic transmission cooling unit — 110
25. V-8 engine with single-exhaust system — 117

26. V-8 engine with dual-exhaust plus resonators 118
27. Typical heat-riser valve as used on six-cylinder engine 119
28. Cutaway view of muffler 120
29. The drive train 132
30. How the clutch operates 133
31. Manual-transmission gear ratios 138
32. Exploded view of cross and roller-type universal joint 152
33. The rear-axle assembly 153
34. The suspension system 159
35. Independent suspension 163
36. The steering mechanism 171
37. Positive and negative wheel casters 172
38. Positive and negative camber 172
39. Wheel toe-in 173
40. Tire-carcass construction 182
41. The meaning of tire sizes 186
42. Conventional and low-profile tires 187
43. The hydraulic-brake system 200
44. Dual, or divided, master cylinder 206
45. Exploded view of wheel cylinder 207
46. Effect of undersized brake linings mated to oversized brake drums 211
47. Self-adjusting brake mechanism 212
48. Power-brake assembly 214
49. Disk-brake assembly 215
50. Engine lubrication system 222
51. Open crankcase ventilation 226
52. Positive crankcase ventilation 227

Introduction

When I discuss mechanical car problems with motorists, frequently they throw up their hands and say they just cannot understand the mechanical functions of their automobiles.

A few years ago I delivered a customer's car. Coffee was ready, and the lady invited me to join her and at the same time discuss the major surgery I had just performed on her vehicle. After pouring me a coffee, she turned dials, pulled levers, pushed buttons on her stove, and placed a roast in the oven. She then turned more dials and made more adjustments to put her washing machine through its paces.

As she picked up her needle and a complicated piece of smocking she had been working on, she told me how much she admired those who were "mechanically inclined." She and her husband knew nothing about cars, she said. While I marveled at her control of the arts and science of the household—all of them a puzzle to me—she told me how she could not fathom the simple principles of a car.

Do you understand why a paddle propels a canoe? Do you know why the pedals on a tricycle move it along the sidewalk? If these are not beyond your comprehension, then neither is the working of a car. The science and principles of the automobile are almost as old as civilization.

The first cars produced were basic and simple. While today's modern chariots are far more sophisticated, the basic principles remain much the same as those of the first cars that appeared on the road.

This book has been written in nontechnical terms to provide the average driver with a better understanding of his car. After reading through these pages you will have a better knowledge of what makes a car tick, and you will be in a better position to communicate with your mechanic, which in itself can save you a lot of money.

Also, you will appreciate that operating a car on a rigid preventive-maintenance plan is safer, more convenient, and more economical than avoiding necessary repairs until sudden failure occurs.

While the car's operation depends on the coordination of many individual systems, all of which are explained in detail in the following chapters, here is a brief summary of what happens as we place the key in the ignition and go through the starting procedure.

As the driver engages the starter, a small gear in the electrically operated starter motor meshes with a much larger gear attached to the flywheel, which in turn is bolted to the engine's crankshaft. The twisting force of the starter sets all the moving parts of the engine into motion, which has the effect of drawing a mixture of gasoline and air through the carburetor and on into the engine's combustion chambers.

Depending on whether the engine has four, six, or eight cylinders, this mixture is ignited at precisely the right moment by the four, six, or eight sparkplugs. It is the burning of this highly combustible fuel/air mixture that generates the engine's power and keeps it operating after the starter has been disengaged.

A series of spring-loaded linkages connects the accelerator pedal to a control mechanism on the carburetor. The farther the gas pedal is depressed, the greater the volume of fuel/air mixture that goes to the combustion chambers. When the gas pedal is released, the engine automatically returns to a normal idle.

There are a number of systems that contribute to the operation of the engine:

The fuel system—gasoline tank, gas lines, fuel pump, and carburetor—ensures a supply of fuel adequate enough to satisfy the demands of the engine under all driving conditions.

The ignition system—points, condenser, coil, high-tension wires, distributor cap, rotor, sparkplugs, etc.—provides the necessary high voltage to fire the fuel/air mixture in the combustion chambers.

The exhaust system—exhaust manifold, exhaust pipe, muffler, and tailpipe—silences the spent gases as they leave the combustion chambers and expel the gases to the atmosphere through the rear tailpipe.

The cooling system—radiator, water pump, radiator hoses, thermostat, fan and water jackets inside the engine through which the coolant (antifreeze mixture or water) flows—controls the engine's temperature.

The lubricating system consists mainly of several quarts of oil stored in the engine's oil pan, and an oil pump which circulates the lubricant under pressure through various oil passages.

The electrical system—the battery provides the electrical energy to operate the starter motor, ignition system, lights, signals, horns, radio, heater, air conditioner, and the various other electrical accessories. The alternator or generator replenishes the electrical energy drawn from the battery when the car is being driven. Depending on the volume of current being drawn from the battery, a voltage regulator ensures that the alternator or generator delivers just the right amount of current to the battery to keep it fully charged.

With the engine running, the next step is to transmit its power to the driving wheels. This is accomplished by several components in the drive train. Coupled to the engine's revolving crankshaft is either a torque converter that operates an automatic transmission or, with manual shift, a clutch to which a standard transmission is attached. A long driveshaft and one or more universal joints relay the transmission's driving force to a set of gears in the rear-axle assembly.

At this point the rear-axle gears turn the twisting force of the driveshaft at a 90-degree angle to supply an equal amount of power to the left- and right-side axle shafts that turn the driving wheels. Thus the turning motion of the engine's crankshaft is converted into the turning motion of the driven wheels.

With the car in operation, the next important step is to be able to steer and stop the vehicle. The brake pedal is attached to a master cylinder that is filled with hydraulic brake fluid. Applying the brakes moves a plunger device in the master cylinder, which forces the brake fluid through a network of steel and rubber brake lines. Built into the brake mechanism of each road wheel is a smaller hydraulic cylinder, the wheel cylinder, to which a brake line is fastened.

The hydraulic pressure generated by applying the brakes causes a mechanism inside the wheel cylinders to push hard against the brake shoes, which in turn press against the brake drums to slow or stop the car.

The steering wheel is fitted to a shaft that operates gears in a steering box. Protruding from the steering box is an arm that is coupled to a series of linkage which is attached to the front wheels. The front wheels are hinged onto their supports in such a manner that they can turn left and right to steer the car. It is important that the steering mechanism be lubricated at recommended intervals.

Strong springs are placed between the road wheels and the body to cushion and minimize road shock in the passenger area. Four hydraulic shock absorbers are used to control the rebound action of these springs. As well as providing traction to propel and stop the car, the tires also play a vital role in absorbing road shock.

Regardless of whether we drive a current luxury liner or a modest vehicle with five or more years on the road, we can all run into major or minor problems.

In the interest of safety as well as convenience, every driver should have a general idea of what makes a car tick. For example, many nuts that attach the road wheels to the car are of lefthand thread. This simply means that when loosening these nuts to remove a flat tire, the rim wrench must be twisted clockwise.

Most people do not study the owner's manual that comes with all new cars. They should, however, because it is loaded with valuable information about their own particular make of vehicle.

To understand and follow the instructions in the owner's manual can save hundreds of dollars in repairs. Half the repairs done today could be avoided if the cars had been taken in for inspection at the recommended intervals. Motorists frequently forget to read or do not understand the conditions of their new-car warranty. Failure to have the car serviced at intervals spelled out by the manufacturer can result in cancellation of the warranty.

Before taking delivery of a new vehicle, make certain that you fully understand the terms of your warranty. If in doubt, seek advice from your salesman. Failure to do so could cost you hundreds of dollars.

When trouble strikes, the more familiar we are with our cars the more likely we will be to make the right decision as to the next step. Some simple problems will be easy to diagnose; others will require the knowledge of a skilled technician. But finding the right mechanic may be a bit of a problem. The man who works on your car must be well-trained, reliable, and honest, and you may have to look long and hard to find him.

Make as much effort to find a reliable mechanic as you would to find a doctor or dentist. In a lifetime we are likely to spend a lot more money for a car doctor than for either a dentist or physician. Remember that your life is as much in the hands of the mechanic as it is in the hands of the surgeon.

When you do find the right man, get to know him and, above

all, stick with him. A steady, friendly customer gains far more personal attention than one who drifts from one shop to another.

Throughout this book frequent mention is made of Emil. Emil was one of a rare breed of craftsmen who love cars. There was nothing he liked better than to tangle head-on with a hard-to-diagnose car problem. He was my righthand man for many years. I still frequently consult him, and he sometimes assists me in my accident-investigation business.

One morning a lady drove into my garage and asked me to check a bad vibration in her car which tended to increase with road speed. She had been told that the automatic transmission needed an overhaul at a cost of about $200, but she found this hard to believe, as the car had been driven only 21,000 miles.

I examined the car and found that two universal joints had burned out. The automatic transmission was perfect. The repairs she actually needed cost $35.

While I don't believe many problems in the garage business stem from outright dishonesty, it must be remembered that wherever a service is rendered, there will be some people who will abuse the trust of their customers and engage in fraud or cover up their mistaken diagnoses at the customers' expense.

I doubt if in this particular instance there was any intention of dishonesty on the part of the mechanic who condemned the transmission. But suppose it had been dismantled and there was found to be nothing wrong with it? This could be a test of the mechanic's integrity—and of his ability to resist the temptation to cover up his improper diagnosis by charging for a transmission overhaul that was not necessary.

The problem of finding a good mechanic is also faced by garage operators. In desperate need for good men, I've offered parts salesmen and delivery men a $200 cash reward if they could find me a good mechanic. My intention was to entice a man away from another garage with the offer of a bigger salary. This sometimes worked, but the price was high, and good men don't stay with you always. It took years off my life every time one of my mechanics told me he was emigrating to the sunny south or opening his own garage. One of the problems of having a good man is that he is likely to branch out for himself. Then he, too, has the problem of finding the right men to keep his business flourishing.

Practically all garage operators have to take a chance occasionally and hire a man on a trial-and-error basis. As a rule of thumb, though, the better the garage, the fewer the new faces and mechanics on trial. Familiar faces, coupled with cleanliness, organization, courtesy, and good equipment, are dependable yardsticks of a garage's reliability.

A good example of the risk posed by mechanics on trial was given by a man I hired some years ago. He had a good tool kit, had operated his own garage until it was expropriated for a highway development, and seemed quite promising when I interviewed him.

On the second day in the shop I put him to work on an electrical-wiring job. He worked for a couple of hours and then called me to have a look. I found, almost unbelievably, that he had the rear license-plate light flashing together with the left parking light for a righthand turn signal.

It turned out that the mechanic was an alcoholic who was also addicted to tranquilizers, and he seemed to be in a permanent trance. I paid him off and suggested he seek professional help.

The problem of finding a good mechanic is sometimes compounded by low wages and poor working conditions. Many mechanics leave the business because they don't like the money and feel they are not respected as skilled technicians. They resent being paid less than tradesmen in other fields. Some people may contradict me when I say mechanics are underpaid, and point out that they know men who come home with as much as $12,000 per year or more. But to get into this bracket a man must be far above average, or lucky enough to run a front-end alignment machine or the tune-up department. The mechanic of average ability has a rough row to hoe.

Often mechanics can make more money attaching the left front wheel onto new cars at the factory than they can in the trade to which they have dedicated many years. This is not the problem of mechanics only. It's your problem, too, and it's the main reason why there is such a chronic shortage of mechanics in the United States and Canada.

According to my accident-investigation files, an alarming number of brake failures occur not in new brake systems or even in neglected ones, but in brakes that have been worked on just prior to the failure. This provides a frightening insight into the need for conscientious mechanics who know how to do the job properly.

Car manufacturers are concerned about the shortage of mechanics and are trying to upgrade the trade with special training programs. We can only hope they are successful.

Millions of dollars are being spent on scientifically planned diagnostic centers that use the latest in computerized and automated equipment. Thank goodness electronics engineers have turned their talents to designing equipment that minimizes human error in diagnosing—the major stumbling block and source of misunderstanding between the motorist and the repair shop.

However great this improvement may be, the repairs will still have to be made by skilled personnel. Repairs themselves cannot be automated.

When repairs are needed, don't be misled by rock-bottom estimates. Seldom is it possible to accurately predict how many parts will be needed to correct a problem in the automatic transmission or the engine until the unit is torn down. A motorist's insistence on a "firm quote" is a source of constant grief. When an honest garageman quotes "anywhere from $100 to $150" for certain repairs, the motorist sometimes rushes off to find a fixed low quote of $100 which can lead him into the hands of fast-buck "gimmick" operators.

In order to get the job, some garages make a practice of promising to do a transmission reseal or a brake job for a ridiculously low figure. Invariably, you will get a call telling you that, regrettably, there is unforeseen damage to a number of parts, and the price is going to be twice that of the original estimate.

An angry reader told me of an experience he had with an old car worth about $150 which he kept as a "second" car. The automatic transmission had failed; he took the car to a "transmission specialist" who offered full repairs for $50, and he was assured that it could be done for that price. A few hours later he got a phone call and was told that a number of other parts in the transmission were "shot," and the job was going to cost $160.

When a motor or transmission fails or makes expensive noises, it is hard for any mechanic to tell you exactly what is wrong until he has taken it apart. Certainly, he can diagnose the fault, but there may be many reasons for the failure, and sometimes several components need replacement at the same time.

The only way a garage can give an exact estimate is to quote on an exchange unit. But this is another area where we have to exercise great caution because of the questionable parts and workmanship in some of the "bargain" exchange assemblies. It must also be remembered that the price for an exchange unit does not always include related parts. For example, some exchange services quote on replacement automatic transmissions but do not include such parts as the torque converter. These parts cost more—sometimes *much* more. Similarly, a "rebuilt" motor may include only such parts as the block, crankshaft, and pistons, but may not include the cylinder heads, oil pan, manifolds, carburetor, starting motor, or other parts. These may also need overhaul or replacement, and the quoted exchange price is meaningless. When quoted on such a replacement, be sure the estimate spells out the least you could pay and the most, according to how many parts are found to need replacement.

When repairs to any part of the car are necessary, ask for a complete general checkup and get an approximate price for repairs to the entire car. If too many things are wrong and the cost of properly restoring the car is too high, scrap it. Some cars are not worth repairing.

A contractor once came into my garage with a seven-year-old station wagon. It was in rough shape and couldn't have been worth more than $300. He wanted the engine rebuilt, and despite my best efforts to talk him out of it, he insisted he wanted to keep it going. When he asked how much the job would cost, I refused to give a firm estimate, saying it might cost $500 or more. When stripped, the engine proved that my worst fears were well-founded. The valves, crankshaft, connecting rods, and pistons were beyond repair, and even the heads were beyond rescue by machining. I gave him half the parts at cost, but even then the bill totaled $640.

He wrote out his check without question and seemed very happy with the way the car ran. But since the rest of the vehicle was in rough condition, I'm sure he'd have been further ahead if he'd made a trade.

Any car must wear out eventually, and there comes a time when the over-all condition of the vehicle makes it impractical to spend volumes of money on it.

The timing of repairs is very important. I do not recommend having major surgery performed on a car shortly before heading off on a long trip. Something can always go wrong after major repairs, and if the work you have just spent a lot of money for fails when you are 500 miles from home, it will be just about impossible to get any remedial action or reparation from the garage that did the work. You will probably have to have the work done all over again and pay the bill a second time. Plan to have the work done two to three weeks before you go away.

When major breakdowns occur far from home, it will often pay to have the car shipped back rather than have it repaired on the spot. Three years ago a neighbor was 500 miles from home when his V-8 engine broke down. He and his family stayed in a hotel for a full week while the engine was overhauled and he paid $600 for a supposedly "guaranteed" job. He limped into my shop after barely making it back. The engine was hopelessly shot, and he traded the car.

It's not wise to authorize major overhauls when stranded hundreds of miles from home. Even when the work is done in a reliable shop, things can go wrong, and how on earth can you return for warranty adjustments? It's hardly fair to expect your local garageman to accept the word of another garage hundreds of miles away, particularly if everything seemed all right when the car left his shop.

Many haulage firms deliver new cars to various parts of the continent and are happy to pick up stranded cars on the return trip. One concern quoted me $85 for a distance of 500 miles. If the car is wrecked or a wheel is off, there might be an additional charge for lifting the vehicle on and off the tractor-trailer. Most motorists don't realize that this service exists. The cost of a tow truck for a comparable distance would be prohibitive.

By making use of this service, the car can be returned to your home town, where you have a choice of garages and can take advantage of the usual warranties extended on repair work.

However, we seldom are faced with out-of-town breakdowns if a vehicle is checked at six-month intervals and maintained properly. I have preached the virtues of care and maintenance all through this book, and I know my emphasis on preventive maintenance may sound expensive, but repairs resulting from lack of maintenance run even higher.

A neighbor of mine dropped over to my house one day to say, "Ray, I read your column, but if I followed your advice I would spend far too much money." A couple of weeks later the same neighbor dropped into my garage to complain about a scraping noise when he applied the brakes. It had been there for a while, he said, but hadn't sounded too bad. Now there was a heavy vibration too.

We pulled off the wheels and found that the brake linings were worn down to the rivets, and the brake drums were scored beyond repair. The drums alone added $100 to a job that could have cost about $50 if he had checked his car before it had started making horrible noises. I diplomatically explained this to him when I gave him the bill. He is now a firm believer in preventive maintenance and early diagnosis of a problem. His final comment when leaving the shop was, "It's a pity we sometimes have to learn the hard way."

I recommend taking a tip from pilots who "fly by the seat of their pants" and rely on their senses as well as the gauges and instruments. It is surprising what your ears, eyes, nose, and touch can tell you about the condition of your car. Pull off the road the moment you hear a strange noise or a change in the customary rhythmic sound peculiar to your car. If in doubt about the trouble, don't drive. Have the car towed to the nearest repair shop.

The ever-increasing cost of car repairs has made it necessary for a number of motorists to buy a modest tool kit and do some of their own maintenance work. Provided they learn how to do it properly and do not go beyond the limits of safety, I can see nothing wrong with doing it yourself. It is pathetic how little the average motorist knows about the mechanism of his vehicle. Just a trivial failure can leave him stranded. In addition to saving money, most men who probe into the innards of their vehicles find it an enjoyable hobby.

Many Europeans make a point of acquiring a good working knowledge of their vehicles. Apart from economics, it's a matter of personal pride not to have to rely on a garage for every minor detail.

The first and most important step is to buy a master manual for your particular make of car. These manuals are available through the parts department of your franchised dealer. Everything from minor adjustments to major overhauls is clearly defined, and diagrams give the names of all components and the order in which they are assembled.

Before starting, remove wrist watch and rings. Metal objects can become jammed between a live wire and a ground and are soon red hot, resulting in serious burns to the fingers or wrist.

Remove such items as tools, cigarettes, or pencils from shirt or outside coat pockets. They may fall out when you are leaning over the engine. When I was in my teens I learned this lesson the hard way. A small screwdriver dropped out of my upper pocket, hit the revolving fan blades, bounced back, smashed my glasses, and cut a deep gash in my eyebrow.

Never work with loose clothing that may get caught in the fan belt or pulleys. It's dangerous to walk away and leave the hood open with the engine running. Children may climb up on the front of the car, and little hands can be severed in split seconds. Gasoline should never be used to wash parts. Cleaning solvent is recommended for this purpose.

An extension light should not be placed on top of or around the area of the radiator. If the engine is running, the vibration can cause it to drop into the fan and be ejected in a shower of metal pieces flying in all directions.

Before raising the car with a bumper jack, block the front and rear of one of the wheels. Never leave the car suspended on a jack. Before crawling underneath the car, be sure it is supported by solid wooden blocks or recommended stands. Bricks or cement blocks can crumble and collapse.

Before working on the electrical system, especially under the dash, disconnect one of the battery cables to avoid the possibility of a short circuit. And, remember, no good mechanic performs a tune-up without first washing all the oil and grime from the engine and ignition components. Dirt on the ignition is a prime cause of starting failure in damp weather.

A word of warning: Without the guidance of a confident mechanic, it is dangerous for the uninitiated to become involved in brake and steering work. Just a slight oversight in these areas can prove disastrous.

When you do take your car into a garage for repairs, it helps if you can describe the problem to the mechanic. I noticed around my shop that customers used such words as *grind, grumble, moan, shatter, shriek, squeal, bang, clunk, thud, bash, smash, knock,* and *shake* to describe a multitude of noises and vibrations. Sometimes they held their noses, assumed pantomime positions, and uttered weird, guttural noises in tones ranging from baritone to soprano to duplicate a noise they heard in the car and thereby helped me to diagnose the problem.

While I sometimes found it difficult to stifle a chuckle, I don't knock those sound effects. They often helped me to pinpoint the exact source of the noise and locate the problem.

With this in mind, I have prepared a trouble-shooting guide at the end of the book. Because drivers recognize noises in their cars as howls or groans, I have used these and other similar expressions as reference terms for a problem. If, for example, you hear a squeal when the brakes are applied, look in the index under "Brakes Squeal."

The Engine

The engine of the car is basically a converter of energy. It converts the energy of heat into the energy of motion. The conversion begins when you engage the starter. This action turns the crankshaft, to which each piston is attached by a connecting rod. (*See Diagram* 1.) Each piston, in turn, is pulled to the bottom of the cylinder. As the piston is drawn down, a vacuum is created and the intake valve opens, allowing a mixture of air and gasoline into the cylinder. As the piston returns to the top of the cylinder, the gas and air mixture becomes compressed in the small area at the top of the cylinder, known as the combustion chamber. A sparkplug fires this compressed mixture and drives the piston down in the cylinder.

The connecting rods in the engine are attached to the crankshaft, which is much like multiples of the bicycle pedal. Each of the four, six, or eight connecting rods—depending on the number of cylinders in the car—is attached to the crankshaft.

As the connecting rods turn the crankshaft, the heavy flywheel attached to the rear of the crankshaft also rotates, and its momentum aids in keeping all the moving parts turning smoothly. The piston is again forced up the cylinder, but this time the exhaust valve opens and the piston expels the spent gases from the engine.

These are the "four cycles" that we sometimes hear mentioned: the intake stroke; the compression stroke; the power, or firing, stroke; and the exhaust stroke. (*See Diagram* 2.) Regardless of whether the engine has four, six, or eight cylinders, this operating principle remains constant. The engine diagrams will give a clearer understanding of how the motor functions, and as we go through this chapter the purpose and operation of each component will be explained.

The Block

The block is the foundation, or the body, of the engine. Every other component of the motor is mounted rigidly to this large casting,

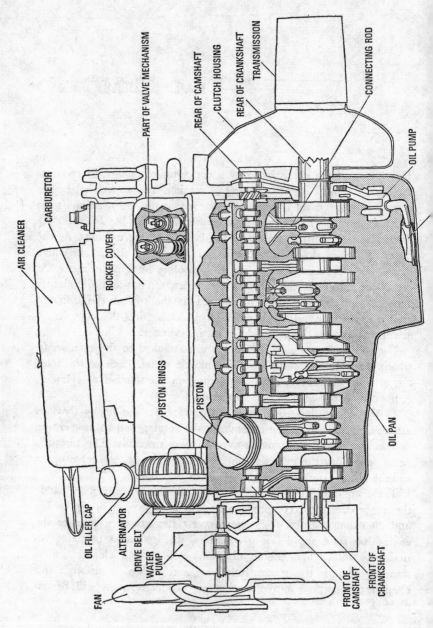

AIR CLEANER

CARBURETOR

ROCKER COVER

PART OF VALVE MECHANISM

REAR OF CAMSHAFT

CLUTCH HOUSING

REAR OF CRANKSHAFT

TRANSMISSION

CONNECTING ROD

OIL PUMP

OIL FILLER CAP

PISTON RINGS

PISTON

OIL PAN

ALTERNATOR

DRIVE BELT

WATER PUMP

FAN

FRONT OF CAMSHAFT

FRONT OF CRANKSHAFT

Diagram 1. *Cutaway side view of engine*

The Engine

The engine of the car is basically a converter of energy. It converts the energy of heat into the energy of motion. The conversion begins when you engage the starter. This action turns the crankshaft, to which each piston is attached by a connecting rod. (*See Diagram* 1.) Each piston, in turn, is pulled to the bottom of the cylinder. As the piston is drawn down, a vacuum is created and the intake valve opens, allowing a mixture of air and gasoline into the cylinder. As the piston returns to the top of the cylinder, the gas and air mixture becomes compressed in the small area at the top of the cylinder, known as the combustion chamber. A sparkplug fires this compressed mixture and drives the piston down in the cylinder.

The connecting rods in the engine are attached to the crankshaft, which is much like multiples of the bicycle pedal. Each of the four, six, or eight connecting rods—depending on the number of cylinders in the car—is attached to the crankshaft.

As the connecting rods turn the crankshaft, the heavy flywheel attached to the rear of the crankshaft also rotates, and its momentum aids in keeping all the moving parts turning smoothly. The piston is again forced up the cylinder, but this time the exhaust valve opens and the piston expels the spent gases from the engine.

These are the "four cycles" that we sometimes hear mentioned: the intake stroke; the compression stroke; the power, or firing, stroke; and the exhaust stroke. (*See Diagram* 2.) Regardless of whether the engine has four, six, or eight cylinders, this operating principle remains constant. The engine diagrams will give a clearer understanding of how the motor functions, and as we go through this chapter the purpose and operation of each component will be explained.

The Block

The block is the foundation, or the body, of the engine. Every other component of the motor is mounted rigidly to this large casting,

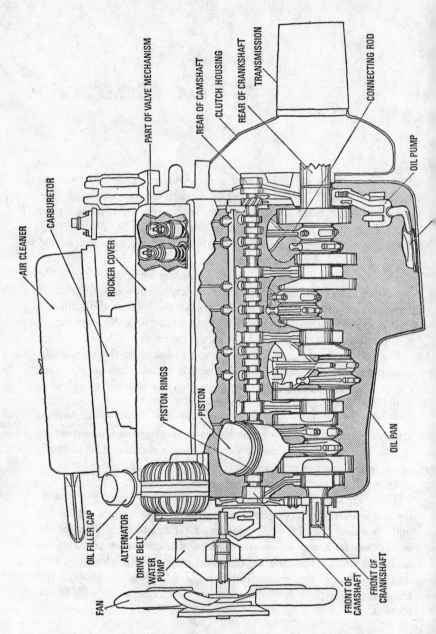

Diagram 1. *Cutaway side view of engine*

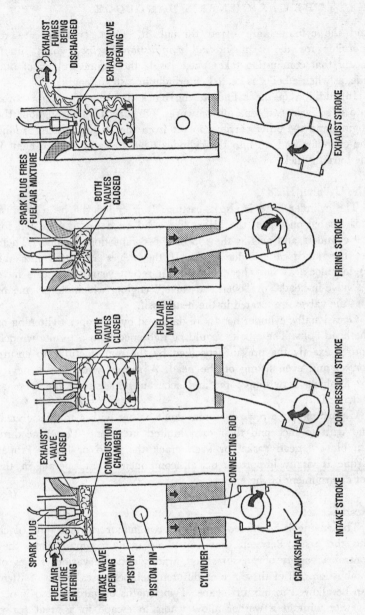

Diagram 2. *The four cycles of internal combustion*

INTAKE STROKE

SPARK PLUG
FUEL/AIR MIXTURE ENTERING
INTAKE VALVE OPENING
EXHAUST VALVE CLOSED
COMBUSTION CHAMBER
PISTON
PISTON PIN
CONNECTING ROD
CYLINDER
CRANKSHAFT

COMPRESSION STROKE

BOTH VALVES CLOSED
FUEL/AIR MIXTURE

FIRING STROKE

SPARK PLUG FIRES FUEL/AIR MIXTURE
BOTH VALVES CLOSED

EXHAUST STROKE

EXHAUST FUMES BEING DISCHARGED
EXHAUST VALVE OPENING

and the cylinders are bored through it. These cylinders are responsible for the term *internal combustion engine,* which simply means that combustion takes place inside the engine instead of outside, as when a boiler is heated externally in a steam engine.

In addition to the cylinders, the block has other passages bored into it to form two separate networks. One feeds oil throughout the engine, and the other carries coolant from the cooling system around the cylinders and up into the cylinder head to carry off the heat of the burning fuel.

The Cylinder Head

The cylinder head is also a casting. It is called the head because it is located on top of the block, like a lid on a tin. It is a seal for the cylinders and acts as the top of the combustion chamber. There are two kinds of cylinder heads. If the valves are fitted into the engine block, a "flat" head is used. In recent years, most cars have a "valve-in-head," or "overhead-valve," engine, which simply means that the valves are located in the head itself.

Occasionally, cylinder heads are damaged by improper tightening of the head bolts. These bolts should be tightened with a torque wrench and to exactly the pressure specified by the manufacturer to ensure correct and even fitting of the head. A torque wrench is a device for applying a twisting force and accurately measuring the force as it does so.

Unfortunately, a few mechanics don't bother with a torque wrench and trust to luck and their own limited judgment. This procedure can blow a head gasket or even crack the head or block. Proper torque is vitally important on all components that operate in the hot environment of the engine.

Head Gasket

The engine is composed mainly of two major castings—the block and the head. Between them, in their many compartments, they control a variety of pressures: oil, water, and the various stages of combustion. All of these are at different temperatures. None of them can be allowed to mix or escape. Two lengths of garden hose joined together without a washer allow water to escape in a great spray. The same would happen if the block and the head were to be joined without the equivalent of a washer between them. In this case, the washer is called a head gasket.

Years ago, head gaskets were formed of asbestos sandwiched between two pieces of metal, or a composition material pressed onto a sheet of steel.

Most engines now use a single thin sheet of crimped steel which is very intolerant of sloppy installation. When this gasket is being replaced, it is essential that the mating surfaces of the head and block be scrupulously cleaned and checked with a straightedge for warpage. If coolant was mysteriously disappearing prior to removal of the head, it is wise to send the head to a machine shop where it can be tested for cracks. If the head is cracked, it must be repaired or replaced. Warpage can usually be corrected by machining to restore the proper surface. If this is not done, the thin steel gasket may fail. (The block, cylinder head, and head gasket are also discussed in the *Cooling System* chapter.)

Pistons and Piston Rings

The pistons and piston rings absorb tremendous pressures and tolerate fantastic heat. (*See Diagram 3.*) When the engine is turning

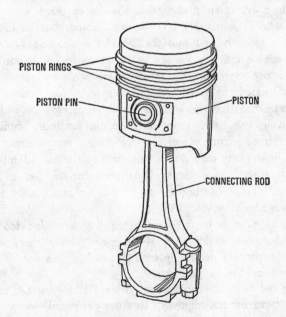

PISTON RINGS

PISTON PIN

PISTON

CONNECTING ROD

Diagram 3. *Piston, piston rings, piston pin, and connecting-rod assembly*

over at 3000 rpm, the fuel ignites in each cylinder 1500 times every minute, and the temperature at the core of the burning mixture can reach over 4000 degrees F. However, the cooling system dissipates much of this heat. It has to; the tops of the pistons would melt if they reached anywhere near this temperature.

Several piston rings, snugly fitted into grooves in the side of the pistons, press out against the cylinder walls to ensure good compression seal and oil control. While these rings are exposed to all the tortures and heat that occur in the combustion chamber, they seldom give trouble in a well-maintained engine. When they finally do wear out, usually the whole engine is due for major surgery. However, when piston rings and/or pistons fail due to poor lubrication, overheating, abuse, or high mileage, oil consumption can increase considerably; the compression will drop, reducing horsepower output; and the engine oil may become contaminated with combustion gases. Worn pistons and/or rings usually show up as puffs of smoke from the oil filler tube and blue smoke from the tailpipe, especially when decelerating from high speed.

Piston rings are often plated with chrome or other materials to minimize wear. It sometimes takes several thousand miles of operation before they fully seat into the cylinder walls, and during this period the engine may burn a few extra quarts of oil. Regardless of precision factory tolerances, there will be miniscule variations on the mating surfaces of the rings and cylinder walls (and other engine components) which have to seat in. To drive at close to wide-open throttle during this breaking-in period could result in scuffing or, in extreme cases, seizure of certain close-fitting components. In my opinion, a little extra care during the first few thousand miles can determine how the power plant will perform for the rest of its life. Many a good engine has become an oil burner at an early age because of savage break-in practices.

At the same time, it must be remembered that driving too slowly can prove harmful. Don't baby the engine. The owner's manual spells out the proper break-in procedure; and if this advice is followed, there should be no problems.

A young lad who is privileged to drive Dad's new car may be tempted to head for the highway, floor the gas pedal, and push the speedometer needle right up to the top—just to see what she'll do. If you are not dead certain you can convince him that such a practice could prove disastrous, in more ways than one, DON'T hand him the keys.

Piston Pins (or Wrist Pins)

Made of case-hardened steel and machined to a mirrorlike finish, piston pins are used to attach the pistons to the connecting rods. Like the pistons and piston rings, they work mighty hard and are subjected to much stress. But they seldom give trouble unless starved for lubricant. Defective piston pins show up as a constant light clatter as the engine idles. The noise usually starts as a whisper, and gradually becomes more noticeable as mileage increases. Seldom is a little piston-pin noise dangerous, but be guided by your mechanic's advice.

Connecting Rod

As the name would indicate, the purpose of the connecting rods is to attach the pistons to the crankshaft. As mentioned, the upper ends of the connecting rods are fastened to the pistons by means of piston pins, and the lower ends are bolted to the crankshaft.

Connecting-rod Bearing Inserts
(*See Diagram 4.*)

The energy the piston picks up from combustion is transmitted to the connecting rod, and that energy, in turn, is transmitted to the crankshaft. If the metal of the connecting rods were in direct contact with the crankshaft, the two would be rapidly destroyed. For this reason, a specially formulated bearing is inserted between the rod and crankshaft. These insert bearings are among the most critical parts of the engine and are usually among the first components to fail if starved for lubricant. As you will see in the *Lubrication* chapter, oil not only lubricates and cleans, it also cools, and adequate temperature control is essential in the area of the connecting-rod bearings. If the bearings overheat, they will disintegrate in seconds, and a loud knock will be heard. This can require anything from the installation of a new rod and insert bearing, plus grinding of the crankshaft, to the purchase of a new engine.

A rod knock is most likely to be heard when the engine is suddenly revved up from idle, or just at the point of deceleration when traveling at about 40 mph. Even if you only *think* there might be a rod knock, shut off the engine fast and consult a mechanic. One

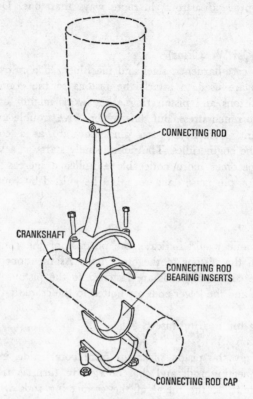

CONNECTING ROD

CRANKSHAFT

CONNECTING ROD
BEARING INSERTS

CONNECTING ROD CAP

Diagram 4. *Connecting-rod bearing inserts*

more minute of driving may result in the defective rod crashing through the side of the block, and then you've really got troubles.

The Crankshaft

The crankshaft converts the up-and-down reciprocating action of the pistons into a steady rotary motion to spin the flywheel. Activated by the flywheel, the transmission relays the engine's rotary force to other components, which in turn transmit the power to the driven wheels.

The crankshaft also plays a vital role as part of the lubrication system. Passages are placed in the shaft in such a manner that oil is forced under pressure throughout its entire length to lubricate the main and connecting-rod bearings.

Main Bearings

A series of metal bearing caps, or saddles, hold bearing inserts which, between them, secure the crankshaft to the engine block. The upper halves of these bearing inserts are recessed in the block. These bearings are placed at both ends of the shaft and at various points along its length.

Main-bearing Insert Bearings

As with the connecting rods, the main bearings also have specially formulated insert bearings to minimize friction between the crankshaft and the main-bearing caps. One of these insert bearings, called the thrust bearing, is designed and shaped to prevent the crankshaft from moving forward or backward. If the thrust bearing fails, the shaft can move forward or backward, throwing the connecting rods, pistons, and various other parts out of alignment. Main-bearing inserts are one of the last parts to fail in a well-maintained engine. However, if for some reson they do become worn, a deep thudding will be heard when the engine is under heavy strain.

Rear Main-bearing and Front Timing-cover Seals

The ends of the crankshaft are fitted with seals to prevent oil from leaking out of the engine. One is called the rear main-bearing seal; the other, located at the front of the shaft, is called the timing-cover seal. Occasionally they will fail and allow some oil to leak, but in my experience they are blamed far too often for leaks that have their beginnings at the top side of the engine. The reason these seals, especially the rear main seal, are condemned is because oil frequently does drip from the rear of the oil pan. The reason for this is the fact that the rear of the pan is the lowest part of the engine; obviously, oil leaking from any upper section of the motor will gravitate to that point. (*See also* the *Lubrication* chapter.)

Timing Gears and Chains

A timing gear, or sprocket, is attached to the front of the crankshaft. Driving either another gear or a chain, this unit is responsible for turning the camshaft in synchronization with the rest of the engine to open and close the valves at exactly the right time and for the right duration. Occasionally a timing chain can stretch and slip and throw out both ignition and valve timing. When this happens, the motor will be lazy or quit entirely, and a number of expensive parts can be damaged.

A loose timing chain or worn gears are usually indicated by a rattling sound when the engine is idling. Repairs should be made immediately.

Crankshaft Pulleys

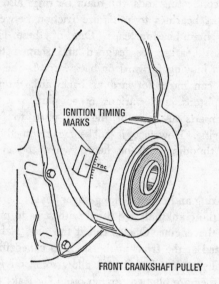

IGNITION TIMING
MARKS

FRONT CRANKSHAFT PULLEY

Diagram 5. *Front crankshaft pulley*

A pulley is fitted to the front of the crankshaft (*see Diagram* 5) to drive the belts that operate the water pump, generator, or alternator, and such options as power steering or air conditioning. Frequently the ignition timing marks are stamped on this pulley. In rare instances the pulley will become loose on the crankshaft; this can be detected by shaking the assembly by hand or by a characteristic jingling noise when the engine is idling. On many cars the inner hub of the pulley acts as a seat for the timing-cover seal. When a leak develops in the timing-cover seal, it is necessary to replace the pulley as well as the seal if the hub has been scored or grooved.

On some cars the pulley also functions as a damper to reduce torsional vibration in the crankshaft. This damper is of two-piece construction—an inner and outer ring of metal held together by a rubber center core. Sometimes the outer section loosens and changes position in relation to the inner section of the damper. When this occurs, the timing mark is thrown out of line and it is extremely difficult to set the ignition timing. When an engine is hard to time, this may be the problem.

The Camshaft

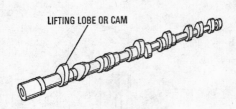

LIFTING LOBE OR CAM

Diagram 6. *The engine camshaft*

The camshaft (*see Diagram* 6) is located in the engine block and named for the series of "cams," or raised irregularities, along its length. These cams push directly against the valve lifters to open and close the valves. On most domestic engines, the camshaft also operates the ignition distributor, the fuel pump, and the oil pump.

Rotating once for every two turns of the crankshaft, the camshaft is of sturdy construction, and the cam surfaces are case-hardened to minimize wear. However, if not properly lubricated or if there is excessive clearance in the valve mechanism, the case hardening can be penetrated on one or more of the cams, and the softer metal underneath soon wears away. When this occurs, the valve action on one or more cylinders ceases to function, and you are headed for major surgery. The camshaft must be replaced—an expensive job in terms of both labor and parts.

Overhead Camshaft

Some high-performance engines (mostly imports) are equipped with an overhead camshaft. Located in the cylinder head, it eliminates such parts as rocker arms and push rods as used with the conventional type of camshaft. However, the camshaft in most domestic cars is located in the block.

Camshaft Bearings

The bearings supporting the camshaft seldom give trouble, but they should be carefully examined and usually replaced when the engine is being completely rebuilt. Worn camshaft bearings can cause a drop in oil pressure, resulting in inadequate lubrication throughout the engine.

The Valve Train

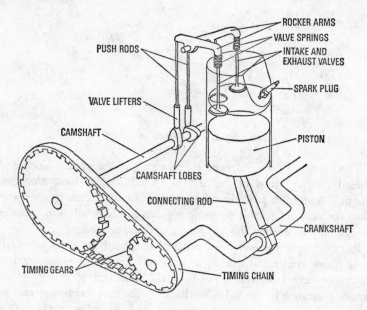

Diagram 7. *The valve train*

The valve train (*see Diagram* 7) is a system of lifters, push rods, rocker arms, valves, valve guides, and springs, and is activated by the camshaft. In some cars the rockers pivot on a long shaft called a "rocker shaft," while on others each rocker pivots individually.

In operation, the lobes on the rotating camshaft push against the lifter, which, in turn, forces the push rod against one side of the rocker arm. The other side of the arm seesaws against the valve stem, forcing the valve to move through the valve guide and open into the combustion chamber. As the camshaft continues to rotate, the pressure of the lobe against the valve lifter is removed, and the valve spring pulls the valve back onto its seat.

Over the years, the valve train has evolved into a highly efficient system which facilitates proper valve operation at the high engine speeds common in the modern car. However, the system is totally reliant on proper lubrication, and any neglect of this area can lead to major, costly repairs.

Hydraulic Valve Lifters

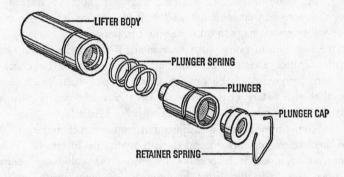

Diagram 8. *Exploded view of hydraulic valve lifter*

Valve lifters used to be solid mechanical devices which did their job but tended to get a little noisy once in a while. When they did, it was usually possible to adjust them to decrease the clearance and noise. However, some noise was unavoidable, and their operation contributed several harmonies to the symphony of the engine in operation.

Hydraulic valve lifters (*see Diagram* 8) were designed to do away with this noise once and for all, and if properly lubricated, they usually do. Machined to the closest tolerances, they are cylindrical devices (about ¾ inch wide and about 2 inches high) and consist of an inner and outer sleeve. A valving arrangement permits the entry of oil, which forms a hydraulic cushion and eliminates clearance and noise in the valve train. When working properly, they are extremely quiet and minimize wear on the camshaft, push rods, rocker arms, and valve stems. But there is a catch: they are precision devices, and tolerances are extremely close. If the engine oil becomes contaminated, hydraulic lifters can stick and create a terrible clatter, which often spells trouble.

Short-run, slow-speed, city driving, coupled with inattention to the demands of the lubricating system, are usually to blame for noisy hydraulic lifters. The high-speed highway driver who changes oil as necessary rarely has this problem.

I am sometimes asked if engine-oil additives will silence noisy hydraulic lifters. I can recall occasions when additives worked, but once a lifter is badly stuck and making a lot of noise, major surgery in generally the only permanent cure.

Low oil pressure can cause noise from hydraulic lifters. In this respect, the noisy lifters can sometimes give a note of warning—telling the motorist that all is not well with his oil circulation—in time to forestall severe damage to other engine components.

At the first sign of noisy valve movement, if the engine oil is clean and the dipstick shows "full," the oil pressure should be checked with a master gauge. If the pressure is up to par, then you can assume that the lifters or other parts of the valve mechanism are faulty. If the oil pressure is low, find out why and fix it fast.

I am sometimes asked if adjustment can correct noise in the valve mechanism on cars equipped with hydraulic lifters. On many engines so equipped it is possible to adjust the valve mechanism. But since the hydraulic lifter is designed to compensate hydraulically for normal wear and to take up the slack, inefficient operation and noise usually mean that something is radically wrong. Adjustment may bring temporary relief, but it will not solve trouble caused by a faulty hydraulic lifter or other defective parts in the valve mechanism.

When an engine is given a valve job, be sure that the hydraulic lifters are removed, dismantled, cleaned, and tested along with all the other parts of the valve train. If mileage is high or the lifters were noisy before the engine was dismantled, it pays to replace them. After all, the time, effort, and money spent to do the job can all go down the drain if the mechanism is damaged again by faulty lifters.

While most cars now use hydraulic lifters, some smaller engines and high-performance units still use the solid type. When solid lifters are employed, it is important that adjustment be made periodically to maintain the correct clearance and avoid damage from hammering.

One small part of the valve train which is sometimes overlooked is the seal fitted to the top of the valve stem in most overhead-valve engines to prevent oil from running down the valve guide into the combustion chamber. This seal should always be replaced when a valve job is done. It should not be overlooked as a possible cause of heavy oil consumption.

Motor Mounts

Until the late twenties, most engines were mounted solidly to the frame. Then, to overcome noise and vibration, rubber mounts were inserted between the frame and engine.

A motor mount is a hard block of rubber which has a steel plate bonded to its top and bottom. One steel plate is attached to the engine, and the other is attached to the car's frame. If one of these plates tears loose from the rubber block, and the driver pulls away sharply from a stop, the engine can twist sideways and jam the gas-pedal linkage in the wide-open position—a terrifying experience. And it's an experience that not one driver in ten would recover from quickly enough to turn off the ignition in time to quiet all those runaway horses. Savage acceleration when pulling away from a stand-still is the most likely cause of motor-mount failure.

Another dangerous aspect of worn mounts is that the gearshift on an automatic transmission can drop into gear all by itself if the engine is being revved up. I know of such an instance. A mechanic was working on a huge truck in front of his workbench, and as he revved up the engine, it suddenly dropped into gear and surged forward. It tore through two heavy partitions and came to a stop as its bumper nudged the front of the superintendent's desk, while he sat petrified in his chair.

Some years ago I knew an elderly man who was making a U-turn when his gas pedal locked solid because of worn mounts. The car jumped the sidewalk, went through a jewelry-store window, and cleaned out the front of the store to the tune of $8000 before it stopped.

Worn motor mounts can also give the exhaust system an awful beating and can tear the exhaust pipe apart at the exhaust manifold. On a steep upward incline, the engine can drop back and make it impossible to change gears. Going downhill, the engine can shift forward far enough to push the rotating fan blades into the radiator.

If the mounts are loose and a car is parked on a steep hill, the driver may find it impossible to pull the automatic transmission out of "Park" unless the car is pushed uphill.

Be sure to include motor mounts on your safety checklist.

The Oil Pan

The oil pan has no mechanical function and simply serves as the reservoir for the engine oil. But plenty of trouble can start right in this pan. Sharp stones or other road obstructions, for example, can put a hole in the bottom of the pan large enough to drain out the oil in seconds.

The gasket between the pan and the block can leak, leading to confusing situations. I was once called in by an insurance company to act as referee in a dispute between the company, a car owner, and a garage operator. When I got to the garage, all communication among the three had broken down. The garage owner was mad, the car owner was furious, and the insurance adjuster, (smack in the middle) was distraught.

It seemed that the car had been involved in a front-end collision and the oil pan had been damaged. The garage had removed, straightened, and reinstalled the pan. Now, claimed the car owner, the pan was leaking. Sure enough, there was a definite drip of oil from the rear of the pan, which the garage operator maintained was a leaking rear main-bearing seal. A mechanic prepared to remove the pan and attack the rear bearing—the idea was that if the replacement seal cured the leak, the motorist would pay the bill. The motorist was far from pleased with this arrangement.

I decided to step into my role as referee and suggested cleaning the engine thoroughly before removing any parts. After this was done, there was no problem pinpointing the true cause of the leak, which was about eight inches from the back of the pan and a long way from the rear main-bearing seal. The mechanic who had straightened the pan in the first place hadn't done a good job, and the oil was seeping past the gasket. Gravity was carrying it down to the back of the engine, where it dripped off the rear main-bearing housing. The pan was removed and straightened out properly, and a new gasket was installed. The story ended with the motorist and the insurance adjuster going happily on their ways, and the garage owner grumbling about the lack of intelligence of some mechanics.

I have long ago lost track of the number of cars I have checked whose owners had been told they needed a new rear main-bearing seal or pan gasket when, in fact, there was nothing wrong with either. Mechanics, and motorists too, should keep in mind the fact that engine oil, when leaking, always follows the law of gravity and runs down. Many of the gaskets in the upper sections of the engine, especially the rocker-cover gaskets, are affected by heat and can buckle or shrink. Sometimes, too, these gaskets are not aligned properly when installed. Leaking oil from the gaskets usually runs down to the rear of the engine and drips off the pan or rear main-bearing housing, giving no clue as to its real origin.

Other units, such as oil filters, fuel pumps, oil lines, and even the oil-gauge sending unit can leak. The proper method of tracing an oil leak is to first clean the engine, top and bottom. After the engine is dry externally, place the car on stands and run it at approximately 1000 rpm. Then, and only then, can the source of the leak be correctly established.

Plugged breathers or a malfunctioning positive crankcase ventilation system can also cause leaks by building up enough pressure in the engine to blow the oil out of the front timing-cover seal and the rear main seal, or a number of other vulnerable points. (Crankcase ventilation is also discussed in the *Lubrication* chapter.)

The Oil Pump

The oil pump is gear-driven from the camshaft and very seldom breaks down mechanically. The most likely cause of trouble here is a plugged oil-pump screen which, designed to keep debris out of the teeth of the pump, occasionally becomes plugged with sludge.

If there is any doubt about the efficiency of your engine's lubricating system, have the oil pump tested. Your mechanic can do this by hooking a master gauge into the system. This test is particularly valuable in cars without an oil-pressure gauge. If the pressure test is O.K., you can be reasonably certain that there is nothing seriously wrong with the pump.

Other remote causes of low oil pressure are: a cracked or loose pipe inside the oil pan that is feeding lubricant to various engine components, a worn camshaft and/or crankshaft bearings, or a sticking pressure-relief valve or broken pressure-relief-valve spring in the oil pump.

The Flywheel

The flywheel is a large, round, heavy piece of metal that makes it possible to idle the engine smoothly at reasonably low speeds. Without its inertia, it would be impossible to smooth out the firing impulses as the fuel/air mixture is ignited in each cylinder.

It is attached to the very rear of the crankshaft, and a large gear, called a "flywheel ring gear," is fitted to its outer circumference. A smaller gear located at the rear of the starter motor engages with the flywheel ring gear to rotate the crankshaft and start the engine. If the ignition-timing marks are not on the front crankshaft pulley, they will be on the flywheel.

In cars with standard transmission, a clutch assembly is bolted to the flywheel to transmit the engine's power to the transmission. In cars with automatic transmission, the engine has no flywheel. Instead, a unit called a driveplate is attached to the rear of the crankshaft. The transmission's heavy torque converter is attached to the driveplate, and their combined weight acts as a flywheel. In this case the flywheel ring gear is attached to the driveplate.

And that, from beginning to end, is the story of the internal-combustion engine. As I said at the beginning, all that's new is that our technology has wrapped much of mankind's knowledge gained over the past five thousand years into a well-groomed powerhouse.

The Fuel System

Gasoline

One of my most fascinating experiences in Detroit was when I first saw a car assembled from start to finish. The components came from all directions, each arriving at the proper spot on the line with amazing precision, and gradually a car took form and rolled off the assembly line. As it stood there waiting for the next move of the assembly man, I was struck by the helplessness of this large mass of technology and engineering skill. It wasn't until a couple of gallons of fuel were poured into the tank and a technician turned the starter that the newborn car gave a healthy roar and was driven away under its own power.

Witnessing this birth of a car, I couldn't help reflect on the importance of that harmless-looking fluid—gasoline. Defined in the dictionary as a "low-boiling fraction of crude petroleum consisting of a variety of hydrocarbons," gasoline is accepted as the most efficient and economical fuel for the automobile. Properly handled, it is a safe and reliable servant. But gasoline has a treacherous and deadly side!

I know a woman who poured two gallons of gasoline into her washing machine, dropped in a bundle of dirty clothing, and turned on the switch. A moment later there was a violent explosion and a raging fire. She was rescued, but she had suffered first-degree burns over 60 percent of her body.

It surprises me how many experienced mechanics and garagemen treat gasoline as though it were as safe as water. Since they do not see the full Jekyll and Hyde sides of its personality every day, they forget that it can be so dangerous.

One summer, after gassing up, I was driving along a road under construction—all washboard and potholes—at about 35 mph. Suddenly I heard a loud scraping noise and thought my tailpipe must have dropped down. I stopped and found that the gasoline tank had dropped off and was being dragged along under the car by the gas line. I don't know why it didn't burst into flames; the tank was drenched in gasoline, and there must have been thousands of sparks from the tank as it scraped over the gravel. A passing motorist sent a tow truck from the nearest town, and when it arrived, the driver disconnected the gas line and dragged the tank out. He was about to lift it onto the back of his truck—which was oozing heat and smoke from its tailpipe—when I humbly suggested he first dump the gasoline into the sand on the side of the road, where it would safely evaporate. "Heck, no," he said. "This gas cost you money, and it's a shame to waste it." He set the tank down on the worn wooden floor of the truck, and the gas promptly began seeping down all over the hot exhaust system.

By this time my nerves were more than a little edgy. I knew the small fire extinguisher in my own car would be useless if this thing ever went up. The truck pushed me into town—amazingly, with no explosion. Examination at a garage showed that the hidden supports holding my gas-tank straps had corroded, and the combination of the heavily loaded gas tank and my bouncing car had caused the straps to tear away.

However, this discovery did not end my ordeal. "Don't worry, sir," the mechanic assured me. "We'll have you on the road again in an hour or so." With that, he promptly dragged a 25-gallon drum from the gas-pump island. Clearly printed on the drum were the words EMPTY ASHTRAYS HERE. He upended the drum, gave the insides a quick swipe with a rag (he didn't want to dirty up my valuable gas, I guess), and proceeded to drain the gas from my tank into it.

To my further alarm, he left the drum uncovered and right out in the open. When he began to reinstall the tank, I prowled around the garage looking for something to cover the exposed fuel. I was afraid somebody might follow the instructions on the drum and dump an ashtray with a live butt into it. I couldn't find a thing, so I finally decided on a restaurant two blocks away as the safest place to wait. There I sat and meditated on the fact that just a few days earlier I had read about a man who had been killed in that same district when a chance spark ignited gasoline that had seeped into his service-station basement.

I returned an hour later, hoping it would be all over—one way or another. But, unfortunately, they were just ready to pour the gas back into the tank. They had the 25-gallon drum perched on top of a stepladder with a broken leg. Both mechanics were smoking. When I appeared, they casually asked me to hold the ladder steady while they syphoned the gas into the tank. I stepped forward gingerly. One of the mechanics put the hose in his mouth and tried to draw the gas through. After several attempts, the gas began to flow—all over him and the floor. By the time he had the stream directed into the tank, at least a pint of fuel was washing around under the car, and he himself was a living torch waiting to be ignited. Finally, when the ordeal was over, I thanked them, paid my bill, and hit the road!

While most of us are spared direct contact with the volatile side of gasoline's personality, the stories of its destructive nature are legion.

I remember during my Navy days in World War II how several Canadian torpedo boats were destroyed by fire at Ostend. A careless stoker had pumped a mixture of gasoline and oil out of the bilges of his boat. It floated on the surface of the water until an unexpected spark sent it skyward—together with millions of dollars' worth of much-needed naval equipment.

Even in the absence of an open flame or a carelessly handled cigarette, there is danger of fire from flammable mixtures. Safety experts call the three elements to creat fire "the combustion triangle." The triangle consists of fuel, air, and ignition. Air is usually available in abundance, and ignition can even be provided by static electricity. Anytime these three elements come into contact, the situation is dangerous. Yet, I have seen gasoline tanks being soldered by mechanics who insisted it was perfectly safe because they were not working with an open flame. Besides, they add, they put some carbon tetrachloride in the tank "to be on the safe side." People have been seriously burned or killed taking the same chance.

Even when a gasoline tank has been drained and cleaned, the danger of explosion remains. When I was seventeen I dented the gas tank on my motorbike. I removed the tank to beat out the dents. Knowing the dangers posed by gasoline, I took the tank down to the laundry room, put it in the tub, and ran hot water through it for more than an hour. Then I left it under a running cold-water tap overnight. Next morning I put a torch to it to heat the metal. There was a blinding flash, and the gasoline tank flew out of my hands. It turned out that I was doubly lucky—only my eyebrows were singed, and all the dents in the tank had been blown out. Later, it was explained to me that enough gasoline had been left in the pores of the metal to vaporize on heating and explode.

If your car must go into the garage for work on the tank, try to burn most of the gasoline first. This will at least minimize the problem of draining large quantities of fuel from the tank before it is removed. Should you be in the garage when the tank is being removed, and you see the mechanic working under the tank with a wrench in one hand and an extension light in the other—get out in a hurry. If you're really attached to your car, you might pause long enough to tell him he is courting disaster. If the extension light drops to the floor, the bulb can shatter and ignite the fumes. If fuel spills from the tank, as it is removed, and splashes onto the bulb, it is also dangerous. A few years ago I saw the remains of a service station that burned down as a result of raw gas dripping onto and cracking an extension-light bulb.

When refueling your car, switch off your ignition and refrain from smoking. In some areas this rule is now mandatory, and the attendant will request that you follow it. A chance spark or backfire through the tailpipe could ignite the gasoline. Furthermore, the attendant does not appreciate the unpleasant exhaust fumes from the tailpipe.

The Gasoline Tank

Once we have gassed up, we are all set to drive hundreds of miles. But first the fuel has to find its way into the car's combustion chamber. That is why the car has an entire system devoted to the storage, cleaning, mixing, and delivery of fuel. (*See Diagram 9.*)

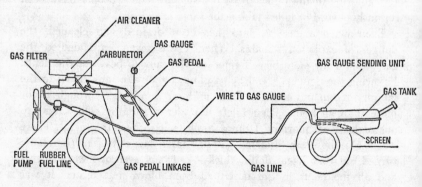

Diagram 9. *The fuel system*

Frequently the gas tank is regarded as merely a storage container for the fuel. But it is actually an integral part of the fuel system, and its condition can affect all the other components, including the gas lines, the fuel pump, the filters, and the carburetor.

Because of the explosive nature of gasoline, the gas tank is made of reasonably thin-gauge steel. If the metal were of much greater thickness, and if the explosive "triangle" were present inside, it could explode with the force of a bomb. Rust from either side of the tank can cause the formation of holes, loss of fuel, and danger of fire. Rust inside can also result in other problems which can cause complete failure of the fuel system.

Water in the Gasoline Tank

A question I am often asked is: "How does water get into the gasoline tank?" Condensation forms inside the gas tank just as it does on the windshield, but, while it is a simple matter to wipe it off the windows, it cannot be wiped out of the gasoline tank. Being heavier than gasoline, water collects in the bottom of the tank and has several damaging effects. (*See Diagram* 10.) The water may

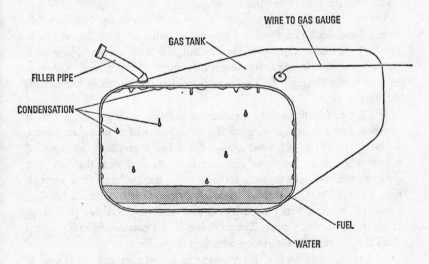

Diagram 10. *The gasoline tank*

form a rust that can eat right through the tank or combine with the water to create a thick sludge. This sludge can block the outlet pipe of the tank and starve the rest of the system. When this happens, the problem is too often not recognized, and the fuel pump is needlessly replaced. If the sludge gets beyond the outlet pipe, it can foul up the fuel pump, filters, and carburetor.

In freezing weather, water in the gas tank can cause ice crystals to form in the gas line, restricting or stopping the flow of gasoline to the carburetor. These ice crystals can be a hazard, especially when a motorist attempts to pass another car and the engine cuts out just when he urgently needs acceleration.

There are several ways of ridding the gasoline tank of water and avoiding its entry in the first place. Air, drawn into the tank through the vented gas cap or a breather pipe fitted to the top of the tank, replaces fuel as it is burned in the engine. On damp days, moisture enters with the air. It is wise to keep the gasoline tank as nearly full as possible; it is no more expensive to drive off the top of the tank than it is to drive off the bottom. The more gasoline in the tank, the less room there is for formation of condensation. Another way to prevent water from entering the tank is to replace a lost gas cap immediately. Driving in rainy weather with no gas cap can allow enough water into the system to stall the engine.

Water formations of an ounce or so that have inadvertently entered the tank can usually be removed with an additive available at most service stations. Mainly alcohol, the additive combines with water, prevents it from freezing or forming sludges, and allows it to flow freely through the fuel system, where it eventually burns with the gas.

If your car stalls in cold weather, make sure it isn't just a frozen gasoline line before agreeing to the installation of a new fuel pump. Leaving the car in a heated garage for a few hours will take care of a frozen gas line. Once the line has been thawed out, the use of a de-icing additive will prevent recurrence of the problem. But remember, the ice must be melted in the gas line *before* an additive will prove effective. When placed in the gas tank, the additive just drops to the bottom of the tank. The additive is not capable of creeping up from the gas tank to the frozen area of the gas line.

However, allowing the ice to melt is sometimes not the cure. If there are excessive quantities of water in the gas tank, it is usually necessary to remove the tank and send it to a specialist for steam cleaning.

There are, of course, other ways than condensation whereby water can enter the gas tank—sometimes in large quantities! A service-station operator told me that he once towed in a lady's car and found a gallon of water in the tank. He was at a loss to know where it came from, but since he had filled the tank the previous day, he cleaned up the mess and returned the car to its owner without charge. A week later, the same car was towed back in, and this time there were three gallons of water in the tank.

After much research, it turned out that the lady's young son was the culprit. It seems that the little guy decided to "play service station," and in his enthusiasm he had removed the gas cap, grabbed the garden hose, and loaded the tank with water. A locking type of gas cap was installed, and there was no further problem.

When water collects in the gas tank, many motorists assume that it came from the underground tanks of their service station. While this problem must head the list of aggravations experienced by service-station operators, very seldom are they responsible for the accumulation of water in the fuel system.

Other Problems with the Gasoline Tank

The following problem, which can occur in gasoline tanks and have quite a baffling effect, is often diagnosed as a faulty fuel pump. If the hole in the gas cap becomes plugged, or if an unvented cap is installed in error, a vacuum forms inside the tank as the fuel level drops and air cannot enter to take its place. A tug-of-war commences in the fuel system: The pump is desperately trying to draw the fuel from the tank, and the vacuum in the tank is just as stubbornly trying to draw it back from the pump. Usually such a contest ends in a dead heat with equal suction on both ends; the gasoline refuses to budge, the carburetor starves for fuel, and the engine quits. But if the fuel pump wins, the vacuum buildup can collapse the gas tank, reducing the fuel capacity by as much as half, and throw the gas gauge completely out of kilter.

The following is a letter from a reader of my column:

"I drive a V-8 station wagon, and one day I began to hear strange metallic noises from the rear. I tightened everything in sight, wrapped my jack and tools in wads of cloth, but the noises continued, and even my local service station couldn't find the cause.

"The engine began to lose its pep and started to stall frequently, so I figured I needed a tune-up. The service station agreed with me and they gave it the works—new plugs, points, condenser, and scads of other parts. The very next day the darned engine began sputtering desperately, and again I heard the loud metallic clinking from the rear as the wagon breathed its last. It appeared, for the first time ever, that I had run out of gas.

"I was pushed to the nearest pumps, but it only took three dollars' worth to fill it. Right away I knew something was wrong, because it usually cost about seven dollars. I decided to put the wagon on a hoist and have a look myself. I immediately discovered what was wrong—the gasoline tank had buckled inwards and had collapsed from all sides, reducing its capacity.

"Then I remembered I had gassed up the day before the peculiar noises started, and the attendant had forgotten to put my gas cap back on. When I returned to the station it could not be found, but the attendant obligingly put on another one at no charge. This turned out to be a dubious favor, since in error he had installed an unvented cap, which caused a buildup of vacuum and the collapse of the tank. The flexing of the metal during collapse accounted for all the funny noises. Now I've got to buy a new gasoline tank and who knows what else."

If your cap is unvented, don't be unduly alarmed. Many cars are deliberately equipped with unvented caps because breathing is provided by a tube from the top of the gasoline tank. The unvented cap prevents water from entering the tank, and a vented cap should not be installed on such a car. A catalogue that indicates the correct cap for every model car should be consulted.

On some cars a rubber hose connects the filler pipe to the gasoline tank. After a few years, this hose sometimes deteriorates and collapses. When this happens, it is difficult to pour gas into the tank. If the attendant complains that the fuel spurts back, or takes a long time to go into the tank, have the hose checked.

Fuel Tank Vapor Emission Control Systems

As well as allowing air to enter the gasoline tank to displace the fuel as it is slowly burned by the engine, the gas tank's breathing system plays another important role.

An increase in temperature inside the gas tank results in expansion of the fuel, which in turn builds up internal pressure. To avoid excessive pressure buildup the fumes (hydrocarbons) that form inside the tank are expelled to the atmosphere through the breathing system.

To prevent these harmful fumes from polluting the air the Fuel

Tank Vapor Control System was introduced. With this new system, instead of escaping to the atmosphere, the fumes are drawn from the tank by the engine's vacuum and burned along with the fuel/air mixture in the combustion chambers.

All cars sold in Canada and the United States from 1971 on were equipped with this anti-pollution device, and all 1970 models sold in California had been so equipped.

While all these systems function on much the same principle, depending on the maker there are some variations. It is claimed that little servicing is necessary to keep them operating efficiently, and that what little service is needed is simple and inexpensive.

However, it is essential that they be included in a routine checkup and inspected as spelled out in the Owner's Manual.

The Gasoline Lines

The steel gasoline lines, which lead from the gasoline tank, have quite a narrow inside passage. They can be plugged by sludge or ice, and they are prone to develop holes from rust, flexing, or friction. Fuel-system troubles that occur in the lines are often blamed on the fuel pump or carburetor.

For example, a small hole in the gas line will admit air but will not necessarily show telltale drips of raw gas under the car. This is especially likely if the hole is high up in the fuel line, where it curves up over the rear axle. Air can then enter the gas line, allowing the fuel to gravitate back into the gas tank. Then, instead of drawing fuel from the tank, the fuel pump sucks only air through the hole in the gas line. When this problem exists, the fuel pump is sometimes tested, and if there is no delivery of fuel, it is promptly condemned, when in fact there is nothing wrong with it.

I have heard of as many as three pumps being installed in rapid succession for reasons such as this. When there are other defects in the fuel system, a new pump may work at first because, being new, it will overcome the existing deficiencies, but it will soon weaken to some degree and fail again.

If you are ever plagued by engine stalling caused by water in the fuel pump and/or the carburetor, and no water is found in the gas tank, check the fuel line, particularly in areas adjacent to the rear wheels. The water thrown up by the wheels can be drawn into the system through a pinhole in the fuel line.

The steel gas line is connected to the suction side of the fuel pump by means of a flexible rubber hose. Should this hose become twisted, pinched, or blocked internally, the fuel pump may cease to function. This hose can also perish, allowing fuel to leak out, or air to enter the system. (*See Diagram* 11.)

Diagram 11. *Badly twisted flexible gasoline hose*

The Fuel Pump

The fuel pump, pulsating heart of the fuel system, supplies gasoline to the carburetor. Like the human heart, it performs an indispensable task; and when it fails, there is real trouble. By and large, the fuel pump is a dependable unit which is too frequently blamed for all the ills of the fuel system. (*See Diagram* 12.)

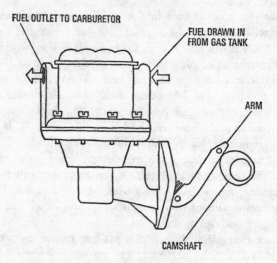

Diagram 12. *Typical single-action fuel pump*

When a fuel pump is being tested, too much emphasis is frequently placed on pressure reading, and volume of fuel being delivered is ignored It must be remembered that if the flow of gas between the tank and the fuel pump is severely restricted, the pressure reading may be normal, although the actual amount of fuel being delivered to the carburetor is insufficient to meet the demands of the engine at high speed. Volume should be checked by disconnecting the gas line on the discharge side of the fuel pump. While the engine is idling, visually check the volume of fuel being delivered as it flows into a container. If a solid body of fuel squirts out each time the fuel pump pulsates, there is nothing seriously wrong with the pump. If, however, there is not a solid body of fuel, further checks should be made to determine the cause of the problem.

Many imported cars have electrical fuel pumps; most North American cars, however, are equipped with a pump which is operated by a lobe on the camshaft. A diaphragm is compressed and expanded, and a simple valving arrangement allows gasoline to be pumped to the carburetor.

On rare occasions the cam on the camshaft that drives the fuel pump wears away and the pump stops feeding gas to the carburetor. When this occurs, to avoid the expense of replacing the camshaft, especially on older engines, some people prefer to install an accessory electric fuel pump, which is available at reasonable cost.

Some cars are equipped with a double-action fuel pump, whose dual purpose is to pump fuel from the gas tank and generate vacuum to operate vacuum-operated windshield wipers. Should the diaphragm that operates the wipers on this type of pump become ruptured, the engine may suddenly start to use as much as a quart of oil in 50 miles. This oil-burning problem is sometimes wrongly diagnosed as worn piston rings.

To test for a ruptured diaphragm, have your mechanic remove the vacuum lines from the pump and check for a coating of raw engine oil inside the lines. If they are not perfectly dry, you can be almost certain that the diaphragm is ruptured. A ruptured diaphragm may be the problem if the wipers stop operating when you are climbing a hill with open throttle. This, of course, does not apply to vehicles equipped with electric wipers.

Fuel Filters

Many cars have a fuel filter in the gasoline line between the pump and the carburetor. These filters are most effective in keeping the carburetor clean. However, if they are not replaced at proper intervals, the accumulated dirt on the inside element will restrict or even stop the flow of fuel. This condition can be dangerous. There may be enough fuel passing through the filter to satisfy the carburetor at low speeds, but let's say you are driving at 50 mph and want to pass the car ahead. You floor the gas pedal, and the maximum amount of fuel pours into the engine. Then, just as you are abreast of the car you are trying to pass, the gas cannot pass through the filter fast enough to meet the much higher demand of the carburetor, and the engine "starves" for fuel. This happened to a man I know, and he had to steer off the pavement onto the left-hand shoulder to avoid a head-on collision.

In addition to this type of filter (depending on year and make of car), there can be other filters almost anywhere. They can turn up inside the carburetor, built into the fuel pump or inside the gas tank. Make sure your filters have been eliminated as a source of trouble before investing in a new pump.

Other things to watch with the "in-line" fuel filter are the connecting hoses. Just like the hose at the gas tank, these hoses can soften or swell up to restrict or block the fuel flow.

A truck driver who used to come to my garage regularly (but not regularly enough, as it turned out) had his $10,000 truck reduced to cinders because of such a soft hose. During one of his trips a new fuel pump had been installed, but the hose connecting it to the "in-line" filter was not replaced. As the truck was barreling down the highway at 60 mph, the hose on the pump side of the filter slipped off and began spewing gasoline all over the engine compartment and through convenient holes in the firewall. As it splashed over the distributor and coil, it ignited, and the driver had to lock on the emergency brake and bail out of the cab to save himself from being barbecued.

The Carburetor and Choke

If straight gasoline were poured into the engine without the proper mixture of air, the engine would fail to start. Even a suitable mixture of gasoline and air must be metered and controlled; otherwise, the engine would be unmanageable. This is the purpose of the carburetor. (*See Diagram* 13.)

The function of the carburetor in mixing air and gasoline in correct proportions is highly demanding, since these proportions vary with engine speed, engine load, and temperature. The carburetor

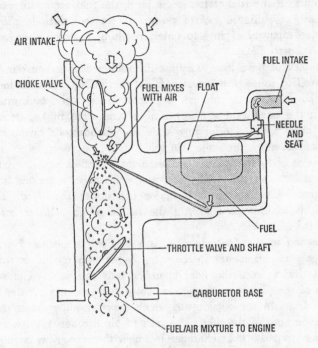

Diagram 13. *Cutaway view of single-barrel carburetor*

is a complex arrangement of needles and seats, high- and low-speed jets, adjusting screws, pumps, diaphragms, air passages, springs, vacuum-operated devices, check valves, and other bits and pieces.

The base of the carburetor is mounted to the top of the intake manifold. Attached to the top throat of the carburetor is a filter that cleans the large volume of outside air that is drawn down through the inside bore of the carburetor.

One of the most important areas of the carburetor is the *float chamber,* which is simply a container for the gasoline that is pumped into the carburetor by the fuel pump. (*See Diagram* 13.)

It is called a float chamber because it contains a float, whose buoyant action opens and closes a valving device (the *needle valve* and *seat*) which, depending on engine speed, controls the volume of fuel that flows into the float chamber and also maintains proper fuel level. The float and the needle valve and seat play a vitally important role in the engine's performance and economy. If a maladjusted float cuts off the fuel at too low a level, the fuel/air mixture will be too lean, resulting in loss of power. If set too high, it allows an excessive quantity of fuel to enter, resulting in too rich a mixture and poor gas mileage.

Many of us have had to adjust the rubber plunger on our household toilets to stop the water from continually running into the toilet bowl. When the plunger is properly seated, the tank gradually fills, at the same time slowly raising a large float that shuts off the water supply. On a miniature scale, the carburetor's float chamber functions on much the same principle.

A piece of foreign matter less than the thickness of a human hair jammed between the needle and seat, will cause a serious flooding condition which can start a major fire under the hood. This is why it is so important to run the fuel through a filter before it enters the carburetor.

Attached to the float chamber is a vertical tube-shaped arrangement, about two inches in diameter. When the engine is running, fuel is drawn from the float chamber into this tube. The suction action of the pistons as they move down the cylinders on the intake stroke draws in the outside air, which moves rapidly down through the inside bore of the tube. The rush of air through the tube draws gasoline from the float chamber in much the same way as liquid is drawn from the lower container of an atomizer as we squeeze the rubber bulb.

The intake manifold then directs the fuel/air mixture into the combustion chambers, where it is ignited by the sparkplugs. Inside the bore of the carburetor is a shaft and gate (the throttle shaft and throttle valve) which, through a series of linkages, is attached to the gas pedal. Depressing the gas pedal opens the gate or throttle valve, allowing the correct volume of fuel/air mixture to enter the combustion chamber.

There are various makes and designs of carburetors. Depending on such factors as engine size and the kind of performance expected, carburetors can have one, two, or four tubes, or bores (technically known as "barrels"). Each barrel contains a throttle valve or gate.

An engine must idle properly; to accomplish this, there is what is known as an *idle circuit,* which is a series of parts to provide enough fuel and air to keep the engine running at low rpm. In order to run at high speeds, the engine needs a much greater volume of fuel and air. To accomplish this, there is a separate *high-speed circuit,* which progressively increases the volume of mixture as the engine increases speed.

Between these two circuits there is a pump connected to the carburetor linkage which pumps in extra fuel to avoid *flat spots,* or momentary lack of power, during acceleration. Other carburetor components ensure that the fuel-to-air ratio and volume are correct, whether the car is pulling a heavy load or operating in extreme cold.

When an engine and the air entering the carburetor are both cold, considerable difficulty may be encountered in starting. To overcome this problem, a choke is used. The choke restricts the flow of air and provides a rich fuel mixture until the engine starts and warms up.

Most chokes today are automatic, although some motorists argue that the old-style manual choke is better. While both can do an equally good job of enriching the fuel/air mixture to the engine, manufacturers have found that people often did not use the choke correctly. Some omitted to use the manual choke and could not start their cars. Others forgot to push the control back in again after the engine had started. Gasoline consumption soared, and the engine stalled or idled roughly. Also, a rich mixture pouring into a warm engine can do great harm, washing lubricant off the moving parts. A warm engine is also extremely hard, if not impossible, to start if the choke is on.

When you observe what a few drivers do with the manual choke, it's easy to understand why car makers install the automatic choke. I remember one woman whose car had been in my garage for a major tune-up. When the car left my shop, it was running like a clock, but a few days later, the lady was back complaining of heavy fuel consumption and rough idling. I checked all the work we had done and found nothing wrong.

I told her to take the car out and try it again. She was back later with a repetition of her tale of woe. But this time I had seen her drive in with great clouds of black smoke pouring from the tailpipe. I found she had the choke pulled full out and was using it to hang her handbag within easy reach. I don't know how long she had been doing this, and even when I explained the hazards of driving with a hot engine in warm weather with the choke full out, I don't think she fully understood why she couldn't continue to use the choke as a purse peg.

In addition to controlling the fuel/air mixture, the choke, through a series of linkages, increases the idle speed to avoid stalling while the engine warms up. A frequent cause of engine stalling while warming up is improper adjustment or sticking of this fast-idle mechanism. If it is set too high and the car is put into gear while the engine is racing, it can damage an automatic transmission and other drive-line components.

Car manufacturers usually recommend that the gas pedal be depressed once—and once only—to the floor before attempting to start a cold engine. This is sufficient to lift the linkage enough to allow the choke to close and shoot a rich mixture into the engine. However, I have found it is sometimes necessary to pump the gas pedal two or three times when starting a very cold engine. This should not be overdone, as raw gasoline washes the lubricant from the cylinder walls and leads to a dry start.

The engine can become flooded from excessive choking (automatic or manual). When this happens, the more you try to start, the more you flood the engine. In order to allow sufficient air to mingle with the raw fuel in the flooded engine, the gas pedal should be depressed all the way to the floor and held there while you attempt to start the engine. Then, and only then, does it have a chance to start. After the engine starts, release the gas pedal most of the way to avoid excessive racing of the motor during the warm-up period. The alternative is to let the car sit for ten minutes or more before trying again.

The automatic choke does a good job, provided it is working properly. When malfunctions set in, however, they can play havoc with fuel economy, cold starting, hot starting, and general engine operation.

The automatic choke is opened by heat from the engine, which takes the tension out of a delicate bimetal spring. Little pressure is needed to open or close the choke valve, which is partially forced open by the air flow when the engine is running. When the engine is not running and there is no air flowing past the choke valve, it is the job of the bimetal spring to open and close the valve.

It is therefore important to have the carburetor stripped and cleaned occasionally. Otherwise, gummy deposits can cause jamming of the choke and other carburetor components. External linkage, which can be cleaned and adjusted without dismantling the carburetor, should be given this service periodically.

Black clouds of smoke from the tailpipe after the engine has been running for a few minutes are a clue to automatic-choke troubles.

Many cars are equipped with a little unit on the carburetor linkage called the *dash-pot,* which is designed to prevent stalling due to sudden closing of the throttle. It operates much like the device installed on doors to keep them from slamming, and if leaks develop in it or if it is improperly adjusted, the engine can stall when you take your foot off the gas pedal. This device is often overlooked. You might remind your mechanic to check and adjust it if you have a stalling problem.

Flat Spots and Hesitations

I receive volumes of enquiries from readers as to the cause of their engines' coughing, stalling, hesitating, or developing flat spots when pulling away or when accelerating at higher speeds.

When the gas pedal is depressed, a series of linkages operates the carburetor's accelerator pump, which in turn instantly forces a stream of raw gas into the manifold. This momentary rich mixture keeps the engine operating smoothly when pulling away or during high-speed acceleration. When there is wear in the various pivot points of the linkage, the gas pedal must move down a considerable distance in order to take up all the slack. Under these conditions, there is little or no movement of the accelerator pump, and stalling, coughing, flat spots, and general lack of power result.

All makes of engines, regardless of whether they are fitted with single-, double-, or four-barrel carburetors, can develop flat spots, but the problem seems more chronic with six-cylinder engines equipped with single-barrel carburetors.

In many instances, when a motorist complains of these problems, the carburetor's accelerator pump is immediately blamed, and the installation of a carburetor "parts kit" is recommended. Sometimes this is the cure and sometimes not; but should this procedure fail, it does not necessarily eliminate the carburetor as the culprit. The parts kit most commonly used includes but a few of all the moving parts—usually the needle and seat, accelerator pump, and gasket set. Considerable wear can occur on many parts of the external linkage. The external linkage is *not* included in a minor-parts kit, and, in some cases, it is not available at all. It is then necessary to install a new carburetor or an exchange unit produced by a reputable company that specializes in rebuilding carburetors according to manufacturers' specifications.

Frequently, with single-barrel carburetors, a brand-new unit costs only a few dollars more than a regular parts-kit overhaul job, and often an exchange rebuilt carburetor is cheaper than repairing the original unit. Some taxi operators find that with single-barrel carburetors it is more economical to install brand-new units.

Other causes of hesitations and flat spots are: a sticking heat-riser valve, ignition timing improperly adjusted, a weak coil, stale fuel or fuel of the wrong octane rating, ignition points too close, worn sparkplugs, too cool a running engine, high-tension cables burned away internally, poor compression. These are but a few of the points that must be checked before condemning the carburetor.

Flooding

Many things will cause a carburetor to flood—excessive fuel-pump pressure, dirt in the gasoline, or a gas-logged float (a hole or crack in the float will allow fuel to enter, and the float will sink, holding the needle valve wide open). The float may also be improperly adjusted, or the automatic choke may be too rich, or the choke heat-control mechanism may be faulty. A dirty, plugged air filter will restrict the carburetor's air intake; loose insulation from under the hood can drop down on the air cleaner with a similar effect.

Sometimes the steel needle in the needle-and-seat assembly will become magnetized and attract particles of foreign matter, preventing proper seating. In some instances, the manufacturers have modified this needle, making it of neoprene or nylon to eliminate the problem of magnetism.

A clogged carburetor air bleed can cause fuel to be siphoned from the carburetor when the engine is shut off. This floods the intake manifold and makes starting difficult.

When the carburetor needs repairs, it is wise to dismantle the whole unit and have it soaked in a cleaning solution. Bear in mind that the modern carburetor is sensitive and should be overhauled and adjusted by a skilled technician, to manufacturer's specifications.

Carburetor Icing

I often receive complaints of chronic stalling problems which persist after complete carburetor overhauls and full tune-ups. A typical complaint is that the engine stalls easily until it has been running for about fifteen minutes. This is usually an icing problem and will crop up when the humidity is high and the temperature hovers between freezing and approximately 54 degrees above zero.

In operation, a carburetor is somewhat like a mechanical refrigeration unit. A temperature drop occurs as the rush of outside air is drawn through the carburetor throat. The moisture in this air freezes, and solid ice crystals form on the throttle valve and bore. When the throttle valve returns to the "idle" position, the ice blocks the flow of air past the throttle valve, and the engine stalls. At this point the car operates only when the throttle is opened beyond the "idle" position, and it is impossible for the engine to idle.

Several years ago I owned a car which persistently gave me this trouble. When I left for work in the morning the car ran fine for the first few blocks, then would intermittently stall when I removed my foot from the gas pedal. One damp evening when the car had been standing all day in a temperature of some 35 degrees, I decided to get to the bottom of this thing. I removed the air cleaner, started the engine, and ran it up to about 1500 rpm. After it had run for about five minutes, I shut off the ignition and shone a flashlight down the throat of the carburetor. Ice had formed, blocking off the idle circuit.

The oil companies are constantly at work in their laboratories testing gasoline additives which retard ice formation or prevent ice from adhering to carburetor surfaces. These additives are currently used in gasoline to combat carburetor icing. The car manufacturers have been designing carburetor preheating devices and thermostatically controlled air-intake devices operating from either the exhaust system or the cooling system. Many cars are so equipped today. These devices further reduce the icing problem.

Vapor Locks

Vapor locks are caused by excessive heat which vaporizes the fuel in the pump or lines. This usually occurs when the car is bogged down on a hot day in heavy traffic, or shortly after the engine has been stopped for a few minutes and restarted. In normal high-speed driving, the gas tank is cooled by the air, and the fuel passes through the lines rapidly enough to keep the lines cool. Little gas is required to keep the car idling in heavy traffic, and the lines can become sufficiently heated by the hot engine compartment to cause the slow-moving fuel to boil. Similarly, if the fuel lines are too close to the exhaust system, the same condition will result. When this condition is chronic, I have overcome it by insulating the fuel lines with asbestos or electricians' loom covered with tinfoil.

I remember taking my family on a camping trip one summer when this was brought forcibly to my attention. We left on a steaming-hot day, and it was bumper-to-bumper crawl most of the way, with temperature and tempers getting hotter each mile.

Dozens of cars were bogged down on the roads, suffering from vapor locks. We were climbing a grade when the car in front of us, with a heavy house-trailer in tow, gave up the struggle and panted to a halt. We couldn't push the heavy weight uphill, and couldn't back up because of the traffic behind us.

Eventually, I went back to my trailer, where I had a cooler full of cold pop. I took two bottles back to the stalled car and poured them over the fuel pump and gas lines. The driver stared in disbelief, but after he turned the key the engine burst into life.

I repeated the procedure with four other cars before we reached our destination, ended up with a big hole in my pop supply, and thought the blackest thoughts about motorists who neglected their cars. What hurt most of all was the fact that only one of the five motorists I had rescued offered to replace the pop.

Every summer, vapor locks play havoc on our highways, and it takes only a few breakdowns to bog down miles of cars. Emergency vehicles can't get through, and lives may be placed in jeopardy.

Before setting out on a trip, have the fan belt examined to make sure it is in good condition and is adjusted properly. Check the upper and lower radiator hoses, and replace them if they are cracked or soft. If you use a cardboard baffle in front of your radiator in winter, remove it when the weather warms up. Make sure that your engine is properly tuned. These precautions will keep your engine running at its coolest and minimize the possibility of stalls due to vapor locks.

The Intake Manifold

The intake manifold is a casting containing several passages which carry the fuel/air mixture from the carburetor to the combustion chambers. Since it has no moving parts, it is usually trouble-free. However, it can warp or work loose and allow the engine to draw air. This extra, or "secondary," flow of air to the engine can cause rough idling, stalling, sparkplug fouling, and loss of power. It is more apt to happen on a V-8 engine, especially during an overhaul, if the mechanics do not check the manifold for warpage, position the gasket properly, or correctly torque down the manifold bolts.

The possibility of a leaking intake manifold should not be overlooked when there is difficulty getting the engine into proper tune.

Air Cleaners

Most cars today have a highly effective dry-cartridge-type air cleaner mounted on the carburetor. (*See Diagram* 14.) It is im-

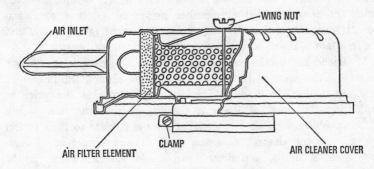

Diagram 14. *Dry-cartridge-type air cleaner*

portant to check the cartridge element at recommended intervals, as it may clog with dust and mudspray and block the passage of air. Oil-bath air cleaners also require periodic servicing, and if used without sufficient oil, do not act efficiently and allow dirt into the carburetor and engine.

Although it may not seem very important, the air cleaner is vital to the efficient and safe operation of the car. A friend of mine, a self-appointed diagnostician, had read somewhere that a plugged air filter makes a car very hard on gas. Examining his own air cleaner one day, he discovered it was plugged almost solid. With his typical brand of lightning-fast calculation, he figured he didn't really need the air cleaner anyway, as he was only driving on clean, well-paved roads. (He didn't stop to ponder how all the dust and dirt got into the filter in the first place.) Deciding to save the price of a new unit, he simply removed the old one and threw it in the back of his car.

Shortly after this, he went on deliveries for his hardware store. As he started the engine, there was a loud bang, but our hero didn't let this bother him—at least not until he stopped at the first traffic light down the road. Then he noticed that the white paint on the hood of the car was slowly turning dark brown. He jumped out, threw open the hood, and found flames belching from the carburetor. Rising to the occasion, he tore off his jacket and threw it on top of the engine. This put out the fire quite effectively, and put my friend in the market for a new jacket.

He asked me to check over his car and find out why it had a tendency to burn gasoline on both sides of the carburetor. The moment I started the engine, it burst into flames again, and only quick action with a fire extinguisher prevented a major conflagration. It turned out that the engine had a burned intake valve, and the resultant backfires were shooting flames into the carburetor.

My friend had overlooked the fact that the air cleaner also acts as a firetrap in the event of backfiring and, to save himself the price of a new air cleaner, he had put himself out of pocket the price of repainting the hood of the car, not to mention the new jacket.

One problem with air cleaners that does not relate to their proper operation is the chance of broken studs or mounting bolts. I have seen these shear off and drop down inside the carburetor. If the carburetor gets jammed by these broken pieces, it can cause a runaway car, or ruin the engine if they are drawn into the combustion chamber along with the fuel.

Emil once loaned his car to a friend who tended to have a heavy right foot. As the friend pulled away from a traffic light, he jammed the gas pedal to the floor. With a noise like an angry airplane, the car hurtled almost the full length of a city block and attained a speed of 60 mph before he had the presence of mind to turn off the ignition and apply the brakes. Shutting off the ignition while the engine was under load blew out the muffler, but this was certainly better than running wild in the middle of city traffic.

The air-cleaner support stud had worked loose and dropped down inside the carburetor, jamming the throttle wide open. If handled roughly, the air cleaner can also tear away at the base and become useless. Since most air cleaners are expensive, they should be handled with care and properly anchored and supported.

Gasoline Mileage

In the cooler times of the year I receive many complaints about poor gas mileage. "My dealer promised I'd get eighteen miles to the gallon, and I'm only getting twelve," is a typical lament.

Unless your dealer makes a complete study of your driving pattern, it is impossible for him to predict the gas mileage of your car accurately. If you are a "drive a few miles, park the car for an hour, drive another few miles" motorist, you can't expect to set any economy records. Even a brief warm-up period before leaving your driveway can gulp down a good quantity of gasoline. It takes up to twenty miles for the car to come to full operating temperature in cold weather, and if your driving pattern is strictly stop-and-go, you can't expect good gas mileage.

A heated garage or block warmer helps when parking overnight at home. (See *Accessories* chapter.) Few of us, however, have inside parking at our places of business. If the engine is already in proper tune, there is little that can be done about heavy winter fuel consumption.

I would venture to say, however, that millions of gallons of fuel are wasted from improper ignition timing—not just in winter, but all year round. Depending on carbon accumulation in the combustion chamber, many mechanics may stray away from specifications and retard or advance the ignition timing according to individual driving habits. I go along with this and have done it myself, particularly on older cars. But remember that on cars fitted with an exhaust-emission system it is vitally important to stick rigidly to the manufacturer's recommendations; otherwise, the emission system can be thrown badly out of kilter. (See *Exhaust System* chapter.) Any motor can be severely damaged if the timing is advanced to a point where the engine knocks or "pings."

Most cars are equipped with a vacuum advance mechanism and centrifugal weights which, after the timing has been set correctly, adjust the ignition timing to suit engine speed and load. Defects in either of these automatic advance units will drastically reduce power and fuel economy.

Underinflated tires can also contribute to a drop in gas mileage, as can heavy lubricants in winter, power accessories, and the "heavy footed" driver; who forces the gas pedal all the way to the floor when accelerating.

Miles per Gallon

In order to conduct an accurate mileage test the first thing to remember is to ignore the gas gauge. The gauge reading is no indication of the exact number of gallons left in the tank. Modern gas gauges cannot be relied upon for that degree of accuracy. For example, take my own car: With a full tank the gauge reads "full" for about 75 miles, and then within a few more miles it drops to ¾. From this point down to "empty," the gauge drops gradually. Even so, on one occasion when I couldn't find a service station, I ran on the "empty" mark for 20 miles without running out of fuel; so, obviously, there was a gallon or two in the tank.

Before making a mileage test, be sure that the odometer (mileage indicator) is accurate. Some highways have measured miles for testing odometers. If in doubt, have it tested by a speedometer specialist. The vehicle should be accurately tuned and serviced, including tire inflation to suit the load being carried. Observe approximate wind direction and speed—direction of smoke from chimneys or angle of trees is a good clue. Much more fuel is burned when bucking a strong headwind, whereas a lively tailwind can result in excellent mileage. Jot down the odometer reading and be sure the tank is completely filled before leaving, record every ounce of gasoline purchased at each refueling during the trip, and fill the tank again upon completion of the run. Depending on area, the price of fuel can vary, so record gallons purchased rather than dollars spent. Remember that a U.S. gallon is only ⅚ of a Canadian gallon.

To establish miles per gallon, divide total miles traveled by number of gallons purchased on the trip (including last tankful). For example, if 10 gallons of fuel were burned on a 200-mile trip, the average would be 20 miles per gallon. Many other variables affect gas mileage, such as the number of passengers, the weight of luggage, the frequency of stops and starts, or speed changes due to heavy traffic. Excessive high speed or constant pumping on the gas pedal waste a lot of fuel. Try to maintain a steady speed and, above all, avoid pumping the gas pedal. Actually, the average miles per gallon of four individual tests would give a more realistic figure of true mileage.

Choice of Fuel

Many motorists are confused as to whether they should use regular or premium gasoline in their cars, and some seem to think that the choice of a high-octane type will automatically give better performance. This is not true.

Performance depends on the engine's compression ratio, displacement, horsepower, ignition timing, and other variables. Some engines are built with a high-compression ratio; some are not. Some engines have lots of displacement and horsepower; some do not.

While it sounds quite technical, the term "compression ratio" simply means the amount of compression taking place when the piston moves up the cylinder against the fuel mixture. The engine's operation results from burning a mixture of gasoline and air, which is drawn into each cylinder, compressed by the piston and fired by the sparkplug. In most engines, combustion takes place when fuel mixture has been compressed to a little more than one eighth its original volume. (*See Diagram* 15.)

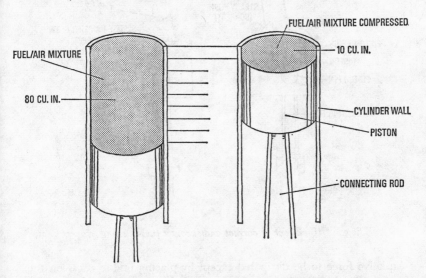

Diagram 15. *Compressing the fuel/air mixture*

If we are talking about a nine-to-one compression ratio, common in high-compression engines, this would mean that the mixture had been compressed to one ninth its original volume before being fired. High compression engines do run better with premium, or high-octane, fuel. In fact, they usually need it to run properly and avoid engine damage.

As a result of the higher compression in a high-compression engine, there is a danger that the combination of heat and pressure will cause a portion of the fuel-air mixture to explode during the burning process following ignition. The greater resistance of premium gasoline to the effects of the increased temperature and pressure in the high-compression engine reduces the chances of explosion. Its energy is applied to the piston evenly and smoothly during the power stroke. But a regular fuel burned in a high-compression engine can explode—delivering a smashing sledge-hammer blow instead of a steady push. (*See Diagram* 16.) There is no way for this

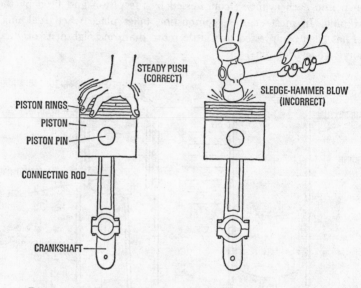

Diagram 16. *Effect of correct and incorret fuel-burning process*

explosive force to be dissipated except by placing undue stress on the engine. The severe shock from the explosion is transmitted through the engine, and you will notice the telltale knock or "ping." Usually piston heads are burned and eroded, and valves can also be burned or warped.

Most six-cylinder domestic engines and "two-barrel carb" V-8 engines are regular fuel users. Don't waste premium (higher-octane) fuels in low-compression engines that don't need them, and don't ruin a good, high-compression engine by burning fuel with too low an octane rating. The type of gas you use depends on the type of driving you do, as well as on the compression ratio of your engine and the manufacturer's recommendations.

Even when regular gas is recommended for your car, if you do not drive a few miles at a good clip on the highway a couple of times a week, you may have to switch temporarily to premium gas. The reason for this is that carbon deposits build up quite rapidly in the combustion chambers when the car is driven only at low speeds on city runs. In time, these carbon deposits will increase the compression ratio of the engine.

If your engine gets loaded with carbon deposits sufficiently to alter the compression ratio, you will hear the "pinging" noise, which forewarns of potential damage to the engine. The proper way to get rid of this carbon is to remove the cylinder head and scrape it out, but this is expensive. A more economical solution is to switch to a higher-octane gasoline until a few fast runs on the highway have blown out the carbon and returned the compression to something like normal. Chemical additives are also available to help loosen the carbon.

No-lead and Low-lead Gasoline

Since they were not formerly available at all service stations, the introduction of no-lead and low-lead fuels (to help control air pollution), has resulted in confusion for many motorists. Most car makers indicated in the Owner's Manual that their 1970 and later engines would operate on unleaded fuel, but there was no clear ruling whether it must or must not be used.

In some cases the car maker recommends using a tank full of leaded gas at regular intervals to break a steady diet of unleaded fuel. If in doubt about your choice of fuel, consult your dealer or contact the oil company from whom you buy your gasoline. (More on no-lead gasoline in the *Exhaust System* chapter.)

The Electrical System

The electrical system is comprised of literally thousands of parts. The foremost component of the system is the battery. Then, amidst a long tangle of wiring, there is an assortment of motors, switches, relays, condensers, fuses, circuit breakers, generators or alternators, and up to fifty or more lamps, ranging from sealed-beam headlights to tiny indicator bulbs.

It is interesting how readily we adjust to modern improvements, and how quickly we take them for granted. This century was into its second decade before there was any way to start a car other than by pushing it or using a large, cumbersome handcrank, which was carried in the tool kit. Today, few drivers would even recognize a starting handle.

Some early cars had a choke control out in front of the radiator to save the driver from constant trips back and forth to the controls inside the car, as he made desperate attempts to adjust the gas mixture to suit the temperamental brute. Then, of course, if he forgot to retard the spark, the engine would kick like a mule, spin the crank handle backwards, and sometimes break the arm of the pioneer motorist.

I remember one cold day when I was a little guy, I watched a farmer attempting to start a Model T Ford. After trying all the starting tricks then in vogue, such as placing a pail of red-hot coals under the oil pan, heating the block with a blow torch, trying the choke in numerous positions, courageously advancing the spark bit by bit toward the danger point, and kicking the tires, he gave up in despair and had his wife tow the monster with a team of horses.

"Son," he told me, "these critters are ten times more ornery than them horses ever knew how to be."

Nowadays you would have a hard time duplicating that scene on the farm. They just don't make cars like they did "in the good old days."

One of the major breakthroughs in North American automobile history was the introduction, around 1913, of the electric self-starting motor. In those days it was offered as the latest revolutionary option.

With the self-starter came such things as storage batteries, generators, electric lighting, and battery ignition to replace the magneto. That, I believe, is when the blacksmith-turned-mechanic began to cuss the horseless carriage and long for a return to the old hay burner with his modest need of new shoes. Even today, some good mechanics would agree with the blacksmith. They are possessed with some sort of mental block when it comes to servicing the electrical system. A mechanic who has not had special training in this field may do more harm than good—groping in the dark while hoping to stumble on the answer to the problem.

Some of the car's electrical troubles can be compared with human emotional problems. In both cases, very strange behavior can be the result. Defective electrical components can impair operating efficiency, pose severe danger (such as fire), or lead to a complete "nervous breakdown." Locating the causes requires much probing by a skilled analyst; an automobile electrical specialist is truly an "automotive psychiatrist."

When failure does occur in the electrical system, it is not enough to replace worn or damaged parts, such as sparkplugs, points, or condensers. The reason for the failure must be established and corrected; otherwise it may recur. Without proper testing equipment and training, a mechanic cannot hope to track down electrical failures. If you are not connected with a garage where the mechanics are thoroughly familiar with the electrical system, look for a specialist.

The Battery

Have you ever wondered what goes on inside that little bundle of mystery called the battery? Actually, there are no complicated moving parts; the battery's construction is quite simple. (*See Diagram 17.*)

The 12-volt car battery is composed of six compartments, or cells, each containing about seven to fifteen plates. There is always one less positive plate in each cell than there are negative plates. That is, in

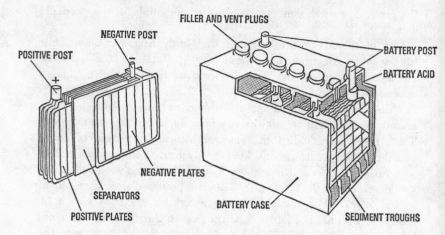

Diagram 17. *Cutaway view of battery*

a cell with fifteen plates, there are seven positive plates and eight negative plates.

The 12-volt battery with seven plates to a cell has a total of 42 plates, and one with 15 per cell has 90 plates. Premium batteries have the most plates. As well as the number of plates, their height, width and thickness are quite important.

The plates are filled with a specially formulated lead and are submerged in a mixture of sulphuric acid and water. This solution is called electrolyte. The reaction of electrolyte on the plates causes a flow of electrical current.

As this current is needed by the car, it is drawn off and the battery *discharges*. To compensate for this loss of current, the alternator or the generator supplies new current to the battery during the *charge* cycle.

A battery cannot last forever. With every discharge and charge cycle, the lead material in the plates sheds to some extent, forming a sediment at the bottom of the battery. Eventually it will shed enough to render the battery inoperative or to develop an internal short.

Troughs are built into the battery case below the plates to keep this sediment clear, but, being conductive, when it does build up enough to touch the plates, it soon discharges the battery, and replacement is necessary. Sometimes a buildup of sediment will cause only a minor short and the battery will keep operating, provided it is kept charged by regular use of the car.

This latter point reminds me of some of the additives that have shown up through the years—"guaranteed" to revitalize the ailing battery. To my knowledge, there is no additive that will replace the lead that is shed from the plates and drops to the bottom of the battery case.

Batteries must wear out, but it is surprising how long some batteries will last. A doctor once brought his car to my garage for a checkup. His battery, he said, was over six years old and had never let him down. He wanted to know how much longer it was likely to last.

I asked his permission to take the battery apart and check the plates, with the understanding that I would sell him a new one at cost if there was any serviceable life left in it. When I got it apart, I found that most of the plates were more than two thirds worn out. Both the doctor and I were happy with the outcome of this bit of practical research. I still gave him a new battery at cost, and he invited me to his cottage for several skiing weekends.

Even when the plates have not shed sufficiently to cause an internal short, gradual plate wear can result in sudden failure on a cold morning. A new battery at 80 degrees F. is just about 100 percent efficient; at 0 degrees F. the same battery has only about half its normal capacity. When the plates are half worn away and the mercury drops to zero, there is only one quarter of the normal reserve to do a lot more work than it would have to do if the temperature were still in the 80s. Much more electrical energy is required to turn an engine that lies in a bath of oil which has thickened from the cold. If it doesn't start immediately, there is no reserve, and the battery quits.

Ratings of Batteries

Batteries are rated by ampere hours, or the time it takes the battery to discharge to a level where it is no longer effective. Usually, the more plates a battery has, the greater its ampere-hour rating. The higher the ampere-hour rating, the greater reserve the battery has. For instance, a 12-volt battery rated at 60 ampere hours should be able to discharge 3 amperes for 20 hours before the charge drops to the point where the battery is no longer serviceable.

Some motorists believe that if the generator or alternator suddenly quits, they must stop driving immediately. However, the average fully charged battery should operate the starter motor several times and power the headlights for about three hours before running down.

With no lights or accessories operating, the engine could run for possibly 24 hours or more, but before continuing to drive, the defective charging unit should be checked to assure that no further damage could result. A cheap or partially discharged battery would run down proportionately faster.

The older the battery, the lower the ampere-hour reserve and the greater the chance of failure when it faces heavy electrical demands.

Replacing the Battery

To avoid the irritation of sudden failure, I replace the battery in my car at the beginning of every third winter. It may be possible to save a few dollars by flogging the battery to the point of failure, but knowing there is an abundance of reserve energy when the engine fails to catch right away is mighty reassuring. I'm sure that no motorist whose car battery has suddenly failed during the season's first cold snap or when he is out in the wilderness, will dispute this point.

When replacement becomes necessary, select a unit that is at least the equivalent of the original battery. A car loaded with extra electrical accessories may require a premium high-capacity battery.

Usually, the longer the guarantee, the better the quality and the greater the capacity and reserve power of the battery. Keep in mind, however, that most warranties are on a pro rata basis. If, for example, a $27 battery is guaranteed for three years and fails after two years, the warranty will be worth about $9 toward a new unit.

Filling the Battery

The periodic addition of water is necessary to ensure that the electrolyte stays at the proper level. If the battery is underfilled, the exposed parts of the plates will harden and become chemically inactive. If the battery is overfilled, the electrolyte can spill out, resulting in severe corrosion of the battery's support mechanism and other vital components.

At one time it was recommended that only distilled water be used in batteries, but today a good grade of drinking water is considered satisfactory. However, water with high mineral content should be avoided. Some motorists argue that the impurities in the water in certain areas are damaging to the battery and insist that distilled water be used. Nevertheless, I can't remember when I last saw distilled water available at service stations or garages.

Battery Failure

Batteries, even new ones, which remain in a semidischarged condition, are a major cause of starting failure, especially in cold weather. The plates can harden, reducing the desired chemical reaction. If this happens, it may be difficult, if not impossible, to fully charge the battery, and replacement is the only cure. The electrolyte can also freeze in a badly discharged battery, destroying the plates and cracking the case.

Overcharging the battery is just as deadly. The electrolyte becomes overheated and, among other damaging effects, the plates will buckle and disintegrate. Ignition points that need frequent replacement, or a battery that frequently requires water, indicate overcharging. To avoid premature battery failure, it is essential that the current output of the generator or alternator be checked and, if necessary, adjusted during the routine engine tune-up.

The best way to charge the car battery is the natural way—with the car generator or alternator. Low-output chargers which can be plugged in overnight are available at most accessory stores at modest cost. They supply only a few amps, keep the battery full charged, and are a good investment for the short-run, stop-and-go driver.

An astonishing number of batteries fail because of obvious neglect. In a neglected battery, mounds of corrosion collect on and between the battery posts and cables. I have seen this corrosion build up to such an extent that it almost completely insulates the battery cable from the post. When this happens, the starter starves for current and refuses to budge.

A puzzling thing can happen at the same time. The starter won't turn, but lights and horn will work. Don't be deceived by this and blame the starter motor. The reason the starter won't work is that it draws about 200 amps, compared to something like 20 amps needed by the horn and lights.

Worse things can happen if a neglected ground strap corrodes all the way through and snaps off. I found this out the hard way when I was in my late teens.

Driving down a winding road late at night, I was surprised to see my headlights flare out brightly into the distance. Then, before my eyes could even adjust to the glare, total blackness. Completely blinded, I wound up in the ditch on the left side of the road.

My battery ground connection had broken off, and the full charge of the generator had overloaded the lighting circuit, brightening the lights to many times their normal brilliance and burning them out.

The cable doesn't have to break right off to cause this failure. All it needs is sufficient corrosion between the battery posts and cables. Merely cleaning the outside of the connections is useless. The top of the battery must be cleaned and the cables removed with the proper puller, and the inside of the cables must be scraped clean with a cleaning tool. The same must be done to the battery posts.

The connections on the other ends of the battery cables should also be cleaned and tightened. Headlights that flare up when the engine is raced, as well as erratic or sluggish starter-motor action, are clues to electrical corrosion problems.

Battery Checks

Establishing the capacity or condition of a new or old battery is really quite simple, provided the technician is familiar with the testing procedure. Involved in a thorough battery check are the following points:

Inspection of the entire case for cracks or leaks.

Inspection of battery posts, clamps, and cables for breakage, loose connections, corrosion, or other faults obvious to the eye.

Making sure the top of the battery is clean and dry. Dirt and electrolyte on top cause a constant discharge.

All cell vents must be open.

The battery carrier must be solidly anchored, and the hold-down mechanism tightened properly. A loose battery can become damaged by vibration and jarring. If the hold-down mechanism is too tight, it may cause the battery case to buckle and crack.

Raised cell covers or a warped case usually mean that the battery has been overheated or overcharged.

Inspection of the electrolyte level. If it is below the top of the plates, add water. If it is not below the plates, a hydrometer test should be made before the level of the liquid is adjusted.

In order to make further tests, it is necessary to note the ampere-hour rating of the battery—sometimes printed on the case. If not shown, the serviceman must refer to the manufacturer's specifications to establish the capacity of the type of battery in your vehicle.

Any battery that is less than three-quarters charged should be recharged. The serviceman should then make a load test. This simply means the use of high-discharge-rate test equipment, which subjects the battery to a severe discharge for fifteen seconds.

Right after this test, a 12-volt battery should not show less than three-quarters charged.

Any battery that passes this test is usually O.K. A battery that doesn't pass the test should be replaced.

Care in Handling a Battery

The battery can be dangerous. As well as being loaded with highly corrosive acid, the chemical reaction inside the battery generates oxygen and hydrogen gases. This explosive mixture fills the space above the plates, and sometimes the atmosphere immediately surrounding the battery. Never place an open flame near your battery; the resulting explosion could spatter sulphuric acid over you, causing severe burns and possible blindness.

If battery acid does come in contact with your skin or clothing, immediately flush the affected area with large amounts of water.

Be very careful in handling the battery. Emil once had a close call with a battery. He was installing a new battery in a car; as he was picking it up, the carrying cable snapped and the battery crashed to the floor. Corrosive acid splashed up onto his face and hands.

Fortunately, Emil was well-versed in the safety procedures for handling acids, and he immediately grabbed a hose, doused himself with water, and escaped with only minor burns.

The Generator

The conventional generator has been doing a good job of keeping batteries charged for many a decade. However, the unit is not capable of high-current output at low engine speeds, which accounts for the number of flat batteries in cars which crawl around the city, often at night, with a heavy load on the battery and an insufficient supply of electricity from the generator.

Think of your battery as a bank account. If you have $100 in the account and write out checks for $120, your account "goes flat" and, unless you have a friendly bank manager, the check will bounce. As you withdraw electrical "funds" from the battery, your generator, like the friendly bank manager, puts them back again. But there is a limit to what the generator can do—when the demand gets too high, it may let you down. Then the battery becomes "overdrawn" and refuses to keep your lights burning or start your car.

The generator is driven by a V-belt from the engine crankshaft pulley, and it is important that this drive belt be properly adjusted and in good condition. If the belt breaks or slips, the generator does not turn, and no current can be produced.

The Alternator

The alternator, found on most North American cars, is just another kind of generator. One of the major advantages of the alternator is that, even when the engine is idling, it charges to some degree. The conventional generator does not begin to charge the battery until the engine is above idling speed.

Despite its over-all efficiency, the alternator cannot begin to produce electricity if the battery is completely dead. Even with cars that can be push-started (many cannot), if the battery is completely dead, the car with an alternator will never start. It can only be started with booster cables from another battery or with a recharged battery. On the other hand, a generator will generate current when a battery is completely dead, if the car is pushed a short distance.

But a note of caution: If booster cables are used, make sure that you connect the *positive* post of one battery to the *positive* post of the other, and *negative* to *negative*. A mismatch of battery terminals will result in a burned-out alternator. Be guided only by the "+" (positive) or "—" (negative) signs on the battery posts. The positive post is usually thicker than the negative post, but if in doubt, leave it alone.

To avoid the possibility of a short circuit when using the battery in another car as a booster, make sure the bumpers of the two vehicles are not touching and that there is no other metal connection such as a tow chain.

The Voltage Regulator

The job of the voltage regulator is to control the electrical output of the generator or alternator. Failure of this unit can cause a battery to discharge itself or become overcharged.

Its operation is quite complex, and its maintenance should be undertaken only by qualified persons. I have seen many generators, alternators, and batteries replaced when the fault lay in the regulator.

Electrical Accessories

Cars have a multitude of accessories which use considerable electricity. They should be used with discretion when the car is driven under stop-and-go conditions. Even the alternator cannot perform miracles and cope with the battery discharge brought on by indiscriminate use of every electrical device.

Unlike the domestic service in homes, where at least two wires are required to operate appliances and lamps, electrical devices in the car need only a single wire; the metal body of the car acts as the ground.

The wires are often broken by the viselike grip of ice, by chafing, or by abuse. When wires break, an open circuit sometimes results, which does no harm other than deprive a component of its operating power. At other times, the broken wire will touch against the body of the car, causing a damaging short circuit and possibly fire.

Fuses and Circuit Breakers

Whenever you buy a car, find out where the fuse panel is before you have trouble. I know a man who didn't. It took him four hours of searching before he eventually found it tucked away under the back seat. (*See Diagram* 18.)

Cars, like houses, are equipped with fuses or circuit breakers to safeguard against serious damage when a short circuit occurs. The fuse burns out when too much current passes through. The circuit

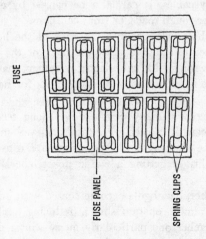

Diagram 18. *Typical fuse panel*

breaker, usually installed in the headlight circuit, opens and closes the circuit to guard against system damage, while still providing the driver with enough illumination to bring his car safely to a halt.

If the lights suddenly begin to blink on and off, it indicates that your circuit breaker has come into operation because of a short circuit. The lights should be turned off as quickly as possible, and the car taken in for repairs.

Circuit breakers are frequently used in other places, such as the power windows.

A sensible precaution against being stranded by a short circuit is to carry a few spare fuses in the glove compartment. Should an intermittent short occur, a new fuse might last long enough to permit driving to the nearest repair shop.

Headlights

A couple of generations have passed since the driver relied on a flickering oil lamp to guide him down the road. Today's North American cars are equipped with sealed beams—units that combine bulb, reflector, and lens in comfortable isolation from weather and corrosion. Like any lightbulb, they will eventually burn out, but usually they give trouble-free service until old age takes its toll.

Motorists sometimes complain about several sealed beams that have burned out in rapid succession. This is an unusual problem and can be caused by overcharging of the generator or alternator, or by dirty, corroded battery cables. It can also be caused by damage resulting from driving over rough roads, or from collisions.

Sometimes a hole will rust into the back of the headlight housing and permit water to splash against the back of the sealed beam. If nothing seems wrong with the electrical system, have your garageman remove the headlight assembly and check for holes in the housing.

It is surprising how many people drive along seemingly unaware that a sealed beam is burned out; the "one-eyed monster" hurtling toward us on the highway is far too common. To avoid this danger, plus the possibility of getting a traffic ticket, check your headlights occasionally.

In dirty weather, headlights become coated with grime that quickly bakes into an almost opaque shield, reducing visibility to almost nothing. I remember one particularly messy winter day when I had to stop four times on a 50-mile trip to clean my lights in order to see the road.

While glare from approaching vehicles on crowded highways is one of the prime hazards of night driving, seldom do motorists suggest adjusting the headlights when the car is being serviced.

One of the main reasons for rejection in safety spot checks is faulty headlight adjustment. When were yours last tested?

Dimmer Switch

Sealed beams have two filaments, one for high beam and one for low. A dimmer switch allows the driver to switch from one beam to the other. These switches seldom fail, but when they do, they cost little to replace.

Some cars have automatic electronic units fitted to the front of the car to dim the lights at the approach of another car. The dimmer switch also operates the high-beam indicator on the dash.

Turn Signals

Driving can be uncomfortable and dangerous when the turn signals don't function. Although hand signals are still legal in many areas, the man in the car behind you is usually not watching for them— he's on the alert for a flashing light. Besides, putting your hand out the window in the rain or the cold is both awkward and unpleasant.

If the filament in one bulb burns out, the flasher is unable to flash any of the signal bulbs on that side of the car. This condition is usually indicated by a steady glow from the turn-signal indicator light on one side of the dashboard and the absence of a clicking noise from the flasher.

The flasher itself will occasionally wear out or even work loose in its socket, resulting in total failure of the system.

Signal lights are seldom given much thought until they fail, but a little common-sense maintenance can save a lot of aggravation. Salt and moisture can eat away the lamp housings and make the bulb sockets inoperative. To avoid this, at least on older vehicles, remove the lenses or socket assemblies occasionally and check for corrosion.

Interior Lights

In addition to the courtesy lights that turn on when you open the door, there are a variety of other lights inside the car—illuminating the glove box, the ashtrays, and the various instruments and gauges.

Not exposed to the weather, they usually last a long time. But they do burn out, and the switches do sometimes fail. If checking or replacing the bulb does not restore illumination, check for a faulty switch, blown fuse, or broken wire.

Motors

In addition to the starting motor, the car is usually equipped with several smaller motors to drive heaters, fans, defrosters, windshield wipers and washers, and sometimes power windows, power seats, and the power top on convertibles.

These motors seldom fail, but when they do, it is wise to check for a poor connection, a faulty switch, or a blown fuse before buying a new one.

Switches

Depending on the number of lights, motors, and other electrical devices on the car, the number of switches can run from two to twenty.

The headlight switch can turn on headlights, parking lights, courtesy or dome lights, and, when equipped with an integral rheostat, can lower the brilliance of the instrument panel lights.

Motors and other lights are operated by switches which are sometimes located in out-of-the-way places. The switch for a heater motor may be hidden behind the dashboard. Courtesy lights that go on when the doors are opened are operated by a switch mounted in the doorpost. The glove-box light is operated by a similar switch.

Devices which may not be thought of as switches include the horn ring and the directional-signal lever. Do not punch or stab the horn ring. It is generally made of die-cast metal and can break—as can the signal-switching mechanism inside the hub of the steering wheel.

The directional-signal lever is a switch which allows the driver to signal a turn, keeps the signal lights flashing while the wheel is turned, and then turns itself off when the car has turned the corner. To do this, it relies on a small ratchet assembly on the steering column, which can be broken if abused.

When making a lane change, sometimes the mechanism does not move sufficiently to allow it to cancel the signal after the lane change has been made. If this happens, cancel it manually to avoid confusing the driver behind.

Many cars are equipped with an emergency switch, which flashes all the signal lights simultaneously. These lights are useful when you are stopped on a busy highway.

The Horn

The horn can sometimes stick—usually at the most embarrassing moment. There is no point in cringing behind the steering wheel hoping to become invisible—you don't have to if you know how to turn the horn off.

Have your serviceman show you how to remove the fuse or disconnect the horn relay. The relay itself seldom fails, but if it does, you have no horn. This is simple to diagnose and can be repaired at modest cost.

Gauges

Several gauges on the instrument panel are there to relay urgent messages when necessary. Keeping an eye on the speedometer is just common sense. On the other hand, keeping an eye on an inaccurate speedometer isn't going to do much good. I've seen speedometers off by as much as 15 mph. If you doubt the accuracy of your speedometer, have it checked by a specialist. Few traffic courts will sympathize with your claim that the speedometer showed you were traveling at the legal speed limit.

The Oil Gauge

There are two types of oil-pressure gauges. One uses a pressure tube through which the oil travels directly to the gauge; the other employs an electrical sending unit. The electrical type is most commonly used today.

Many cars have a red warning light that comes on only when the oil pressure drops and does not indicate the amount of pressure. The engine should be shut off the instant this red light shows, because the engine can burn out almost instantaneously without lubrication.

The Temperature Gauge

The heat gauge or red warning light (depending on the make of car) is actuated by a heat-sensitive unit fitted into the engine block. With the regular "needle" type of heat gauge, as the engine temperature increases, a message is transmitted from the block to the gauge in the instrument panel, which, in turn, moves the needle to indicate the temperature of the engine.

The red warning light is also activated by a heat-sensitive block unit, but it must be remembered that this warning light comes on only when the engine is already overheated—it does not indicate a "Cold" or "Normal" engine.

In addition to the red warning light, some cars have a green light which comes on when the car is started and the engine is cold. This green light goes out when the engine reaches a temperature of about 120 degrees F. But beyond that temperature, there is no further warning until the engine overheats, at which point the red signal light warns the motorist.

Since the coolant under seventeen pounds of pressure does not boil until the temperature reaches about 263 degrees F., it is conceivable that the engine temperature may reach 230 degrees F. before the red warning light comes on. This does not necessarily mean that you have a serious problem; it could merely be temporary trouble. For example, if your car is bogged down in heavy traffic on a hot day, your cooling fluid could become hot enough to actuate the red warning light.

If the light does not soon go out, the car may be overheating due to insufficient cooling fluid. If in doubt, it is best to pull off the road, shut off the engine, and wait for a few minutes. Then, when you are *sure* that the engine has cooled sufficiently to remove the pressure cap safely, check the height of the coolant in the top tank of the radiator.

Ammeter and Generator Light

Again, in many instances, a red warning light has replaced the ammeter. The red light only warns of trouble, or discharge, while an ammeter indicates degree of charge and discharge of the battery. If the red light should flash on, or if the ammeter needle shows "discharge," it is not as serious as a danger signal from the oil or water system. Nonetheless, it should be checked immediately at the nearest garage.

The Gas Gauge

The gas tank contains a float which sends an electrical signal to the gauge on your dashboard, indicating the amount of gas in the tank.

The sending unit can fail or a wire can break, leaving the gauge showing full as the tank gets closer and closer to empty. If you seem to be getting miraculous mileage, gas up. If the tank takes several gallons and your gauge showed full before filling up, have it checked. In some areas you can be fined for running out of fuel in tunnels or expressways.

Red Warning Lights

The major danger posed by red warning lights is failure, or even removal, of the bulb. A friend of mine was driving on a highway when his oil-gauge light flashed on. The car seemed to be running properly, but he pulled into a service center just to make sure. An enthusiastic apprentice asked if he could help, and my friend asked for a mechanic. The apprentice explained that they were all busy, but that perhaps he could take care of it. My friend left the car and went to have a fast cup of coffee, then returned and was told it was just a simple adjustment and was "all fixed up" at no charge.

A few miles down the highway, the engine began making expensive noises, and the mechanic at the next service station confirmed that the engine was burned out. It turned out that the oil-pump screen was plugged and there was very little circulation. The "helpful" apprentice had simply removed the warning-light bulb to eliminate the annoyance of the flashing red light.

To make sure something like this doesn't happen to you, check your warning lights occasionally. When you first turn on your ignition, the red oil light should glow until the engine is started. If it does not, there is trouble in the circuit, or the bulb has failed. Get it fixed—it could save your engine.

The Starter Motor

The hardest-worked and heaviest-current-consuming electric motor in the entire car is the starter motor. Without it, we would be back with the handcrank—not a very cheerful prospect with today's massive, high-compression engines. For one thing, it would be almost impossible to turn over the engine fast enough to start it, and for another, arm-fracture and heart-attack statistics would soar.

Buried underneath the car, the starter is often forgotten as we casually twist the ignition key and listen to the roar of hundreds of horses coming to life. When the starter is engaged, a small gear at its rear is meshed with a considerably larger gear which is attached to the flywheel.

When trouble in starting does occur, the starter is sometimes condemned when, in fact, there is nothing wrong with it.

Cars with automatic transmission can only be started in Neutral or Park, because of a safety switch attached to the linkage. This switch shuts off electricity to the starter when the car is in reverse or one of the forward gears. It can sometimes fail and shut off electricity to the starter in any transmission setting. Many starters have been replaced because of failure in this small, inexpensive part.

Teeth stripped from the flywheel ring gear can also cause the starter motor to spin uselessly. The condition of the flywheel ring gear should be checked when a starter is being repaired.

The starter is usually engaged by an extreme righthand turn of the ignition key. On older models it is sometimes actuated by depressing the gas pedal or by a push button on the floor or dashboard. Any one of these mechanisms can fail, and again the starter may be blamed.

The Starter Solenoid

When you turn the key or engage your starter in some other way, what actually happens first is that you actuate another switch—the solenoid switch. This is an electromagnetic switch which supplies current to the starter. If the solenoid is not working properly, it may cause the starter motor to fail.

Ignition

As explained in the *Engine* chapter, when the fuel/air mixture has been compressed in the combustion chamber, it has to be ignited. This is the job of the sparkplug. But with as many as eight cylinders to be fired in rapid succession, the right plug must fire at the right time—with split-second efficiency. The 6 or 12 volts available from the car battery is nowhere near sufficient to fire the sparkplug. Much higher voltage, usually about 20,000 volts, is needed. (*See Diagrams* 19 and 20.)

Other components of the ignition system, the distributor assembly and coil, provide this acute timing and high voltage.

The Coil

When the electricity leaves the battery, it flows through the ignition coil and builds up to the needed voltage, which is then fed to the distributor.

The coil seldom fails and needs little attention. For this reason, it is often overlooked as a trouble source, and is frequently ignored during an engine tune-up. It should be tested when the ignition system is under repair.

Be careful of that black, high-tension wire leading out from the middle of the coil. If you handle it when the engine is running, it may give you a severe shock.

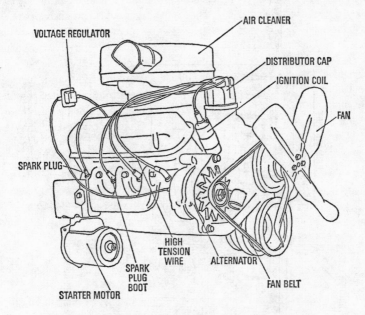

Diagram 19. *Typical V-8 engine*

The Distributor

The job of the distributor is to distribute the high voltage from the coil via the high-tension cables to the sparkplugs, causing them to ignite at precisely the right moment. Driven by the engine's crankshaft, the distributor rotor directs the charge from the coil to one of the four, six, or eight towers in the distributor cap into which the high-tension cables are plugged.

There are two frequent adjustments made to the distributor. One is the actual timing, where the distributor body is rotated around the rotor assembly to either retard or advance the spark; the other is the setting of the breaker points which control the pulses of electricity through the coil.

Motorists sometimes wonder why points have to be replaced periodically. They are one of the hardest-worked components in the ignition system. In addition to handling surges of electricity, they must open and close about 12,000 times per minute on a V-8 engine when traveling at 60 mph. Defective points are one of the most frequent causes of hard starting and poor performance.

In time, these points wear out or, more properly, burn out from the

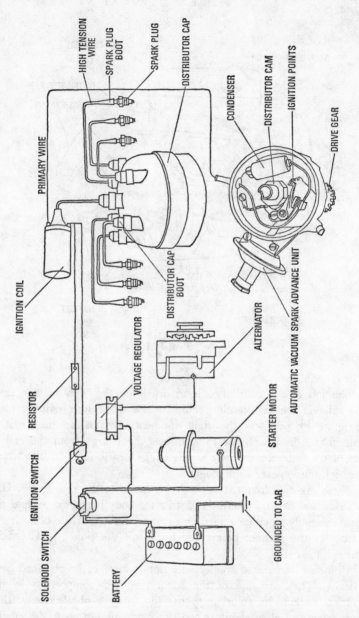

HIGH TENSION WIRE
SPARK PLUG BOOT
SPARK PLUG
DISTRIBUTOR CAP
CONDENSER
DISTRIBUTOR CAM
IGNITION POINTS
DRIVE GEAR
PRIMARY WIRE
IGNITION COIL
DISTRIBUTOR CAP BOOT
RESISTOR
VOLTAGE REGULATOR
ALTERNATOR
AUTOMATIC VACUUM SPARK ADVANCE UNIT
IGNITION SWITCH
STARTER MOTOR
SOLENOID SWITCH
GROUNDED TO CAR
BATTERY

Diagram 20. *Arrangement of starting system, ignition system, and charging system* constant surges of electricity as they open and close. If these points are improperly adjusted, their life can be seriously shortened—starting will be difficult, and engine performance will suffer.

Points should be checked frequently and replaced at the first sign of deterioration. It is also good policy to check generator or alternator output when installing new points. I have seen points burned out in a thousand miles when too much current was passed through them.

Very often overlooked are the centrifugal weights inside the distributor, which automatically advance the ignition timing as engine speed increases. If they do not work properly, a lot of power and fuel are wasted at higher speeds.

Another type of automatic spark advance is through a vacuum-operated unit which advances the spark at higher speeds and retards it at lower speeds to avoid pinging. The most common cause of failure in this type of unit is a ruptured diaphragm or plugged or broken lines feeding the vacuum to the unit.

I would estimate that in 50 percent of all tune-ups, these two automatic units (the centrifugal weights and the vacuum spark advance) are completely overlooked. Beware of gimmick advertisements offering tune-ups for a ridiculously low figure; tuning a car properly is time-consuming, and prices can vary according to the amount of work required.

The Condenser

The condenser is an integral part of the ignition system. It protects the breaker points from excessive burning and works in conjunction with the coil to build up high voltage for the sparkplugs. Although it is an insignificant-looking metal cylinder weighing about one ounce, if it fails you're grounded.

I had an early eye-opener to what a faulty condenser can do. When I was about fourteen, right after my older brother had bought a used 1924 Star, we set off to visit friends about twenty miles out of town. Halfway there, the car started to miss and backfire violently.

We stopped at several garages, where the points got a filing and adjusting that they had never had before. Eventually, the car just quit. While we sat in the blazing sun outside yet another garage, the mechanic vainly groped about for four hours.

We finally gave up and took a bus home. The next day the car was towed back to the used-car dealer who had sold it to my brother, where a faulty condenser was found to be the culprit.

This was my first experience in learning how much trouble the ignition system can give. I have seen countless cars on which a lot of money has been spent replacing the wrong ignition parts because of faulty diagnosis.

To minimize starting problems and engine emissions, a new type of electronic ignition system was first offered as optional equipment in 1972. It became standard equipment on all 1973 models produced in North America. This device does away with both ignition points and condenser by using the principle of varying magnetic fields in a distributor that has no touching mechanical parts.

The variation is produced as a center unit inside the distributor (known as a reluctor) revolves and induces electrical charges in the circuit leading to a transisterized electrical control unit. This in turn directs the charges to the ignition coil. Here they are amplified up to 4000 times and returned to the electronic distributor, where they are directed to the right sparkplug at the point of firing. The only wear areas in the distributor are simple bearings requiring oil every 24,000 miles.

The Resistor

In the mid-fifties another component, the resistor, was incorporated into the typical ignition system. While it has been with us for all these years, a lot of motorists are unaware of its existence. However, if it fails, the engine can be completely immobilized.

The resistor came into general use with the introduction of the 12-volt battery. After the engine has been started, the resistor cuts in to lower the battery voltage going to the ignition system, thereby protecting the breaker points from burning and pitting.

Ignition Switch

Occasionally the ignition switch can fail and prevent the car from starting. It can also stick in the start position and lead to serious problems.

A young lady came into my garage one day to complain of a funny whirring noise in her car. She had been driving with her ignition switch stuck in the far-right position for more than an hour, and the starter had burned out.

The ignition switch has a spring to pull it back from the start position. If this spring breaks, the switch can jam. When starting your car, be sure that the switch springs back to the left as soon as the engine starts. If it does not, twist it back and then have it repaired.

Never hold the switch in the start position after the engine is running. If you do, you may damage the teeth on the flywheel gear or ruin the starter.

Sparkplugs

How long will sparkplugs last? I've seen some fail at 3000 miles, while others are still going strong at 20,000 miles. Driving pattern is the most important factor in the life of plugs. The stop-and-go, short-run, city driver cannot expect too much mileage from plugs.

I guaranteed my tune-ups for six months or 10,000 miles, whichever came first. But if a city-driven car came in for a tune-up and my records showed that the sparkplugs had already gone about 7000 miles, I would sometimes suggest that the motorist install new plugs. I pointed out to him that the labor involved in properly cleaning and gapping the old plugs was worth nearly half the price of new ones. Then I would offer to install a set at a discount. I did this because I wanted the customer to enjoy the full advantages of his tune-up for as long as possible, and, besides, I could hardly guarantee my tune-up for 10,000 miles if the plugs were good for perhaps only another 3000.

The sparkplug insulators (the porcelain section which sits outside the engine) must be clean and unbroken. A crack in these insulators or a coating of dirt, grease, or salt can offer a convenient path for the high voltage to escape into the engine block without firing the sparkplug. This leads to hard starting, poor engine efficiency, and excessive fuel consumption.

High-tension Cables

Damaged high-tension cables can also rob the sparkplugs of their vital 20,000 volts. Years ago, these high-tension cables were composed of a steel core with a thick coating of insulation. However, with the growth of television and other high-frequency electronic communications systems, it was found that there was too much interference from automobile ignition systems.

A number of governments eventually moved to ban the older type of high-tension cables, and the only kind manufacturers now install is formed of a cloth type of cord impregnated with carbon. This cable does a good job of eliminating radio and television interference, but is more easily damaged by abuse.

If one of these cables is grabbed and given a mighty yank to pull the connector away from the sparkplug, the internal carbon core can be ruptured, resulting in poor transmission of the high voltage to the sparkplug. Engine misses and roughness follow.

When you are handling high-tension cables, treat them with respect. If you get hold of the business end while the engine is running, about 20,000 volts are going to run up your arm and give you quite a shock. Since the amperage is low, this shock is not deadly, but it can make you jump enough to hurt yourself on the hood or fenders of the car.

If you remove the cable, grasp it carefully and firmly by the heavy rubber insulator near the sparkplug connection and pull away gently.

One final note: Keep that engine clean; dampness that clings to dirt in the area of the distributor, coil, high-tension cables, and sparkplugs can steal every ounce of electrical energy from the sparkplugs. This often accounts for the car that refuses to start on damp mornings.

How important is cleaning of the ignition? Ignition cleaning should be included in a tune-up. If I were tuning my own car and I didn't have enough time to do both the tune-up and ignition cleaning, I would skip the tune-up and clean the ignition.

A variety of solvents or cleaning compounds are available, but using them is a messy business. Your local garage is usually equipped to do the job properly at a modest cost.

The electrical system is one of the most complicated aspects of your car. Be sure to ask an expert if you have any doubts about its performance.

The Cooling System

The cooling system is one of the hardest-worked systems of the entire car, and its proper functioning is vital to the operating economy and life of the engine. Automatic transmissions, too, frequently rely on the engine's cooling system to maintain proper operating temperatures. Despite this, I have found that the cooling system is frequently misunderstood or neglected by both car owners and service repairmen. (*See Diagram* 21.)

Failure of any one of the many cooling-system components may be disastrous. Overheating may crack the block, which could mean a whole new engine. Excessive heat may also destroy the cylinder heads. On the other hand, if the cooling system operates at too low a temperature, probably due to thermostat failure, oil circulation may be restricted or completely blocked by the formation of sludge, and the engine will fail.

The things some motorists do to their car's cooling system, either unwittingly or in a misplaced effort to keep costs down, range from the hilarious to the tragic. Shortly after I opened my own garage, an old-timer drove in with great clouds of steam puffing from his car engine. He climbed out and began unscrewing the radiator cap. There was a sudden flash, a loud bang, and the engine caught fire. We pushed the car out to the street and, as the old gent stood there gazing incredulously at the flames, the radiator exploded and the whole car began burning furiously. By the time the fire department arrived, the car had burned to ashes.

It took a while to extract an explanation from the speechless owner, but it seemed that someone had told him that straight coal oil made an excellent antifreeze. They neglected to mention that coal oil is highly explosive when heated.

Oh, well, those were Depression days, and we all tried to save a buck—even if it sometimes wound up costing us more than we had

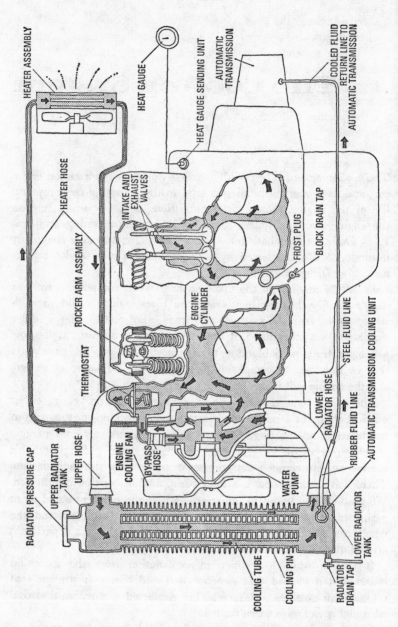

Diagram 21. *Side view of engine cooling system*

saved. Anyway, I'm sure nobody will argue the point when I recommend the use of only ethylene glycol as an antifreeze.

If your cooling system is not abused by the addition of coal oil and is properly serviced at the correct intervals, it is almost foolproof. But neglect can quickly add up to inconvenience and costly, unnecessary repairs.

In warmer climates, if straight water is used, the motorist should remember to use a cooling-system additive that combines a rust inhibitor and a water-pump lubricant. Used at all times, it can prevent rust formation and failure of the water pump. The water must also be clean and free from all foreign matter.

Frequent addition of well water can be quite harmful if the water contains certain minerals. I have seen radiators plugged solid with limestone and other mineral solids when water from high-mineral-content areas has been continually used. If you know the water is loaded with minerals, use rainwater or other soft water.

To avoid problems, repair a leaking cooling system at the first opportunity. An efficient, leakproof cooling system should operate for months under normal driving conditions without adding fluid.

Antifreeze

Motorists who live in the cooler zones where antifreeze is necessary, often ask me such questions as: In warmer weather should antifreeze be drained from the radiator? Left in? Thrown away? Stored until next winter?

Here is what I do with my own car, and I know many others who follow my example: Have the antifreeze tested in the fall; if it is clean and strong enough, no harm will be done by using it for a few years, provided a can of rust inhibitor and water-pump lube is added. If the solution is not up to strength but is still clean, add a few quarts of pure antifreee until the desired degree of protection is reached. All good brands of permanent-type ethylene-glycol-base antifreeze contain lubricants and rust inhibitors, but they deteriorate and must be replaced each year. Most modern water pumps have no grease fittings and require this additive for internal lubrication.

A man who has been a radiator specialist for more than twenty years told me that he drove his last car for four years without once changing the antifreeze. It was, he stressed, just as clean when he traded the car as when brand-new. "All it takes," he said, "is a little common-sense care and maintenance. Changing antifreeze every season is literally pouring money down the drain."

Any brand-name ethylene-glycol-base antifreee is satisfactory to protect the cooling system in cold weather. Equal parts of ethylene glycol and water protect down to 34 degrees below zero. Straight ethylene glycol should never be used. It congeals in extreme cold and prevents proper circulation. For proper "depth" protection, a mixture of 60 percent ethylene glycol and 40 percent water protects to 62 degrees below zero.

When filling the radiator at the end of the winter, many motorists are tempted to add straight water. Then one morning the outside temperature drops unexpectedly to zero, and they worry for fear they might have a cracked block or might split a radiator. Neither of these calamities is likely, provided there is even a very weak solution of antifreeze in the cooling system. As an example, if the cooling system is one of twelve-quart capacity but there are only two quarts of antifreeze to ten quarts of water, the car is protected to 19 degrees above zero. With this mixture, however, the temperature could even drop below zero and it is doubtful there would be any serious damage. It takes the expansion of solid ice to crack the radiator or block, and the coolant will not turn to solid ice provided some antifreeze remains. But it *will* turn to a thick slush, preventing proper circulation through the radiator and engine-cooling jackets. If the engine is started, this slush will melt readily in the block, but will prevent circulation by remaining in the hoses and radiator. The engine will soon overheat as the coolant in the cooling jackets boils, and then there is real danger of cracking the block.

Never one to be satisfied until I have proven a theory myself, I once put one ounce of ethylene-glycol antifreeze and seven ounces of water in a thin glass tube and placed it in the freezer section of my refrigerator, which operates at zero. I checked it twenty-four hours later, and it had turned into a thick slush which I could easily crush with my fingers. There was no evidence of solid ice, which would have cracked the tube.

If the temperature drops well below freezing and you suspect your antifreeze mixture is weak, it is not wise to start the motor until the temperature rises or the car has been towed to a warm garage to thaw out. If you have to use the car at once, there are certain things that can be done. First, remove the radiator cap and check to see if there is liquid or slush inside. If it is liquid, you have no problem—

go ahead and start the engine. But if you see slush, place a thick cover over the front grille area and run the motor for about five minutes or until the temperature gauge reads normal. Then turn off the key immediately. Wait for a few minutes until the heat generated by the engine has had time to melt the slush and restore circulation. Carefully remove the radiator cap and check again. It may be necessary to repeat the process several times, depending on the temperature and thickness of the slush.

Another approach is to pour boiling water down the outside of the radiator core and over the water hoses. This should melt the slush sufficiently to allow safe starting of the engine. I have even heard of electric hair dryers being used to thaw out slush in the radiator core and hoses. But under no circumstances run the engine until the coolant boils.

The logical way to avoid all these problems is to keep your antifreeze up to full strength all winter long. It is false economy to save the price of a quart or two of antifreeze and wind up ruining your motor or radiator.

Alcohol-type Antifreeze

Prior to the introduction of ethylene glycol, alcohol was used to protect the cooling system; even now a few motorists continue to use it. However, I advise against the use of alcohol, as it has a low boiling point, evaporates rapidly, and is highly flammable. Also, a high-temperature thermostat cannot be used with alcohol, because the boiling point of alcohol is too low.

During the Depression, various types of antifreeze solutions were tried, including plain salt with water. One man actually canned and marketed salt water, guaranteeing it as a permanent antifreeze. At a time when people were even prepared to try coal oil, his business began to flourish. But it wasn't too long before he closed shop and left town—the salt in his "antifreeze" had a tendency to devour certain metal components of engines, including cylinder-head gaskets. The briny brew seeped through and coated ignition wiring, and many a car refused to start. Worse, dozens of engines were completely ruined, and many were the lawsuits in progress when our hero discreetly disappeared.

The Radiator

Modern cars, in addition to being faster and more powerful, boast low-slung, close-to-the-road body styling. Because of their low profiles, it is necessary to equip them with smaller radiators than in the past. On the other hand, today's radiators are far more efficient. On many cars the radiator is responsible for cooling the automatic-transmission fluid as well as the engine. The coolant absorbs the heat from engine and transmission and is then returned to the top of the radiator. Here it rapidly dissipates the heat as it descends through a series of cooling tubes. In time, some of these tubes can become plugged with particles of rubber from worn heater and radiator hoses, rust from the block, and impurities in the water.

One summer, a man I know ran into trouble in a tiny town 200 miles from the nearest city. The radiator had plugged up and caused the engine to boil. The local repair shop found that the cylinder head was cracked. The radiator had to be sent to a town 30 miles away to be repaired, and a new cylinder head had to be shipped from the city. My friend was tied up in the town for two days and paid a repair bill of over $200 plus motel expense. The garage would not accept his check, and he had to wait for a bank to open to get the cash. All this annoyance could have been avoided if the cooling system had been properly maintained.

To save yourself a similar headache, have your garageman remove the radiator cap and check for particles of foreign matter on the cooling tubes in the top tank. If necessary, have the radiator removed and sent to a specialist for repairs. If your car is equipped with an expansion tank (similar to the top tank of conventional radiators, but placed behind the radiator), it will not be possible to make a visual check of these tubes. In this case I recommend removing and cleaning the radiator at least every three years for reasonable assurance of 100 percent efficiency. However, if you don't want to remove the radiator, at least take an air hose and blow out the dirt and insects that have accumulated on the outside of the radiator core. Do not attempt to flush the cooling system with harsh detergents or solutions such as lye or baking soda. These solutions can devour certain metal components, loosen all the dirt and corrosion in the block, plug the top tubes of the radiator, and cause overheating. Reliable, flushing compounds are available at most service stations and parts houses.

If, after the cooling system has been cleaned and checked, the engine still tends to overheat or boil, the following difficult-to-diagnose condition may be the culprit. On modern radiators cooling fins are soldered to the cooling tubes. Due to vibration as well as expansion and contraction caused by the pressure within the system, the fins sometimes break away from the cooling tubes and considerably retard heat dissipation. It usually takes a radiator specialist to find this fault, and the only cure is to recore the radiator.

Another tough problem to diagnose is that of the undersized core. Some years ago my foreman, Emil, bought a two-year-old car in the early spring. All went well until he made his first long trip of the summer, when, for no apparent reason, his engine started to overheat and sometimes actually boiled when he was bogged down in heavy traffic. Emil is not easily discouraged, but he was completely floored by this problem. Thoroughly familiar with every detail of the cooling system, he had meticulously gone through the whole circuit, checking all the possible causes, but he discovered nothing that seemed to lead to the trouble.

Eventually, in sheer desperation, he removed both cylinder heads, checked them for warping or plugged water passages, and then sent them to a machine shop to be magnafluxed for minute internal cracks. The machine shop found nothing wrong. As a last resort, although the radiator was spotlessly clean, Emil sent it to a radiator specialist, who discovered that the radiator core was too small to cool the V-8 engine in peak periods.

It turned out that the car had been involved in a front-end collision shortly after it was purchased by the original owner, and a cheap undersized core had been used to replace the original. This core would cool the engine under normal conditions, but the moment it had to idle in traffic for long periods in hot weather, it could not dissipate heat fast enough, and the engine overheated. The proper core was installed, and Emil had no further trouble.

When having a radiator core replaced on either a new or used car, insist on its being the equivalent of the original equipment. If your car is still under warranty, no manufacturer will honor the warranty if your engine has been damaged due to installation of an inferior, undersized radiator core.

When a car is driven in frigid zones, it is sometimes difficult to maintain the normal operating temperature of the engine. Putting a cover over the lower outside section of the radiator can be helpful, but the motorist must be sure to remove this cover when the weather warms up.

Radiator Pressure Cap

It is an established fact that the cooling system operates more efficiently under pressure. Through the years, the car industry has gradually increased this pressure, and modern cars are equipped with a radiator pressure cap of up to (and over) 17 pounds.

Most motorists have only a sketchy idea of the important role played by the pressure cap. I have been asked, "Why do I need a pressure cap? Isn't it just another gadget to go wrong and cost me money?" Others say, "In the old days they didn't have pressure caps, and cars ran fine."

While it's true that in the "good old days" they didn't have pressure caps, today's cooling systems are far more efficient and are called upon to do a lot more work. We don't see nearly as many cars belching out steam on the side of the highway as we did in the "old days."

Every pound of pressure applied to the cooling fluid raises the boiling point by about 3 degrees F. Therefore, with a 17-pound pressure cap the coolant will not boil until it reaches something like 263 degrees F., instead of the normal 212 degrees.

You may have noticed when water is coming to a boil in a glass coffee percolator that small bubbles start rising from the bottom as the boiling point approaches. The water has begun to boil at the bottom, where it is in closest contact with the burner. In your engine the same thing occurs in what we refer to as the "hot spots." One of the most intense "hot spots" is located in the valve seats. When your car is climbing a hill, the exhaust valves can actually turn cherry red. This heat is dissipated through the head or block when the valve closes on its seat. As the temperature of the seat rises, the same little bubbles you saw are generated in the coolant. Under adverse conditions, all the cooling fluid surrounding the value seat may turn to steam and cease extracting sufficient heat from the valve assembly. The metal temperature rises fantastically, and a valve seat can crack. A pressurized cooling system is unquestionably more efficient and offers far greater protection to the engine.

There are also some disadvantages to the pressure system. The radiator core flexes as the pressure rises, and this can sometimes cause an older radiator to spring a leak. If your radiator or hoses have deteriorated, they can be blown open by the pressure. If this occurs on the highway, your engine can be destroyed before you realize you have lost all your cooling fluid. For this reason, it is wise to replace hoses as soon as they begin to show signs of deterioration.

If your car is aging and you are concerned that a high-pressure cap may damage your cooling system, you may exchange your pressure cap for one of a lower rating with no ill effects. But the difference in pressure will certainly lower the cooling efficiency of the system, particularly in warm weather.

To avoid problems with your cap, it should be tested during routine checks or whenever there is evidence of overheating. Service centers have special equipment to test the pressure cap. If defective, it should be replaced immediately.

One final word of caution: NEVER open the pressure cap when the car is overheated. The moment the cap is unscrewed and the cooling fluid is allowed to return to normal atmospheric pressure, it will turn to steam and blow up in your face. A customer of mine was almost blinded, had the skin scalded off his face, and spent many painful weeks in the hospital because he had made this error. *Think before opening that pressure cap*. Allow a few minutes for it to cool, or at least wear a glove or cover the cap with a rag—*lean well away*—before *slowly* unscrewing it.

The Water Pump

Hot water from the engine cooling jackets enters the top of the radiator and, as it is cooled by the passage of air through the core, it sinks to the bottom. Some means of moving this cool fluid back to work in the engine is necessary; this is the job of the water pump. (*See Diagram* 22.) Belt-driven by the crankshaft of the engine, the water pump is literally the heart of the cooling system. Just as your heart keeps your body supplied with blood, the water pump speeds coolant, rust inhibitor, and lubricant through all the passages of the cooling system. If it fails, the whole car can "die."

Failure of the water pump's inner seal (frequently due to lack of water-pump lubricant in the cooling fluid) and failure of the front bearing are two of the most common water-pump failures which cause loss of fluid. The front bearing requires no lubrication on almost all domestic cars. The most likely cause of premature bearing failure is overtightening of the belt that drives the pump.

Some years ago I learned the hard way of another component whose failure can result in a baffling boiling condition. An old neglected car was driven into my shop boiling violently. "I'm in a

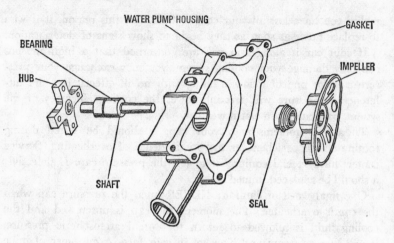

Diagram 22. *Exploded view of water pump*

hurry," snapped the man driving it. "I want this fixed right away. I know it isn't anything serious. How much will it cost?"

I opened the hood, and beneath the Vesuvius-like cloud of steam lay an accumulation of grimy, mushy, seeping heater and radiator hoses and a broken fan belt. Coolant was bubbling out of the radiator core. When I had totaled up all the parts needed (one fan belt, two heater hoses, upper and lower radiator hoses, and assorted hose clamps), I added the cost of antifreeze and labor and gave him an estimate. Doing his best to look the picture of outrage, the motorist began heaping abuse on both my foreman and myself. "You guys are always looking for a chance to do more than is necessary," he accused. "And on top of that, you overcharge."

He grudgingly sanctioned the repairs—only after demanding a written guarantee. We finished the repairs, double-checked our work, road-tested the car, and everything seemed to be in order as we handed him the keys. But the next morning, with a squeal of tires and more steam, he jerked his car to a stop outside the shop just as we were opening up. "You never fixed a darn thing," he charged. "It still boils, and I've lost all my antifreeze. I'm going to tell the Better Business Bureau what a bunch of crooks you guys are. Fix it or I'll sue!"

After several hours of probing while the customer hopped from side to side telling us that it was all our fault, we located the cause of the problem. A water pump contains a round plate attached to the inside end of the driven shaft to which are attached a series of fins. Their function is to circulate the coolant throughout the system. Somehow most of these fins had broken off, severely retarding circulation, so that after an hour or two of driving at low speed the engine would boil. We replaced the pump, and the motorist went on his way after assuring us that he would not sue, because we had chalked the whole thing up to experience and had rung up "no charge." As he left, I asked him when his cooling system was last serviced. "Oh, I don't know," he said. "I just bought the car last week. It used to be a taxi."

I have seen these fins fail on only a few occasions in my thirty years in the garage business, but they're something to keep in mind when every other part of the cooling system checks out O.K.

Heater and Radiator Hoses

The heater and radiator hoses carry hot water from the engine to the heater when required, and to the radiator for cooling. They also allow the cooled fluid to return to its work in the remainder of the system. Nevertheless, in spite of the simplicity of their operation, these hoses can take quite a beating, and a failure in a hose can mean total cooling-system failure.

Subject to the pressure built up within the cooling system, the hoses constantly flex as the coolant is pumped through them. They must be able to take this flexing and pressure without rupturing. And, believe me, worn hoses can swell up like a balloon and burst.

I could not hazard a guess as to how many engines have been ruined because of neglected heater or radiator hoses. Many engines are equipped with a small "bypass" hose between the engine and the water pump, which provides for circulation in the block only. This hose is frequently overlooked, but it, too, can drain the system should it fail.

Many cars are fitted with brackets to support the heater hoses, and it is imperative that they do their job. Otherwise, the hoses will flex at the point where they are attached to the water outlets and gradually tear apart. In cars without brackets, the long lengths of hose must be supported in some way (such as with electrical tape) to prevent undue flexing.

When hoses are being checked, they should first be examined with the engine at normal operating temperature and the cooling system under the full pressure built up by the radiator cap. This pressure makes it easier to check for possible external cracks and ballooning of the hoses. Then the system should be depressurized by loosening the pressure cap (but remember to exercise extreme caution here). The hoses may then be checked by squeezing them between the fingers. If they are soft and mushy and readily crush inwards as you squeeze, they need to be replaced.

Deterioration of hoses usually starts internally and gradually works through to the outside. I have seen hoses so badly worn internally that they blocked circulation of the coolant.

The Block

Although the block is solidly formed of cast metal and does not itself move, it can fail and cause complete engine breakdown. The two big enemies of the block are extreme heat and cold. If the engine overheats, the block can crack. The same thing can happen if there is no antifreeze in the cooling system and the mercury suddenly drops to zero.

Possibly 75 percent of the damage (usually a cracked block) to this unit results from overheating due to neglect of the cooling system. When the block is cracked, it is frequently necessary to replace the entire engine assembly, which on luxury liners could run into a thousand dollars or more.

While a cracked block is a serious matter, some garages are too hasty to recommend a new one. In some instances, depending on the location and severity of the damage, modern electric-welding equipment or a process of drilling a series of holes through the crack and inserting threaded plugs makes it possible to repair the crack permanently. However, this work should be done only by a specialist.

A crack will not always be visible from the outside of the engine, and mysterious problems can crop up. The experience of one of my readers bears this out. He had stored his car for the winter, and when spring arrived he was pleased to find that it started readily. He was going to take it into the service station for a general checkup but decided first to drive to a town about 25 miles away.

After a few miles, clouds of steam came pouring from under the hood. He drove to the nearest service station, where the mechanic found that worn radiator hoses had drained the cooling system. Apparently, coolant had been leaking from his cooling system all winter, or else he had burst a hose during the run down the highway.

The hoses and coolant were replaced, and the motorist paid a modest bill of $10. The next day the engine boiled again, and since there was no sign of external leaks, his local mechanic suggested he had blown a head gasket, which was allowing coolant to leak into the engine.

The mechanic was proud of his instant diagnosis when, on pulling off the cylinder head, sure enough, he found a blown gasket, which was quickly replaced. However, the coolant continued to disappear, and clouds of steam from the tailpipe proved that water was still getting into the engine. The head was again removed, and closer inspection revealed a crack in the block, which probably occurred when the engine first boiled. Had the enthusiastic mechanic looked further on his first inspection, he would have found the crack.

Accumulation of rust in the water jacket when no rust inhibitor has been used in the coolant, or a buildup of solids when water with harmful minerals has constantly been added, will cause "hot spots" in the engine. By far the most serious of these two causes is rust. I have seen rust build up around the cylinder sleeves to a height of four inches in extreme cases. It is not possible to remove this rust merely by flushing the block with water and detergents. While a messy job, on some engines it is possible to remove some of the frost plugs and excavate much of the rust, but usually the engine must be hoisted out, dismantled completely, and submerged in a chemical bath to rout the rust. This is why it is so vitally important to use rust inhibitor in the cooling system at all times.

The top surface of the block to which the cylinder head is attached can warp due to overheating. This can result in a blown head gasket, loss of compression, and leakage of coolant into the engine. When cylinder heads are removed, the top surface of the block should be checked with a straightedge to determine possible warpage or other damage that can result from chemical action from the combustion chamber.

It is not always possible to machine the upper surface of the block back to operating tolerances; replacement may be necessary. The use of rust inhibitor and proper maintenance of the cooling system are invaluable in preventing the disastrous effects of overheating.

Cooling Tubes

Cooling tubes are placed inside the water jackets on many engines to direct the coolant into specific "hot spots." These tubes are practically trouble-free and seldom see light of day unless the engine assembly is completely stripped down for rebuilding. However, they too can suffer from the results of rust and mineral buildup, and fail to protect the critical "hot spots."

Frost or Expansion Plugs

Although they are most commonly referred to as "frost" plugs, I don't think "expansion," "Welsh," or "core" plugs really offer much protection against frost should the block become frozen solid. Every engine is fitted with a number of these plugs, and, while it is generally thought that their function is to relieve pressure on the block by popping out should the water in the head or block freeze solid, this is not their real purpose.

Actually, they are necessary to the fabrication of the block. When the block is cast at the factory, sand is used to form the inside water jacket. When casting is complete, this sand must be removed from inside the block; small holes are left for this purpose. Metal plugs are inserted to seal these holes, and that is the primary purpose of the "frost plug."

The plugs are located in various parts of the engine, depending on the make. Occasionally, after a few years, they rust away and the coolant begins to leak out. This can sometimes account for mysterious leaks that have no other explanation. Some engines have one of these plugs at the very rear of the block, and when this one leaks, it is often necessary to remove the engine to replace it.

I once had a customer who drove in with the telltale drips of coolant falling down in the area of the flywheel housing. His normally bubbling sense of humor deserted him when I handed him a bill for the replacement work. One frost plug: 20¢. Installation of frost plug: $48. It only seemed to aggravate the situation when I jokingly offered to let him have the frost plug at my expense.

Cylinder Heads

In much the same way as the block, the cylinder head can be cracked or warped by frost or overheating. It is exposed to more heat than any other part of the engine, since it contains the combustion chambers where the mixture of gasoline and air is actually ignited. Here, too, the cooling system plays a vital role in temperature control.

When overheating occurs, the cylinder head is frequently the first component of the engine to sustain damage, such as cracked valve seats. The head can also warp from overheating and blow the head gasket. When this occurs, compression is lost and coolant begins to disappear. As with the block, damaged cylinder heads can sometimes be repaired, but when replacement is necessary it is usually expensive —one more reason to guard against overheating.

In fact, overheating of the cylinder head can cause all sorts of headaches. A reader of my column told me how his three-year-old car had overheated and boiled up on the highway. Immediately afterwards, it began to require a quart or so of water every other day. After two weeks of wondering where the water was going, he took it to a mechanic, who found that a valve seat was cracked and the coolant was seeping into the combustion chamber.

The valve seat was replaced, the leak corrected, and my reader paid a bill of $85. A week later, his engine developed a frightening knock as he drove down the highway, and he pulled into another garage. This time a rod had burned out, necessitating replacement of the crankshaft at a cost of $260.

While the mechanic at the first garage had found and corrected the coolant leak, he had overlooked checking the engine oil, which had become heavily contaminated by water and antifreeze seeping past the piston rings into the crankcase. Sludge had formed on the oil-pump screen, severely restricting the flow of oil through the engine. The connecting rod, starved of its vital lubrication, promptly burned out.

When coolant starts to disappear mysteriously, it is very likely going into the crankcase. Stop driving and have it checked immediately. If the volume of the leak is sufficient, just one hour of driving can ruin the engine. If large quantities of coolant have entered the crankcase, just changing the oil may not be enough. It could well be that the oil-pump screen is practically plugged solid, and the only sure way to find out is to remove the pan and check visually. Removing the oil pan is far less costly than replacing the engine.

Head Gaskets

The head gasket is responsible for maintaining a tight seal between the cylinder head and block. It is the job of the gasket to keep compression within the combustion chambers and cylinders and to provide a watertight seal where water passages adjacent to the cylinders run from head to block. A faulty or blown gasket is one of the most frequent causes of coolant mysteriously disappearing, usually into the depths of the engine. When correctly installed, and provided the engine is not overheated, the head gasket will seldom fail. But if it does, it can be extremely damaging and sometimes difficult to diagnose. (The block, cylinder head, and head gasket are also discussed in the *Engine* chapter.)

Diagnosing Internal Coolant Leaks

Prior to the introduction of the pressure-testing machine, it was difficult and sometimes impossible to trace leaks in a grimy engine compartment. Now, by merely attaching the machine to the filler neck of the radiator or expansion tank and pumping up the pressure, seeping coolant can usually be forced out, making it a simple matter to pinpoint an external leak. Unfortunately, too many mechanics immediately fix the obvious leak and forget to make further use of the machine. They send the motorist on his way with possibly further undetected defects—the internal kind.

Whenever it becomes necessary to top up the radiator frequently, head for a service shop immediately and have it remedied. And insist on a thorough pressure test of the cooling system both *before* and *after* repairs have been completed.

If a pressure test shows no external leaks, but the coolant continues to disappear, the leak is probably internal. First, check the engine oil level, and, if it is over the full mark, the coolant is almost certainly leaking into the engine. In this case the oil should be changed before starting the engine. If the oil is clean and the level is correct, start the engine and let it warm up to normal operating temperature. Then turn off the ignition, remove the sparkplugs, and attach the pressure machine to the radiator, pumping it up to at least the same pressure as is stamped on top of the radiator cap.

After the car has remained idle for an hour or two, or even overnight, disconnect the small primary wire that feeds current to the distributor. Turn the engine over with the starter, and usually the coolant will gush out of the sparkplug hole of the faulty cylinder (or cylinders). This pinpoints the defect. Next, the head must be removed to determine if the head or block is cracked or if the head gasket is blown. Make it a point to insist on this all-important pressure test *before* and *after* repairs.

Internal-cooling-system leaks can also cause exhaust fumes to accumulate inside the top radiator tank. Some garages use a chemically operated testing device that draws a sample of the air from the radiator-filler neck and quickly detects the presence of harmful exhaust fumes in the cooling system.

The Thermostat

The thermostat in your car, while small and inexpensive, is the main control center for the entire cooling system. The two most common types are referred to as "bellows" and "pellet." Almost all modern cars are equipped with the "pellet" type, which is far more suitable for pressurized cooling systems.

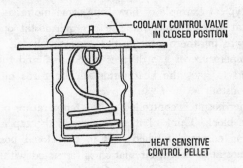

Diagram 23. *Typical cooling-system thermostat*

The thermostat plays two main roles. (*See Diagram* 23.) It supplies adequate hot water for the heater and assures that the engine will reach its proper operating temperature as quickly as possible. Thus, while many motorists may think the thermostat is there only to warm up the inside of the car quickly and save them from the winter chill, its basic function is to regulate the temperature of the engine.

Engineers are primarily concerned with the operating temperature of the engine. Heating the inside of the car for passenger comfort, while important, is still a secondary consideration. To operate a car in winter without a thermostat is to pass a death sentence on the engine—particularly in areas where the temperature drops below freezing.

A car was once driven into my shop in midwinter making noises like a threshing machine. The owner was a health enthusiast, concerned that living in a heated home and working in a heated office were lowering his resistance to every bug around. To offset all this and make sure he got large doses of cool, fresh air, he had removed the thermostat from his car and was driving around with all the windows open. He might just as well have used the open windows to throw his money to the four winds.

When we dismantled his engine, we found the center valve chamber loaded with four inches of thick sludge. The oil passages were plugged almost solid, and the engine was on the verge of seizing up. The only remedy was a rebuilt engine—at a cost of more than $400.

When it was explained to him what had caused his trouble, he confessed that he had been running into nothing but problems and expense all winter, but no one had ever pointed out the true cause.

This is a typical example of how little some motorists know about the thermostat and its function. The car thermostat operates much the same way as the thermostat on the domestic electric range. When a baking temperature of 350 degrees is required and the thermostat dial is turned to 350, the heat automatically turns off and on to maintain a constant level of 350 degrees.

The car thermostat is controlled by the temperature of the coolant in the engine block. Think of it as you would the tap in your bathroom—nothing comes out when it is in the closed position. When the car thermostat is closed, circulation is restricted within the block, and the engine is rapidly preheated. Once a predetermined temperature is reached, the thermostat opens, restoring normal circulation. As previously mentioned, the primary function of the thermostat is to preheat the engine as rapidly as possible to allow free movement of oil and maximum fuel economy.

Water in the crankcase, generated by condensation, rates among the chief enemies of the internal-combustion engine. That is why it is so important to raise the block temperature rapidly to a point where water in the crankcase turns to steam and is expelled through the crankcase ventilating system.

Whether you live at the North Pole or the Equator, under normal driving conditions, replacing a winter high-temperature thermostat with a low-reading summer unit—or removing it altogether—is a waste of time and money. Worse, removing the thermostat from some cars, strangely enough, can cause overheating. Be sure you have a 180–195-degree thermostat in your car (but be guided by the recommendation of the car manufacturer), and let it stay there all year round. Some motorists will argue that in summer the car boils with a high-temperature thermostat. This is not true. Provided the thermostat is functioning properly, some other component in the cooling system must be causing the overheating. Figure it out. Since, even without a pressure cap, water does not boil until 212 degrees F. is reached, how on earth could a thermostat which opens at 180–195 degrees cause the coolant to boil?

Remember, manufacturers' warranties do not cover an engine that has been damaged by the lack of a thermostat or one that is malfunctioning. Whatever you do, don't be like my health-fanatic customer whose expensive engine was ruined for lack of a thermostat worth only a few dollars.

In a surprising number of ways the car engine is like the human body. For example, if our body temperature fluctuates only a few degrees, we are in serious trouble. The "thermostat" within our bodies operates with fantastic precision, usually maintaining an exact body temperature of 98.6 degrees, regardless of the outside temperature. Doctors tell me we either shiver or perspire, depending on outside temperature, in order to maintain our correct body temperature. While the thermostat used in the car engine is not nearly as sensitive as that of the human body, a considerable change either on the low or the high side, as with a human being, can lead to serious trouble. Sometimes the thermostat is blamed for all the ills of the cooling system, and when you report in with a boiling engine a new thermostat is installed with no further diagnosis. Insist that the thermostat be tested before accepting the fact that it is defective. Many a thermostat is replaced when, in fact, there is nothing wrong with it.

Causes of thermostat failure are about the same as those for any other mechanical unit. Abuse or just plain everyday use can eventually wear them out after a few years of average service. Another common cause of failure is an overheated engine. Always have the thermostat removed and tested after an engine has overheated.

Some thermostats are marked "This Side Up," and some have no markings whatsoever. I have seen many thermostats installed upside down—an error which can lead to an almost instant boiling condition.

The Fan

The radiator fan draws cooling air through the core of the radiator when the car is stationary or moving at lower speeds. It is a simple component, requiring little if any maintenance, provided it is not damaged by collision or mishandled.

Because the fan is not really needed at high speeds and its operation steals horsepower from the rear wheels, some cars are equipped with thermostatically or centrifugally controlled fans. Let me explain their purpose:

At high speeds, when natural forces drive air through the radiator and around the engine, the need for a fan is greatly reduced. To cut down annoying fan noises and to conserve horsepower, these thermostatically or centrifugally controlled fans reduce fan speed at a predetermined number of revolutions.

The number of fan blades varies according to the cooling requirements of an engine. Don't be discouraged if, when examining your own fan, you find some of the blades grouped together or spaced unevenly. This is done to decrease the whine at high speeds.

While relatively simple, the fan has many a shock in store for those who abuse it. One of the most dangerous practices when working on an engine is to attempt to rotate the crankshaft by pulling on the fan blades. This can bend the metal of the base of the blade beyond its elastic point and, at the least, result in imbalance and vibration. At the worst, it can lead to that dread enemy of mechanical parts—metal fatigue. In time the damaged fan blade will break loose and fly off with deadly force. I know of a mechanic who was killed instantly when a blade broke away and buried itself in his head as he revved up the engine. I have also seen holes in car hoods where fan blades have sliced clean through the metal.

On some cars there is a metal shield mounted just above the top section of the fan. It bears this warning: "Caution—Beware of Fan." Never place fingers on, under, or around this shield while the engine is running—they can be sliced off in a split second. Never allow children to climb up on the front end of the car when the hood is open and the engine is running, and do not stand in the line of fire of a rotating fan. Keep tools and loose objects out of upper pockets when leaning over a running engine. Never place extension lights where they can drop into the revolving blades.

I once had a green apprentice who set an extension light on top of a car radiator. The vibration of the running engine caused the light to drop down between the fan and the radiator core. Fortunately, the apprentice was not injured, but the radiator core was torn to shreds, and it cost us $80 to repair the damage.

The fan can be lethal. Stay away from it!

Driving Belts

The strength and durability of most fan belts and other driving belts amaze me. They are flexed and stretched and operate in temperatures from far below zero to well above boiling point while driving the generator or alternator, fan, water pump, power steering, and air conditioning. Although these belts drive many essential units, they require little attention and are frequently forgotten entirely. But failure of the belt to drive just the water pump alone can result in a burned-out engine.

It has been my experience in the garage business that one out of every three driving belts is worn to the point where replacement is necessary. Be sure that all driving belts are in good condition and adjusted to the proper tension. Too loose a setting causes slippage and premature wear, sometimes accompanied by a nerve-racking, high-pitched squeal. Too tight an adjustment will damage the bearings in the units the belt is driving. Replacement or adjustment is not costly and usually takes only a few minutes.

Minor Belt Squeals

I am often asked how to cope with a belt which, though appearing to be in good condition and properly adjusted, insists on squealing. In the first place, drive belts are not supposed to squeal, and most of them don't. But there is the occasional stubborn squealer and, although I've searched for years, I have yet to come up with a guaranteed cure for the temperamental belt that howls. I have tried soap (some old-timers swear by a bar of soap), and, while it has stopped some of the squeals for a day or so (and occasionally permanently), for the most part the pesky squeal returned. As a last resort, I have even installed a new belt, which is usually, but not always, the answer.

Sometimes the problem is not attributable directly to the belt. On occasion, I have seen one of the pulleys badly worn or out of line— too far forward or back, putting the strain on the edge of the belt. Sometimes the pulleys on exchange, or even new generators or water pumps, are out of alignment. However, this seldom happens, and we have to accept the stubborn case of a new or old squeaking belt.

The fan belt can also be the culprit in an unusual condition which literally shocks many drivers. If your car suddenly seems to become "fully charged" and you get a static electric shock every time you touch the car, check the inside surface of the fan belt. If it is quite dry and worn down to the fabric, it could quite easily be creating the "powerhouse" responsible for your shocks. I ran into this static trouble years ago, and after much research discovered that a dry fan belt, worn to the fabric, was the offender. Replacement of the fan belt did away with the static buildup.

Automatic Transmission Cooler

On many cars equipped with automatic transmission, an element is fitted to the inside of the radiator tank at the bottom. Its purpose is to cool the transmission fluid which is pumped through the cooling

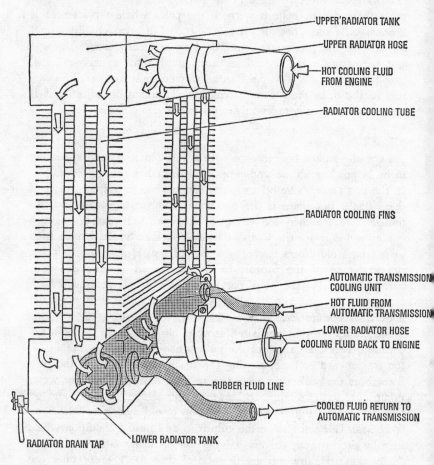

Diagram 24. *Automatic transmission cooling unit*

unit under pressure. (*See Diagram* 24.) This unit seldom causes problems, though I have seen a few of them deteriorate. The cooler can, of course, be damaged in a collision.

Whatever the reason, if a leak does develop in the transmission cooler, serious trouble can follow. Either the coolant in the radiator seeps into the cooling unit and in turn is carried back to the transmission, causing it to burn out, or the transmission fluid leaks into the radiator, polluting the coolant and robbing the transmission of its vital fluid. If the radiator is being repaired, remind your serviceman to test the automatic-transmission-fluid cooling unit for leaks.

The Heater

Although not one of the components essential to the functioning of the car, the heater is a necessity for passenger comfort. It is also a safety aid when freezing temperatures are liable to coat your windshield with ice.

To function efficiently, the car's heating unit depends on the cooling system to provide a constant flow of hot fluid, which is drawn from the engine before being cooled in the radiator. This hot fluid is used to heat an air stream which passes into the car. Many things can affect the serviceability of the heater, and I will outline in detail possible causes of failure. These failings, naturally, will not apply to air-cooled engines.

If the heater in your car does a better job as a refrigerator, first check the thermostat to make sure it is a high-temperature 180–195 degrees F. unit. If you are unsure at what temperature the thermostat on your car opens, have it tested in hot water with an accurate thermometer. If it checks out at the correct opening temperature, look closely at the heater hoses—they may be bent or plugged, blocking or restricting circulation. A malfunctioning pressure cap also can cause a considerable drop in the temperature of the fluid going to the heater.

It's also a good idea to check the heater control knobs. They may move properly on the "On" and "Off" positions, but a broken cable or wire can make the shut-off control valve stick in the "Off" position or fail to turn the fan motor on. There may even be problems in the control valve itself, necessitating replacement of the whole control unit.

To direct heat into the inside of the car or against the windshield, the heater relies on a miniature version of the radiator core; as water is pumped through, it transfers the heat it picked up from the engine to an air stream passing through the core and into the car. This core, too, can become plugged with dirt, internally restricting or stopping the flow of hot fluid through the heater.

Blockage in the heater core can sometimes be cleared by flushing with water and blowing out with air pressure. But in stubborn cases it may be necessary to remove and dismantle the heater unit and send the core to a radiator shop to be boiled out in a chemical bath. Occasionally, the core has to be replaced.

Car manufacturers sometimes use vacuum generated by the engine to operate the heater controls, and here, too, problems can occur. A broken, plugged, or disconnected vacuum hose can cause chilly blasts. The vacuum-operated controls can also become sticky and jam. But often the cure for this is simple lubrication. Some heaters have a control switch which operates very much like the thermostat on a household furnace. Failure of the switch can lead to failure of the system.

Sometimes air gets into the cooling system and reduces circulation to the heater. In rare instances a loose, warped, or cracked cylinder head on the engine itself can be responsible for an air lock in the heater core or hoses. This can be a tough one to diagnose; it calls for a pressure test, with the engine running, by a responsible mechanic. The pressure tester is fixed onto the neck of the radiator and pumped up to a pressure of about 14 pounds. The engine is then run under load for a few seconds. If the head is loose or cracked, a head gasket is blown or, worse, there is a crack in the block; then the pressure gauge will usually climb rapidly.

Before a cold morning and a cold heater drive you to panic, lean under the dashboard and check the fuse for the blower motor. In most modern cars the fuse will be located on a panel mounted on the firewall. You may also find it attached to a pigtail wire running out of the heater motor. If the fuse is O.K., then something else is wrong, and you might need advice from your garageman.

A low coolant level in the radiator can also be the cause of heater failure. This condition is usually indicated by a gurgling sound from the heater as the engine is revved up and air bubbles through the heater.

Finally, don't forget there may be doors or vents which *you* must open to allow heated air to enter the car. In some cars the outside air-duct controls must be operating efficiently, since they control the volume of air that passes through the heater core. Many heaters have doors or control cables which require opening or closing, depending on whether the motorist wants to heat the whole car or just defrost the windshield.

It pays to know how to open or operate these doors. One winter morning, a gleaming new car pulled up to my garage with the windshield and all the windows completely covered with ice. The little old lady who eventually crept from the car, teeth chattering, explained that she had to stop the car every two blocks to scrape the ice off the windshield. I looked inside her brand-new car and found that she simply had not opened the outside air duct and had not manipulated the doors to direct air through the defrosters. The result was that she had practically no heat in the car and was convinced that she had been sold a lemon. I opened the vents and doors and invited her to come into the office to thaw out and have a cup of coffee before leading her out to a nice warm car with the ice falling off the windows.

If shivering on cold mornings until your car warms up gets you down, various models of electrical heaters are now available at reasonable cost. These operate from house current and can be mounted under the instrument panel. Such a unit is particularly helpful when a car is left parked in the driveway overnight. It keeps the interior of the car at a comfortable temperature and prevents ice from forming on the windows in the event of freezing rain. When you are ready to use the car, just unplug the electrical cord from the house and turn on the car heater. These handy heaters are available at most auto-parts stores.

Air-cooled Engines

Some motorists argue that the cooling fan on an air-cooled engine requires more horsepower than the water pump and fan on a liquid-cooled engine. But engineers tell me that there is little difference between the two in horsepower consumption.

While most American car engines are liquid-cooled, there are still a number of air-cooled, rear-engine vehicles. One of the main advantages of the air-cooled engine is that the fuel is not wasted heating up gallons of cooling fluid. The engine rapidly reaches normal operating temperature, which is a particular advantage when your driving pattern is one of many short stop-and-go runs. The possibility of sludging up the engine under these adverse driving conditions is considerably reduced with air cooling. Other benefits are: no antifreeze to buy, no hoses to leak, no engine damage due to internal coolant leakage.

Why, then, are not more cars driven by air-cooled engines? The fact is that they have disadvantages, too—disadvantages which make them unsuitable for many applications enjoyed by a fluid-cooled design. For a start, air-cooled engines are invariably noisy. The fins and ducting necessary to cool the engine also serve as sounding boards to transmit engine noise to the rest of the car. The necessity for fins and extensive ducting would tend to make larger air-cooled engines more space-consuming than a water-cooled engine of the same horsepower.

When air-cooled engines are used, they are usually quite suitable. Unlike the water-cooled engine, in which fluid is pumped to all "hot spots," the air-cooled engine is cooled by a fan. Fins are cast into the cylinders to draw the heat out of the engine. Metal shrouds direct cool air to the engine and fins, and the volume of cool air directed to the engine is thermostatically controlled. Maintenance consists of periodic adjustment and inspection of the belt driving the fan, testing the thermostat for accuracy, and checking the cleanliness of the cooling fins. The inspection periods of the cooling system are spelled out in the owner's manual supplied by the car manufacturer at the time of purchase. Major repairs stemming from neglect or abuse of the air-cooled system can be avoided by following the instructions in this manual. If your car has an air-cooled engine and you have lost this manual, ask your dealer for another. Although the necessary maintenance is simple and the cost usually moderate as long as new parts are not needed, it is vital that servicing be carried out at proper intervals.

Unless you are certain that your mechanic is trained to service air-cooled engines, it is best to look for someone who specializes in your make. Sometimes the "general practitioner" will do more harm than good.

How To Cope with a Boiling Engine

How the motorist copes with an overheated engine often determines whether or not he spends hundreds of dollars on car repairs. If you find volumes of steam pouring from your engine, here is what to do:

Open the hood to hasten cooling. Don't open the radiator pressure cap until you are *certain* the steam pressure has dropped; otherwise you could be severely burned. After the engine has cooled, start it and, if available, add hot water very slowly. *Never* add cold water immediately after the engine has been boiling—wait fifteen to thirty minutes. If you are on the highway and no water is close by, start walking until you find some, or flag down another motorist. When you have added water, drive to the nearest repair shop and have the cooling-system pressure tested for leaks and repaired as necessary. But under no circumstances should the car be driven until the radiator has been filled. If the engine was allowed to cool before you added water, chances are in your favor that no harm has been done. But remember, if after it has boiled over, you find that the radiator needs frequent topping up and there are no external leaks, it could mean that the head or block is cracked internally or that the head gasket is blown. Continued driving will allow coolant to run down into the pan and contaminate the oil and ruin the engine.

Any time the coolant starts to disappear from the radiator, even if there has not been a boiling problem, remember, it has to be going somewhere. Find out why, and authorize repairs immediately.

Stop-leaks and "Witches' Brews"

Are stop-leak additives truly effective in the cooling system? Do they permanently seal external and the more mysterious internal coolant leaks? Can they be harmful? These are some of the questions I am frequently asked concerning what some customers refer to as "witches' brews," often guaranteed to cure all the ills of the cooling system.

In the event of a minute imperfection in any part of the cooling system, such as a radiator or heater hose not completely sealed to its metal connection, a thin spot in the soldered connections of the radiator, slight flaws in the block, cylinder head, or head gasket, stop-leaks can be effective. Some car manufacturers sell them and recommend their use. However, the car makers do not claim these additives to be a complete cure-all.

Modern cooling systems operating under the up to 17-pound pressure created by the pressure cap are far less forgiving of weak spots than older cars, which operated under little or no pressure at all. The addition of a mild stop-leak or "seeping fluid" will frequently take care of some minor defect which passed unnoticed during assembly of the new car, or slight errors made during repairs later on. When it comes to internal leaks such as damages to head gaskets, heads, or blocks, it is not likely that stop-leaks will afford a permanent cure.

I have never been overly impressed with so-called miracle cures sold in cans and bottles. While certain chemicals can help, they are sometimes highly oversold and certainly will not create miracles. Usually, the only practical cure for extensive damage is major surgery. Wishful thinking and the addition of a dollar's worth of stop-leak will not remedy excessive damage and can easily lead to the ruin of the whole power plant. Be cautious of ads which would have you believe that a buck's worth of some miracle product will as good as replace a damaged block or radiator. Be sure the additive you select is manufactured by a reputable company and recommended by the makers of your particular vehicle. Your warranty can be voided if harmful chemical additives are responsible for engine damage.

Heavy Loads

North American motorists frequently overload their cars with trailers, boats, cartop carriers, camping equipment, and other outdoor-living gear. All this gear places an extra strain on the engine and, in turn, on the cooling system. When selecting a new car, if it is to be used for carrying heavy loads or pulling heavy trailers, it is wise to order the heavy-duty package, which includes a heavy-duty radiator. The car manufacturers *do not* extend their warranties to engines damaged by overheating due to overloading, and many insist on the installation of the heavy-duty package whenever a heavy trailer or other heavy load is to be carried.

The Exhaust System

The exhaust system is that part of the car which takes waste products from the chemical-plant-like action of the car's engine and expels them quietly through the tailpipe.

The system begins with the exhaust manifold and ends with the tailpipe. Basically, the exhaust system is comprised of these parts: the exhaust manifold, the exhaust pipe, the muffler and tailpipe.

The exhaust manifold directs the exhaust gases and the sounds of combustion to the exhaust pipe. This pipe is nothing more than the

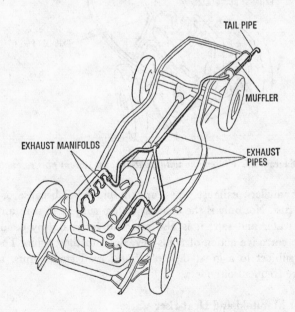

Diagram 25. *V-8 engine with single-exhaust system*

name implies—a simple pipe. Its job is to pass the exhaust gases to the muffler.

The muffler—which quiets the sound of the exhaust—channels the fumes to the tailpipe, and so the exhaust reaches the atmosphere.

In its simplest form, that's the exhaust system, but on V-8s there are two exhaust pipes, one leading from each side of the engine. These two pipes join under the car and then are attached to the muffler. (*See Diagram* 25.) Some cars have a second muffler, sometimes called a resonator. With more powerful V-8 engines, there is frequently a dual-exhaust system. (*See Diagram* 26.)

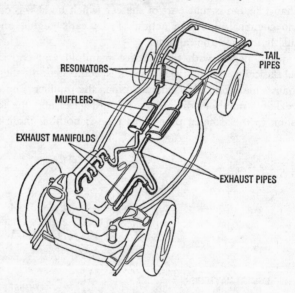

RESONATORS

TAIL PIPES

MUFFLERS

EXHAUST MANIFOLDS

EXHAUST PIPES

Diagram 26. *V-8 engine with dual-exhaust system plus resonators*

Most mufflers, exhaust pipes, and tailpipes fail because of the old curse—rust. Not only is the exhaust system subject to constant splashing by water and salt; it is also attacked internally by condensation and the corrosive action of acids developed in the engine. The system is also subject to a great deal of abuse; road stones, ruts, and potholes are frequent offenders.

Exhaust Manifold and Heat-riser Valve

When the exhaust valves open to rid the engine of spent gases, the exhaust manifold feeds the gases out to the exhaust pipe, muffler, and tailpipe. Like the intake manifold, the exhaust manifold is bolted to the engine; often there is a gasket between these two parts.

Included in the exhaust manifold on many cars is a heat-riser valve which is kept in position by a shaft. (*See Diagram 27.*) When

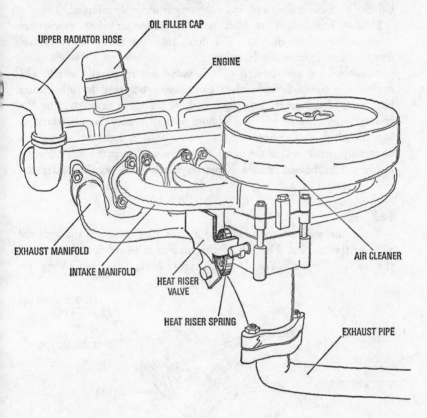

OIL FILLER CAP

UPPER RADIATOR HOSE

ENGINE

EXHAUST MANIFOLD

INTAKE MANIFOLD

HEAT RISER VALVE

HEAT RISER SPRING

AIR CLEANER

EXHAUST PIPE

Diagram 27. *Typical heat-riser valve as used on six-cylinder engine*

functioning normally, the valve pivots on this shaft, which protrudes through the exhaust manifold. Mounted externally on the heat-riser shaft is a bimetal heat-sensitive spring and a counterweight.

In the closed position, the valve directs hot exhaust gases against the intake manifold. The gases preheat the fuel-air mixture before it reaches the combustion chamber, thereby minimizing the engine's warm-up period.

As the exhaust manifold becomes heated, the increased temperature causes the heat-sensitive spring to reduce its tension, and the counter-weight pulls the heat-riser valve open. In time, carbon and gum, heat and corrosion can seize the shaft in the manifold. When it seizes in either the open or closed position, it upsets the delicate balance of carburetion, and fuel economy is seriously affected.

I have found that at least half of these heat-riser valves are seized solid. On my own car, if I don't lubricate the valve every two months or so, it ceases to function.

The checking and freeing of this valve are frequently overlooked during a tune-up. Seized valves can usually be freed by lubricating both ends of the protruding shaft and, at the same time, twisting the counterweight by hand. In stubborn cases, it may be necessary to tap the shaft and counterweight gently with a light hammer. Occasionally, wear causes the shaft to loosen in the manifold, allowing dangerous carbon-monoxide fumes to escape and possibly enter the car's passenger area.

Mufflers

From the exhaust manifold the fumes pass through the exhaust pipe to the muffler. The job of the muffler is to deaden the roar of the exhaust gases. (*See Diagram* 28.) Most quality mufflers to-

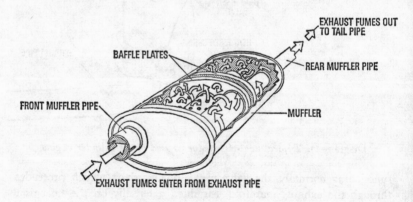

Diagram 28. *Cutaway view of muffler*

day are galvanized or treated to protect them from corrosion by rust or acid. A good muffler is "tuned" to the requirements of the car with the right number of baffles, each designed to dampen sound without unnecessarily obstructing the flow of gases.

Cheap mufflers may be made of untreated metal and are far more susceptible to rust and corrosion. Appearances can be deceptive. The bargain muffler may be the same size and look about the same as a good one, but there can be a big difference on the inside. Often the muffler has few baffles. I remember one salesman who came into my shop with a new line of mufflers which were supposed to be every bit as good as original equipment. I took one and compared its weight with that of a standard unit and found it weighed four pounds less. With that much less material, it's a good bet that the muffler would give nothing like the length of service of the original unit.

Some shops offer bargain prices by installing an undersized muffler. A poorly made, small muffler can throw the entire system out of alignment and cause annoying rattles. It can also lead to excessive noise or serious damage to the engine by increasing the back pressure.

I used to have an account with a small trucking company for routine maintenance and repairs. One of the company's drivers came in one day with a blown muffler. When we quoted a price of $20 to replace it, he said he knew where he could get one for $12. He got it, but he was back at my garage again in about two weeks with a red face and burned-out valves. The bargain muffler he bought was too small and had built up tremendous back pressure.

When there is too much back pressure, several things happen. Spent exhaust gases that cannot escape properly through the valves build up inside the combustion chamber. As the piston moves up on the exhaust stroke to push these gases out, it has to work harder than it should, and the power stroke of another piston is partly wasted on this extra effort, making the engine lose power. Excessive heat is generated, and eventually the strain can prove too much for the valves.

Plugged mufflers can also cause excessive back pressure. I remember one customer who came to my garage complaining of a "sluggish" engine. After exhaustive tests, Emil could find nothing wrong. But there was no doubt that the engine was lazy. Then Emil got one of his inspirations and disconnected the muffler. When he started the engine, there was a temendous surge of power as he pressed the gas pedal. We found that the muffler was almost plugged solid with sticky carbon desposits. This is a rare condition, but it should not be overlooked when there are no other apparent reasons for poor performance.

A similar problem can occur when the muffler, exhaust pipe, or tailpipe are badly dented or bent. Anything that restricts proper exhaust will harm the engine and reduce performance.

I am sometimes asked if the normal "built-in" back pressure that is caused by the operation of the muffler is harmful. Engines would perhaps be somewhat more efficient without an exhaust system and the back pressure that must come with it, but imagine the racket if exhaust noises were not controlled. Besides, engines are designed to compensate for the back pressure.

Motorists have asked me why mufflers are not made with a much thicker gauge of metal to make them last longer. The answer is that it would not be safe to make mufflers of too robust construction. Because they are made of a fairly light metal, they would have very little explosive force if they ever blew up (more on that later).

Mufflers *could* be made to last longer. A good example was the ceramic-coated type introduced by one car manufacturer some years ago. While it has a longer life than the ordinary muffler, it is more expensive. Usually, when replacing a muffler, the motorist is happy to get one that will last for a couple of years or so. The maker who introduced the ceramic-coated type as a long-life feature found that it didn't prove to be a strong selling point and soon discontinued it.

Dual-exhaust Systems

Some motorists feel that a dual-exhaust system, which consist of two complete exhaust systems, is a worthwhile way to cut down back pressure and increase gasoline mileage. Dual-exhaust systems are fine when designed into the car by the manufacturer, who usually specifies them only for large high-performance engines. The dual system is seldom helpful on smaller engines. The single system is capable of handling the car's exhaust at speeds from idle to the top of the speedometer and has no difficulty coping with average highway speed limits.

My nephew asked me if he should install dual exhausts on his convertible with a small V-8 engine. A friend had told him he could expect up to five miles more per gallon with the twin mufflers. Since most of his driving is in the city, I told him it was doubtful if he would enjoy any appreciable improvement in fuel economy, and it would take a long time to recover the cost of installing a new dual system at possibly twice the price of a single-exhaust system. Besides, he would be letting himself in for twice the labor and parts costs when repairs were eventually needed. But I really got through to him when I pointed out that one of our luxury liners with a massive, powerful engine had a dual-exhaust system with four mufflers—which cost approximately $200 to replace. He decided to leave his car the way it was.

The Resonator and the Tailpipe

I am sometimes asked what a resonator is. Quite simply, it is an additional "silencer," or second muffler, that may be found on both single- and dual-exhaust systems. Its primary function is to produce a quieter, more pleasant sound. It is frequently used on imported compacts and domestic V-8 luxury liners.

Finally, there is the tailpipe. Its function is simply to ensure that the now-silenced gases are expelled behind the car. Like the exhaust pipe, it is nothing more than a pipe and the final extension of the exhaust system.

Brackets

The support brackets which keep the exhaust system from touching the car body are important. There must be air space between every part of the exhaust system and the body or frame of the car. Not only may contact cause fire; it may also make funny clunking noises, which in error can be diagnosed as transmission trouble, poor universal joints, or a worn rear end, among other things.

The whole exhaust system is designed to float with the engine. If there is insufficient clearance between the undercarriage and the exhaust system, it will strike against the undercarriage, especially when the engine is first started or under heavy acceleration.

The support brackets should, therefore, be inspected periodically to determine that they are intact and to see that the muffler or pipes have not been bent into contact with the undercarriage.

I had a customer, a young lawyer, who was a devoted classical-record collector. One day he parked his car while visiting a client, and when he came back three hours later there was a wisp of smoke curling from the trunk. When he opened the trunk he found all his Brahms, Beethoven, and Bach, not to mention a case full of valuable documents, representing months of work, burning. Everything was damaged, including the interior of the trunk and the spare tire. We later found that his muffler had been bent up so much that it was resting against the bottom of the trunk. Unfortunately, while his insurance covered the damage to the car, it did not take care of the contents.

An insurance adjuster once told me of an unusual claim he had settled. A policyholder had driven his car onto a hard mound of snow and wound up with all four wheels off the ground. After being towed free, he headed for the highway. Shortly afterwards, he smelled smoke and discovered that the rear carpet was on fire. He poured snow on the smoldering carpet and headed for the nearest service station, where it was discovered that the supporting brackets for the exhaust system had been buckled by the pressure of the snow, and the muffler was locked tightly against the floor of the car, causing it to get hot enough to ignite the carpet inside.

Damage to the Exhaust System

I cannot emphasize too strongly the dangers of a faulty exhaust system. Every motorist should have this system checked at least twice a year, whether he is having trouble with it or not. And I don't mean just the exhaust pipe, muffler, and tailpipe. Points frequently overlooked include the manifold gaskets, worn heat-riser valves, broken bolts, cracked manifolds, and cylinder head gaskets.

Tailpipes are so easily bent that it's wise to be cautious about getting too close to piles of hard snow or ice when maneuvering in tight quarters. Usually a restricted tailpipe can be detected by a loud swishing or whistling sound under heavy acceleration. If you hear such a noise, have the system checked immediately.

The alignment of the exhaust system is important and often difficult to maintain. Maintaining this critical alignment can be doubly difficult when installing a muffler smaller than that specified by the manufacturer. If the muffler is only half an inch shorter, it can pull the tailpipe far enough forward to bring it into contact with a spring or shock absorber or allow it to rattle against the car body or rear-axle assembly. The extra efforts of the mechanic to achieve a reasonable mounting can result in high labor charges—possibly high enough to offset the saving on the price of the smaller muffler. It pays to buy the proper part in the first place.

If there is a leak in your exhaust system which cannot be accurately pinpointed, this is no reason to condemn the whole system and cut off exhaust pipe, muffler, and tailpipe with a torch. Such hasty action may reveal that the leak was in the engine. I have seen the results of a "fast buck" artist going to work with a torch and making a big hole in a motorist's pocketbook when a gasket between the exhaust manifold and exhaust pipe would have stopped the leak.

I have frequently found stubborn leaks by removing the air cleaner from the carburetor, restricting the tailpipe opening, and then letting the engine run at about twice normal idle speed, while I squirted oil into the carburetor from an oil can. With a good volume of oil going through the engine, it usually showed up as blue smoke at the exact point of the leak. Of course, this will also result in great clouds of choking smoke from the tailpipe; it should not, therefore, be done in a garage or other confined area.

Sometimes the exhaust system can drive a motorist to distraction with offbeat failures that occur without any leak or real danger. A good example is loosening of baffles in the muffler. Every time there is a change in engine speed, the baffles rattle and chatter. It is an unusual noise and can be mistaken for a worn water pump or generator, or a loose heat-riser valve. There is usually no cure except installation of a new muffler, but I remember one time when Emil gave such a muffler a clout with a hammer and was lucky enough to bend it in just enough to tighten the baffles without damaging the muffler.

And, as I said earlier, mufflers *can* blow up. All it takes is a buildup of gasoline or fumes in the muffler and a spark or flame from the engine. This is why you should never turn off the ignition when the engine is running fast, or worse, turn it off and then on again while driving. When I was in my teens, I was riding with a chum in his dad's car. I wanted to go back home, and he wanted to keep driving, so I playfully leaned over and turned off the ignition. By the time he turned the key on again, a fair amount of gasoline had been pumped into the muffler. There was a resounding explosion, and the muffler blew apart.

Two petrified kids drove the roaring car to a garage where a friend of mine worked, and had the muffler welded back together again in record time. But, as luck would have it, my chum's dad had his own inspection pit, and he crawled under the car that same day for a routine check. He quickly spotted the fresh weld and, needless to say, my pal was grounded for two weeks.

I have noticed that people usually only think of the muffler when the car develops a noise caused by a leak, but there are many other points where trouble can occur. The exhaust manifold can leak because of cracks, warping, loose bolts, or a blown gasket. In addition, there can be leaks from the heat-riser valve, exhaust pipes, cylinder head gaskets, and the tailpipe.

Repairs to the Exhaust System

Temporary repairs to the exhaust system are sometimes made with a welding torch; but, with few exceptions, this is seldom satisfactory. If the metal has rusted thin enough to break open, there isn't much there to weld to, and new holes are likely to develop around the weld.

Stones or other impact damage which causes a hole in an otherwise sound component can often be corrected by welding, but have the job done by a man who knows his trade. Improper welding can weaken the metal and cause it to break through later.

Various types of patching materials are available, but when any part of the exhaust system has so many holes that it resembles a sieve, the use of these materials may quiet the noise for a short time, but this type of patchwork is not likely to last long.

I have seen people do strange things with their exhaust systems, and some of the things they do are just plain useless, if not dangerous. Shortly after World War II, an old gentleman from the country came into my garage with a loud rattling noise in his exhaust system. He was concerned only with the rattle, but I could hear the rumble of a bad muffler as well. I climbed under the car and found the cause of the rattle—the tailpipe was broken in several places and was banging against the rear-axle housing and gas tank. What amazed me, though, was the "muffler"—or what he had in place of one.

He had taken the cylinder from an old water pump out of his well and had attached it somehow to the rest of the exhaust system with pipe fittings. It was an ingenious installation, and it certainly did lower the noise to an appreciable extent. But when I told him it was extremely dangerous and could explode with the force of a bomb if enough gasoline built up inside, he simply looked me in the eye and said, "Well, it ain't happened yet, son."

Finding and fixing leaks in the exhaust system is not only a matter of convenience in order to cut down the noise and conform with the law, it can also save your life. The exhaust system does not simply keep the car purring quietly; it also carries away large quantities of deadly gas. Many people who do not realize this die needlessly each year from the fumes developed by their own cars.

Carbon Monoxide

This poison is colorless, odorless, tasteless, and lethal. Carbon monoxide is a gas that is generated every moment the engine is running. Because it defies our senses, it claims many unsuspecting victims who are not aware they are being asphyxiated.

In my thirty years in the garage business I have been exposed to carbon monoxide hundreds of times—and have suffered anything from a minor headache to a complete blackout. I know of twelve people who have died from its effects.

Just prior to opening my repair shop, I was working on a friend's car in an unheated garage at the rear of my parents' home. I had the engine running so that I could adjust the tappets. I was fully aware of the dangers of carbon monoxide, but since it was a cold day I left the garage doors closed. Anyway, I reasoned, it would only take a few minutes. Halfway through the adjustment, I dropped over the engine. It's an odd, drowsy, almost pleasant sensation, and the temptation is to just let yourself go.

Although I don't remember doing it, fortunately I was conscious enough to pull out the coil wire and stall the engine, then somehow I managed to crawl over and open the doors. When I came to, I found myself lying in a snowpile, and I haven't a clue how long I was there before finding the strength to get inside the house. I was deathly sick for two days, and my doctor told me I was lucky there was no permanent brain damage. To this day, the slightest whiff of carbon monoxide gives me a violent headache.

A chemical engineer employed by a safety appliance company once invited me to attend a test he was conducting to establish the volume of carbon monoxide within the interiors of their employees' vehicles. Each car was tested on the parking lot by placing a long hose inside the car's body, engine compartment, and trunk. The hose was attached to a sensitive instrument in the engineer's office, which drew the air from the car and recorded the exact amount of carbon monoxide in each location. I was shocked to see, as dozens of cars went through this test, that at least 25 percent of them were defective to some degree. When the hose was placed near the manifold of a six-year-old compact, the concentration of gas was so strong that the graph on the testing instrument jumped beyond its limits, which is a maximum reading of 1500 parts of carbon monoxide to 1,000,000 parts of air.

Examination proved that the gasket had blown between the exhaust pipe and manifold. The owner of this vehicle told us she had wondered why she felt sleepy every time she drove the car, and she said that her two children were soon asleep when driving with her. She thought this was rather odd, as they never normally wanted to sleep during the day. I examined the firewall between the engine compartment and the inside of the car, and there were five holes through which fumes passed into the passenger section. A test was made within the passenger section of her car, and a reading of 75 parts of carbon monoxide per 1,000,000 parts of air was recorded. The engineer explained that the average person is entering the danger point when a reading of 50 parts of carbon monoxide per 1,000,000 parts of air is recorded. But he told me there is no set pattern; some may react at a lower reading, depending on such things as age, physical condition, and one or two drinks of alcohol. Any one, or all, of these things combined can induce sleep, nausea, headache, or a general slowing down of the reflexes.

When inhaled, carbon monoxide is taken up by the hemoglobin (that part of the blood stream whose normal function is to carry oxygen). The hemoglobin has an affinity for carbon monoxide about three hundred times greater than for oxygen; consequently, the absorption of the poisonous gas is quite rapid. As the hemoglobin becomes saturated with carbon monoxide, the oxygen in the blood stream is reduced in proportion. When the brain does not receive enough oxygen, reflexes can be considerably slower. If the air contains sufficient carbon monoxide, death ultimately comes as a result of oxygen starvation.

Carbon monoxide can easily leak into a car even when you are traveling down the highway at 60 mph. Motorists I have spoken to about dangerous leaks in their engine compartment have told me that it didn't matter all that much because they had a thick firewall to prevent gases from getting into the car, and the stuff would be swept away by wind pressure as the car moved. The trouble is that this wind pressure forces the gas right into the car—through the firewall. The firewall is pierced with numerous holes, which are necessary to allow passage of the steering column, brake and gas pedals, and a maze of wires, cables, and hoses. They are sealed with rubber grommets or boots, but rubber can shrink with age and allow any amount of gas to get by. Grommets or boots can also accidentally be pushed out or improperly replaced when work is done on the car.

On older cars, particularly in frigid areas where salt is used on the roads, it is wise to lift the floor mats and check for holes in the floor. Also check for holes in the firewall, through which carbon monoxide can enter. Should your car scrape against an obstruction on the road and make you suspicious of exhaust-system damage, open the windows and drive immediately to a garage to have it checked.

Even if we accept the danger of carbon monoxide, it is important to remember that the exhaust system needs attention. When it comes time to make repairs, it does not pay to save a dollar or two by installing inferior equipment.

Lowering the center of gravity in our modern chariots has done much to improve their handling as well as give them the popular low-slung appearance. But the exhaust system takes a terrible pounding as it rides along only inches from the road.

Exhaust-emission Systems

The average car in its years of operation could generate enough poison to wipe out the population of a fair-sized city. That is why authorities in most countries are so concerned with air pollution caused by car exhaust. After years of research, it was found that 90 percent of the air pollution in the city of Los Angeles was attributable to automobile exhaust emissions.

As a result of this startling discovery in the mid-sixties, California government officials passed a law requiring that engines on all new vehicles sold in that state be fitted with controls to minimize these dangerous emissions.

Since 1968 these controls have been required on all new vehicles sold in the United States. Emission control laws were introduced in Ontario in 1969 and in Canada generally in 1971.

To reduce exhaust emissions to specified limits, various modifications have been made to the engine design, the carburetor, and the ignitions system. These modifications, comprising the exhaust-emission control system, vary depending on the year and make of car and the size of the engine.

Some engines also use belt-driven pumps to inject air into the exhaust manifold. The air injected by this system ignites the gases that are not completely burned in the combustion chamber, thus reducing the hydrocarbons and carbon-monoxide fumes that pour from the tailpipe. To ensure maximum efficiency of this system, it is essential that all control devices be tested and adjusted during a routine engine tune-up, and that factory specifications for ignition timing and carburetor adjustment be strictly adhered to. A mechanic who is not familiar with this system could unknowingly throw the whole mechanism out of kilter.

The following incident illustrates what could happen if inexperienced personnel attempt to trouble-shoot these systems. While in a service station recently, I was admiring the power plant on a new high-powered sports car that was fitted with an exhaust-emission, belt-driven air pump. To some degree, these pumps resemble an alternator. A curious apprentice mechanic, after scanning the engine said, "Well, how about that—she's got dual alternators."

Proper maintenance of emission systems is the responsibility of each owner. During roadside spot checks, mobile equipment is used to measure the volume of combustion gases emitted from vehicles equipped with these systems. Fines may be levied on owners of vehicles whose hydrocarbons and carbon-monoxide fumes exceed the limits of the government exhaust-emission regulations.

In addition to air pollution, malfunctioning emission systems pose numerous mechanical problems such as hard starting, stalling, poor acceleration, and "after-run" or "dieseling"—when the engine continues to run after the ignition key is shut off.

I am sometimes asked why the idle is so rough and also why the engine continues to run after the key is shut off on exhaust-emission-equipped engines. The reason for this is that the fuel/air idle mixture on these engines is considerably leaner (less fuel), and a lean mixture is not conducive to smooth idling. Some motorists, after spending thousands of dollars on a gleaming new chariot, are horrified when they see the engine roughly rocking about on the rubber mounts. To pacify these unhappy people, mechanics are sometimes tempted to increase the idle speed, which will smooth things out a bit. But the problem is that this same increase in idle is the prime reason that the engine does not stop when the key is turned off. To add to all this, the lean idle mixture also generates more heat in the combustion chamber; the carbon then becomes red hot and ignites the fuel, regardless of whether the key is off or on.

Over the past few years intensive research has discovered more and more sophisticated means of cleaning up exhaust gases, and it seems that this is just the beginning of a complex and mighty expensive approach to controlling exhaust emissions.

Designers have been forced to turn to lower-compression engines, producing less exhaust emissions but at the expense of miles per gallon of fuel and decreased horsepower.

It is estimated that up to 1972 emission controls, as required by law, had cut gasoline mileage by 8 percent (using 1970 models as a base). In the 1973 models it is reported that mileage was again cut by another 7 percent. Unless the researchers (and motorists) get lucky, 1976 models are expected to give 29.4 percent less mileage per gallon than the 1970 models.

In addition to devices used on the 1973 models that further reduce harmful emissions by recycling exhaust gases through the combustion chambers, new avenues are being explored to filter emissions through catalytic devices.

At the time of writing, hundreds of different types of catalytic filters to purify exhaust gases are being tested. Engineers feel that it is inevitable that a filter of this type will have to be introduced into the exhaust system if cars are to meet emission control levels projected for the mid-1970s.

A catalyst is an element that produces chemical change. In this case, the change in the exhaust fumes would make them acceptable ecologically before they are released into the atmosphere.

The arrival of a catalytic filter would bring problems with special types of fuels, for the presence of such additives as lead in the gasoline would poison the catalyst, ruining it. It is estimated that replacing a damaged catalyst will cost us about $100.

It is important to refer to the Owner's Manual for guidance as to the right fuel to use and for special treatment of any filtering devices that might be incorporated into the exhaust system.

The Drive Train

Once the engine is running, its power must be transmitted to the "drive train," a sequence of gears and components that finally rotate the wheels to move the car. (*See Diagram 29.*)

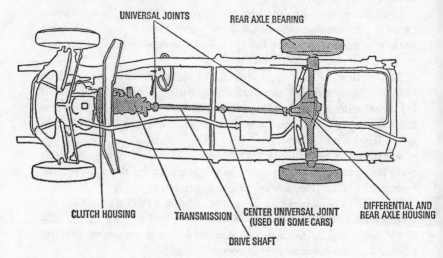

UNIVERSAL JOINTS   REAR AXLE BEARING

CLUTCH HOUSING   TRANSMISSION   CENTER UNIVERSAL JOINT (USED ON SOME CARS)   DIFFERENTIAL AND REAR AXLE HOUSING

DRIVE SHAFT

Diagram 29. *The drive train*

The key to this drive train is a collection of gears of different sizes, called the transmission. When these gears are matched in certain ratios, they permit the vehicle to be moved forward or backward and give the driver a choice of power to suit driving needs. The transmission multiplies the engine's power for starts and for climbing hills. By means of a "neutral" gear, it disconnects the engine from the rear wheels and allows it to run without stalling when the car is standing still.

Before we can use the gears, there must be a means of linking the engine to the transmission. With manual transmissions, this is done by means of a clutch; with automatic transmissions, by means of a torque converter.

In addition to the neutral position of the standard transmission, the clutch is another means of disconnecting the engine from the rear wheels. With the transmission in gear, it allows the engine to run, or idle, while the car is standing still. While the car is in motion, the clutch permits the driver to change gears without damaging them. With automatic transmission, the torque converter does the same job.

The Clutch

Attached to the engine's flywheel, the clutch assembly comprises a pressure plate and disk. The disk is placed between the flywheel and pressure plate; attached to both sides of the disk are asbestos facings. When the clutch pedal is up, or in the engaged position, the spring-loaded pressure plate forces the disk hard against the face of the flywheel, which, when the engine is running, causes the flywheel, disk, and pressure plate to rotate together. With the clutch pedal pressed down to the floor, or in the disengaged position, the pressure plate is pulled away from the disk, allowing the flywheel and pressure plate to turn without rotating the disk. (*See Diagram* 30.) The

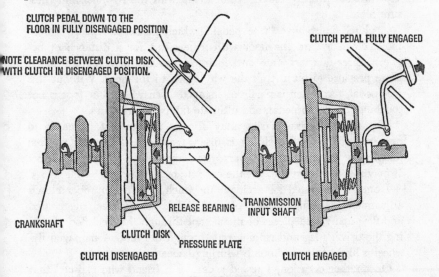

CLUTCH PEDAL DOWN TO THE
FLOOR IN FULLY DISENGAGED POSITION

CLUTCH PEDAL FULLY ENGAGED

NOTE CLEARANCE BETWEEN CLUTCH DISK
WITH CLUTCH IN DISENGAGED POSITION.

RELEASE BEARING

TRANSMISSION
INPUT SHAFT

CRANKSHAFT

CLUTCH DISK

PRESSURE PLATE

CLUTCH DISENGAGED

CLUTCH ENGAGED

Diagram 30. *How the clutch operates*

pressure plate is operated by a clutch-release bearing, which is controlled by a series of linkage attached to the clutch pedal.

After placing the transmission in gear, the driver gradually engages, or raises, the clutch pedal, and at the same time depresses the gas pedal. The flywheel then transfers its rotary energy to the disk, which in turn is connected to the transmission by a steel shaft, and the vehicle is set into motion.

When the car is moving, each time the gears are shifted, the engine's driving force is disconnected from the transmission by disengaging the clutch—if it were not, the transmission gears would be destroyed.

To adjust the clutch costs about two dollars, but to replace one, depending on make of car, can cost over $100. However, motorists seldom ask to have the clutch checked for adjustment, and unless the garageman suggests it be done, it is usually neglected. I am sure that more than half the clutches that are replaced fail as a result of this oversight.

All clutches will wear out in time. In much the same way as brake linings, the asbestos facings inside the assembly wear off as they are squeezed between the pressure plate and the whirling flywheel. The facings wear out a lot faster if the clutch is out of adjustment and slips because proper contact is not made with the flywheel and pressure plate.

A clutch must have "free pedal," which means the pedal should move down toward the floor with little effort for a distance of between three-quarters and one inch. It should then require much more pressure to push it all the way down to the floor. Without this free pedal, the clutch is partly disengaged, even when your foot is not touching the clutch pedal, and ultimate failure soon occurs.

The clutch-release bearing may also be affected. It is meant to operate only when the clutch is disengaged, and if there is no free pedal it revolves constantly, burns out, and makes a grinding noise. It may then be difficult to get the car into or out of gear.

I once investigated an accident in which, due to improper clutch adjustment resulting in lack of free pedal, the flywheel overheated and flew apart, and pieces of metal shot through the steel floor, gashing the driver's leg and ripping out through the roof. A damaged flywheel is like a 20-pound bomb whirling beneath you.

On another occasion, I tested a car for a friend who claimed that the engine was so lazy the car would barely move as he engaged the clutch and attempted to pull away. There was nothing wrong with the engine, but the clutch was so badly out of adjustment that even when fully engaged it slipped, allowing the engine to race up while the car remained almost stationary. Every component in the clutch assembly was burned out and, at only 6000 miles, it was necessary to replace the whole assembly at a cost of over $90.

An engine that revs up ineffectively as the clutch is engaged, or an unpleasant burning odor, are clues to a slipping clutch.

The face of the flywheel may be scored by continued use of a clutch in need of repair. When replacing a clutch, to avoid premature wear to the new asbestos facings, plus the possibility of grabbing or chattering as the clutch is engaged, a scored flywheel must be machined to a mirrorlike finish. Also, the teeth on the flywheel ring gear that engage with the starter-motor gear should be checked for possible damage.

Originally, when overhauling the clutch, it was usually only necessary to rivet new asbestos facings onto the old disk. When a clutch is being replaced today, some motorists cannot understand why the same procedure cannot be followed. For many years now, the disks have been of two-piece construction and are spring loaded to ensure smooth getaways and eliminate sudden grab or annoying chatter as the clutch is engaged.

The heat generated during normal use can weaken or break these springs, resulting in harsh, erratic clutch action. The pressure-plate springs are also subject to heat damage, and the surface of this pressure plate that contacts the asbestos facings is likely to be scored when the facings are worn down. The complete pressure-plate assembly and disk, and usually the clutch-release bearing, should be replaced when the clutch is being overhauled.

On some cold mornings you may hear a loud howl when the transmission is in gear and the clutch pedal is depressed. The most likely cause of this is a dry pilot bearing, which supports the transmission shaft in the center of the flywheel. But if the noise goes away when the car warms up, the problem probably isn't too serious. But when a clutch job is being done, it is important that the pilot bearing be lubricated or replaced as necessary.

Under average driving conditions and with good maintenance, a clutch may be expected to last for as much as 50,000 miles. However, I have seen some that were worn out at 3000 miles, and others still going strong at 100,000 miles.

Manual Transmission

Just as it takes more effort for a person to run a race or to climb a hill, an automobile must have flexibility of power for rapid acceleration from lower speeds and for climbing hills without appreciable loss of speed. Up to a point, the faster the engine turns over the more power it develops. Therefore, in order for the engine to develop sufficient power to climb a steep hill without loss of forward speed, it is necessary for the engine to turn over much faster than would be required to maintain speed on a level road.

While some of this can be accomplished with the accelerator pedal, it isn't always possible, nor is it wise to depend on more gas to do a job that should be done with the gears in the transmission.

So, with manual transmission, when increased power is needed to pull away from a stopped position or to climb a steep hill, the driver selects "low" gear, which, as the clutch is engaged, allows the engine to turn over much faster than it would in "high" gear. Now, while pulling away in "low" gear, the wheels on the road that drive the car are turning quite slowly, but their twisting force, or ability to push the car ahead, is multiplied considerably.

Before discussing how gears in the transmission can multiply the engine's power, let's take a look at the simple gear ratio on a bicycle. In this case, the *driving* gear—the large gear to which the pedals are attached—is turned by the rider's feet and is connected by a chain to the smaller, *driven*, gear on the rear axle.

Because the prime function of a bicycle is to move the rider at a much faster speed than he can walk, it has a "high" gear ratio, that is, the gear attached to the pedals has about twice as many teeth as the axle gear. For this reason, the rear wheel turns two full revolutions for each one turned by the rider's feet.

But when the cyclist starts to ride up a hill, he finds he must pump on the pedals much harder to maintain his momentum. If the hill is steep enough, he will end up by standing on the pedals to apply his whole weight on the downward thrust, or he may even get to the point where he gives up and pushes the bike to the top of the hill.

Now, here's where the transmission comes in. If the cyclist could change his gear ratio (and on some bikes he can), he might select one that would give him perhaps one turn on the pedals for each one on the driven wheel. It would require faster pedaling, but the pressure needed would be considerably reduced, so he could climb the hill, sitting comfortably on the seat.

The application of different gear ratios is perhaps best explained by going back to high-school physics and the principle of the lever. It's the same as using a long bar and a fulcrum to apply pressure beneath an article we wish to move. Many of you will remember that the favorite illustration for this principle showed a man using a lever to lift a one-ton elephant by moving the fulcrum close to the lifting end.

In the transmission, instead of having a lever and fulcrum, gears of different sizes are meshed together. When extra energy is needed, the engine's driving force is applied to a gear in the transmission which meshes with a gear having a larger number of teeth. In this way, the *driven* gear rotates at a slower speed but has more driving force, because it is absorbing more of the engine's power in each turn.

The typical domestic car fitted with standard transmission has four gear selections, or ratios. They are comprised of first (or low) gear, second gear, third (or high) gear, and reverse gear. Protruding from the front of the transmission assembly is a shaft (the input shaft) that is connected to the clutch assembly. Extending from the rear of the transmission is another shaft (the output shaft) that is attached to the driveshaft and other components (discussed later) which, together with the clutch and transmission, transmit the engine's power to the rear driving wheels.

Some domestic sports models, as well as many imports with less powerful engines, offer four forward-gear selections (the popular "four on the floor" stickshift), which provide greater utilization of the engine's power.

Ratios are made up of gears with different numbers of teeth that are matched in certain choices to make up the first gear, or second, etc., as offered by the transmission. Typical first gear is a ratio of about three to one—with the engine turning over three times while the shaft it is driving turns over just once. In this way, you get more power out of the engine by revving it up, but the car moves slowly.

The second gear ratio is something like two to one, and in third (or high) gear, one to one. A one-to-one ratio simply means that the transmission gears are not multiplying the engine's power. Thus, the engine, the transmission's input and output shafts, and the driveshaft are all rotating at exactly the same speed, or revolutions

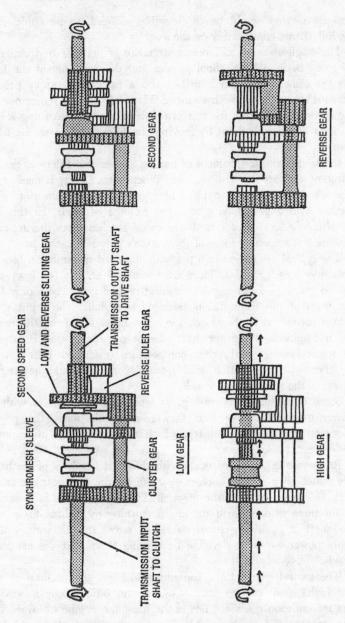

Diagram 31. *Manual-transmission gear ratios*

per minute (rpm). (*See Diagram* 31.) There is a further *fixed* gear-reduction arrangement in the rear-axle assembly that is explained later in this chapter.

While it is relatively easy to mesh two gears when they are both rotating at the same speed, it's a different story when you want to "change" gears—that is, mesh a slow-moving gear with one that is moving perhaps twice as fast. This situation is encountered when the car has gained momentum and you want a higher gear, or when the car is climbing a hill and has slowed to a point where the engine is laboring and you have to shift "down" to use more power to maintain speed.

Many years ago, to prevent damage that might be caused by a clash of the gears, the automobile engineers devised "synchromesh" gears. The synchromesh device assures that when shifting up or down, both gears being mated are turning at the same speed.

Until 1965, most cars had synchromesh only on second and high gears, and while this made it easier to shift gears for general driving, it was necessary to stop the car completely in order to engage first gear. Today, however, most new cars have synchromesh on all forward gears, which is particularly helpful when drivers are "gearing down" for cornering or braking.

Even with synchromesh, care must be taken when shifting up or down. But many drivers don't realize that there is a knack to changing gears properly. A neighbor of mine who drove a domestic car equipped with automatic transmission decided to trade it for a high-powered sports model with standard stick and four forward speeds. On delivery, the salesman asked him how long he had been driving with automatic. My friend told him it was roughly two years, and was taken aback when the salesman casually said, "Well, I'd better take you for a spin and show you how to change gears again." After a little tutoring, my neighbor fully appreciated the necessity for the refresher course.

When changing into low gear on vehicles that do not have synchromesh in that range, it is essential that the car first be brought to a full stop. Even moving ahead at less than 1 mph can damage the gear teeth. On cars with synchromesh on all forward speeds, low gear can be engaged while the car is moving at lower speeds, but a high-speed change may damage any of the components in the drive train.

Since there is no synchromesh on reverse gears, the vehicle should not be rolling even slightly forward or backward when this range is selected. Countless numbers of transmissions have been destroyed when unsynchronized low-gear ratios or the reverse gear have been selected while the car was in motion.

If your car is equipped with a standard transmission, don't be like some members of the "rush-and-push" set who think they are giving Stirling Moss a tip or two by cramming their gearshifts through the full range. No professional driver crams the gears through. He saves time through proper coordination.

Make sure the clutch is fully depressed before moving the gearshift, and then hestitate briefly at neutral before selecting a gear. That way you will save wear and tear on the gear teeth, which, like your own with their enamel armor, are protected by case hardening. Constant clashing of the gears, or even one serious grind, can strip off the case hardening and allow the softer material beneath to wear away in a short time.

Introduction of the synchromesh unit is one of the most worthwhile modifications made to the standard transmission. It takes the guesswork out of changing or selecting gears. Prior to its introduction, shifting from low to high gear, for all but experts, could prove a major chore, and a slip-up could result in stripped gears.

Many drivers resorted to such methods as "double clutching"— releasing the clutch, putting the gearshift in neutral, rapidly engaging the clutch again and releasing it, then cautiously selecting the desired gear and engaging the clutch to complete the change. Others swore that counting to three with the clutch released, before placing the vehicle in gear, would minimize gear clashing, while another school of thought leaned to the "sound and feel" approach to changing gears. But, regardless, in those times the garages did a roaring trade performing major surgery on sick transmissions.

In the late twenties, a chum of mine invited me out for a spin in his dad's luxury liner. It seems he had read somewhere that with proper skill, after using the clutch to pull away in low gear, it was possible to change through second and high without using the clutch. Well, all went well as he used the clutch to get going in low, but the moment he tried for second without the aid of the clutch, there was a deadly crunch from the transmission. The rear wheels locked up, and the car skidded to a stop. Apparently, he hadn't quite mastered the art of a clutchless shift, and had ripped the teeth off most of the gears. The car was towed into the garage for an expensive refit, and to this day I can't remember how long it was before that lad was allowed to drive the car again.

The mechanic said that when he got the transmission on the bench and took off the inspection cover, he was able to remove most of the gears without further dismantling by just shaking the case.

Today, proper handling and maintenance will ensure years of good service from a standard transmission. Should things go wrong, be sure the external shifting linkage is checked before authorizing major repairs. As an example, wear in the steering-column gearshift mechanism can lead to difficulty in changing gears, and this may be improperly diagnosed as clutch or transmission trouble. While on the surface a relatively minor fault, a worn gearshift mechanism makes it all too easy to shift into reverse when trying for second.

Overdrive

Some years ago, a device known as an "overdrive" was offered as a gas stretcher, speed booster, and engine saver. The operation of an overdrive is similar to that of the transmission. It provides an extra high-gear ratio, which reduces engine speed when traveling in excess of a predetermined speed. Thus, wheel speed is increased while engine speed and power are decreased. The idea, basically, is economy. But if there is a strong headwind, if the car is going up a steep grade, or if the car is heavily loaded, the overdrive is of limited value. While still used on some imports, the overdrive has practically disappeared on domestic cars.

The Automatic Transmission and Torque Converter

My first experience with automatic transmission was in 1938 when a wealthy customer pulled into my garage with his brand-new 1938 Buick. Excited as a kid with a new toy, he said, "Take her for a spin; she's got a self-shifting transmission." Sharing his enthusiasm, I got behind the wheel and headed out on a test run. There were four forward-gear ratios and, sure enough, to quite a degree, depending on speed and throttle position, they did shift up and down automatically.

While the clutch had not been totally eliminated, its use was quite limited. Before pulling away, it was necessary to disengage the clutch, place the automatic selector lever in the low position, and re-engage the clutch. The vehicle would then move forward at a touch of the gas pedal.

Without further use of the clutch, and once the car got rolling, the transmission automatically shifted up to second gear. But before it would shift up to the third- and fourth-gear ratios, the driver had to move the selector lever to the high range.

As you can see, in its early stages, while the automatic transmission did much of the work, it was still necessary for the driver to take an active part in manipulating the gear-shifting mechanism.

The "self-shifting" transmission was offered as a mighty expensive option, and it was introduced during the Depression of the thirties. In those years, few of us could afford a new car, let alone consider investing in a new-fangled option that had yet to prove itself a worthwhile, reliable component.

Looking back to that eventful road test, I remember pondering whether the engineers could whittle down the cost to the point where this revolutionary maze of mechanism would fit into the Depression-plagued budget of the average motorist. Then, too, I wondered what on earth it would cost to repair. Would it stand up? Could the average mechanic gain sufficient technical experience and the necessary data to accurately repair it with reasonable speed? This was my main concern.

I finally shrugged it off as being entirely too complicated, a pipe-dream that would probably never get off the ground.

However, determined to eliminate the clutch and come up with a fully automatic transmission, the engineers continued their quest for perfection. After struggling with various designs and countless modifications, they finally produced a transmission that shifted through all the forward-gear ratios with no help from the driver and without the need of a clutch.

In the late forties, optional automatic transmissions were available on the popular production cars, but they were not a big seller. People were reluctant to invest in something that might be expensive to maintain and that few mechanics knew anything about.

More or less happy with the clutch and stick shift, many new-car buyers would say, "I can shift a lot of gears for the extra cost of an automatic transmission." However, automatic transmissions gradually started to sell, and today, even the diehard stick shifters, after experiencing the convenience of an automatic for a few weeks, forget about price just as quickly as they forgot about the gearshift and clutch.

At the outset, with automatic transmission a precision-built device known as a *fluid coupling* took the place of the conventional clutch as used with a standard transmission.

In its early stages, the primary function of the fluid coupling was to transmit the engine's power to the automatic transmission. Later on, however, it was improved to the point where it not only transmitted the engine's driving force but also multiplied the engine's power. This revolutionary modification is fully automatic and provides improved acceleration by going into action when pulling away and when moving at lower speeds.

As a result of this modification, the term *fluid coupling* was changed to *torque converter*. While the word *torque* may sound a little technical, in layman's language it simply means twisting force or power. Thus the torque converter could be interpreted as a device that multiplies power.

For many years now the torque converter has been used on most cars equipped with automatic transmission.

Basically, the torque converter is a cylindrical steel case weighing perhaps 40 pounds and, depending on the make of car, about 12 inches or less in diameter. Hermetically sealed inside the steel case are two shallow dish-shaped metal plates technically known as turbines. Attached to the inner surface of each turbine and positioned at a precise angle are a series of steel fins, or blades. These two turbines, inside the torque converter, are fitted extremely close together, with the steel blades in each section facing each other. The torque converter and the turbines inside are filled with several quarts of light oil. One of the turbines (the *driving* member) is attached to the engine's crankshaft, and the other (the *driven* member) is fastened to a shaft that operates the maze of mechanism inside the automatic transmission.

When the engine is running, obviously the crankshaft and the turbine attached to it are turning together. The angles of the steel blades attached to the rotating turbine are such that they scoop into the oil inside the fluid coupling and force it into the steel blades of the turbine which is attached to the transmission, which causes a pushing or twisting effect on the driven turbine.

While too complicated to explain in detail, an additional mechanism between the driving and driven turbines makes it possible for the torque converter to multiply the engine's power when starting up and at lower speeds.

When the engine is idling, only slight pressure develops between the two turbines, which in effect disconnects the driving force of the engine from the transmission. It is this factor that makes it possible for the car to remain stationary at a traffic signal with the automatic transmission in gear. The torque converter does the same job as the conventional clutch when it is in the disengaged position.

However, the moment the driver depresses the gas pedal, the driving turbine attached to the crankshaft forces the oil hard against the blades of the driven turbine, and it starts to rotate. As the car pulls away and gains reasonable speed, the driving and driven turbines are rotating at practically the same speed.

So, as you can see, rather than a clutch or steel-to-steel connection between the engine and the automatic transmission, there is a yielding cushion of light oil. This cushion of oil in the torque converter, plus automatic gear changing, has done more to simplify driving than any other factor since the inception of the automobile. People who, when learning to drive, had difficulty mastering the art of synchronizing the gearshift, clutch, and gas pedal, will agree that beginners today, with an automatic transmission, never had it so good.

The torque converter is reasonably trouble-free, but like any other mechanical device, normal wear can take its toll. For this reason, if it ever becomes necessary to overhaul the automatic transmission, it is wise to include the torque converter.

Should a well-tuned engine suddenly become lazy when pulling away, it is quite possible that wear in the internal mechanism is preventing the unit from multiplying the engine's power. Keep this in mind if at any time your mechanic cannot come up with the reason for sluggish low-speed acceleration after the engine has been thoroughly tuned and everything else seems to be in order.

Through the years, the types of automatic transmissions have been many and varied. Some had two, three, or even four forward-gear ratios that changed automatically through the full range. Others had two forward-gear ratios; while referred to as "automatics," they would not change gears by themselves, and you pulled away in high gear and relied on only the torque converter to multiply the engine's power. If extra power was needed to get started on a steep grade, the driver had to move the selector lever to the low position. The "semiautomatic" transmission, as used on some compacts, operates on the same principle.

Most automatic transmissions produced in recent years provide either two or three forward-gear ratios which work in conjunction with the torque converter to provide nimble acceleration at all speed ranges. While both these transmissions offer excellent performance, the unit with the three forward-gear ratios provides even faster getaways, especially when it is coupled to a lower-powered engine.

The automatic transmission is as automatic as you want to make it. For nimble acceleration at lower speed ranges, you can put the selector lever in low, where it will remain until you shift to a higher gear. When descending a long, steep grade, to minimize wear on the brake linings and to avoid the possibility of overheating the brake system, selecting a lower gear ratio is also helpful. But a word of caution here. It can be damaging to manually select a lower gear range when the vehicle is moving at a fast clip. Slow down a bit before selecting second gear, and even a bit more when dropping into the low range. When going downhill in a lower gear range, take your foot off the gas pedal. Then, instead of the engine driving the road wheels, the road wheels tend to drive the engine, thus causing a braking action. This slows the car's descent, and frequently it is not necessary to apply the brakes.

To a lesser degree, this braking action is also effective in the "drive" position, but the engine generates considerably more resistance in a lower gear ratio. With a heavy rig, veteran truck drivers always select a lower gear ratio before heading down a long, steep grade. Be sure to shift back to the "drive" position after descending a hill. To continue to drive in the low range at sustained high speeds may possibly burn out both the engine and the transmission.

Under normal circumstances and when driving through reasonably level terrain, it is better to leave the automatic in the "drive" range. Usually the automatic is far more skillful in selecting the right gear at the right time than the driver would be. To develop the habit of constantly switching the gears around, especially flooring the gas pedal in the low gear range, is hard on the engine, the transmission, the rear tires, and many other components.

The device for selecting the various gear ratios in the automatic transmission is either mounted on the instrument panel, or the steering column, or on the floor. Where the floor-mounted method of shifting is employed, the transmission is sometimes referred to as a "stick shift" automatic. Since the term "stick shift" is usually used to indicate a standard transmission, to use the same term with an automatic can sometimes be a little confusing. However, the stick-shift-controlled automatic transmission is just as automatic as any other modern automatic transmission.

The advantage of the stick shift is that the control lever is within easy reach of the driver's hand, and, depending on power requirements, he can shift through the gears in split seconds.

Care and Repair of the Automatic Transmission

The automatic transmission is a complicated maze of parts—gears, pumps, bands, clutches, springs, valves, a valve body (sometimes referred to as "the brain"), and other bits and pieces too numerous to mention. The average transmission contains 250 parts or more. If stripped down and displayed on a workbench, these parts would occupy more than 20 square feet. Putting one together is no easy task.

A word of warning: The average mechanic knows little or nothing about the function of this highly complex unit. When repairs or even minor running adjustments are necessary, it is wise to select an established transmission specialist—unless you are absolutely sure your local serviceman has had special training and really knows his automatics.

When not abused and if properly maintained, today's automatics can last for over a hundred thousand miles or more. The smooth getaway and effortless shifting result in less wear on the engine and all other parts in the drive line. With a standard transmission, a driver who fails to shift gears properly or at the right time overworks both the engine and drive-line components.

In all types of automatic transmission, oil pressure actuates various mechanisms that control the transmission's operation. The circulation of this oil lubricates and also controls the temperature of the transmission.

No other unit works harder or is more taken for granted than the automatic transmission; but, like the engine, it requires periodic tune-ups. Seldom, however, do motorists think to have it checked and serviced at the intervals outlined in the owner's manual. To neglect the adjustment of such things as bands and linkage that play such a vital role in the precise, smooth operation of this complicated unit, can result in expensive transmission repairs.

Also, a transmission that is only slightly out of adjustment can lead to poor gas mileage. For example, I once tested a car for a neighbor who, after spending $80 on a major engine tune-up, was getting only ten miles to a gallon of gas. It turned out that, due to improper adjustment and worn control linkage, the transmission would not shift up into high gear until the car reached 40 mph. Since practically all his driving was in the city at speeds below 40 mph, the vehicle was operating in low gear most of the time, which uses considerably more fuel. After minor repairs, the transmission automatically shifted into high gear at around 18 mph, and normal gas mileage was restored.

For trouble-free operation, preventive maintenance is a must. When checking under the hood, ask your attendant to include the oil level of the automatic transmission. If the oil level is low, find out why and fix it fast. Gear shifting should always be smooth and effortless. Erratic action during gear changing, such as slipping or jerking, should be checked immediately.

Another feature of the automatic transmission that is sometimes overlooked is the "passing gear." This is a special device that causes the transmission to shift down when the gas pedal is tramped to the floor and gives you an extra surge of power and speed for passing or for getting out of a tight spot in an emergency. It is in situations like this that the driver finds an automatic can shift down quicker than he could do it himself, no matter how sharp he might be on the clutch.

I have encountered a number of drivers who did not know their cars had this passing-gear device. They remind me of an uncle who was similarly in the dark when he bought a new car. In his case, the new car was a Model A Ford. For years he had happily driven his Model T with its two forward gears, and he never forgot to change gears at the right time. When he bought his Model A, somebody forgot to tell him he now had three gears to change. After returning from his first weekend trip with the new car, he rushed to the dealer to complain about the "noise" the car had made during his weekend driving. He was quite embarrassed when a salesman diplomatically suggested he try driving in high gear.

The automatic transmission does have its enemies. Excessive heat, usually caused by abuse, is probably the biggest of these. Over half the transmission and drive-train repairs performed in my garage were due to abuse or neglect.

Never place the transmission in "drive" or "reverse" when the engine is revving up too fast. I am amazed at the number of drivers who start the engine, speed it up to the equivalent of 20 mph or more, then slam it into gear. The shock of this is injurious to such parts as the universal joints, rear-end assemblies, and the automatic transmission. In addition, fantastic pressure and heat are generated, which can destroy the fluid and lead to a burned-out transmission.

Fear of stalling seems to be the main reason for this abuse, but if an engine is at operating temperature and in proper tune, it is not necessary to race it to keep it running. It is also very bad practice to hold a car with automatic transmission on a hill by revving up the engine. Use the brake. While stopped in heavy traffic in hot weather, it helps to put the transmission into neutral and rev up the engine slightly to speed up circulation of the cooling fluid through the radiator. This aids cooling of both engine and transmission.

The question of when to change the automatic-transmission fluid seems to be a source of great controversy. The answer can vary considerably, depending on year, model, and make of car. To be absolutely certain, it is essential that the instructions spelled out in the owner's manual are strictly adhered to. The fluid may deteriorate in time and will do so more quickly when overheated by abuse, such as savage acceleration or rocking the car back and forth in snow or mud.

Like the human body, the automatic transmission has to breathe. Many an automatic has been resealed, overhauled, or exchanged at high cost when, in fact, all that was needed was to clean the breather, allowing just plain air to enter or escape the unit.

If your automatic-transmission fluid level drops suddenly, or if you see spots of fluid underneath the car, make absolutely sure the breather has been checked before giving the O.K. for expensive repairs. Normal operating temperatures and fluid expansion build up pressure, and if the breather becomes plugged with dirt or other foreign matter, the fluid will be forced out of the dipstick tube or through the seals. When the fluid leaks out, it can be very damaging to the transmission components, and can even set the car on fire if it pours over a hot manifold.

I remember one time I towed in a customer's car which had burst into flames on the highway. Everything under the hood was burned, and the transmission was ruined. The total cost of repairs ran well over $500. Examination showed the transmission breather to be plugged with mud—a problem that could have been solved in a few minutes at little cost.

Fluid can sometimes disappear mysteriously, leaving no trace of a leak under the car. On some cars there is a vacuum-operated control attached to the transmission case. If the diaphragm in this unit ruptures, fluid can be drawn out of the transmission and into the engine. Besides draining the transmission, this can cause rough gear shifting, an emission of blue smoke from the tailpipe, heavy carbon deposits in the engine, and ignition knock or ping.

When the seals of an automatic begin to leak, it usually means that a reseal job should be performed, but a lot of money is spent on brews guaranteed to remove the curse of an ailing transmission. Sometimes the use of an additive is justified, as when the seals have become hardened. Additives manufactured by reputable companies will sometimes soften the seals enough to restore their usefulness, but don't be misled by some advertising claims that a certain additive will practically rebuild your transmission. It won't.

Towing or Push Starting

Before towing a vehicle equipped with automatic transmission, read your owner's manual carefully for proper towing procedure, and stick rigidly to those instructions. If in doubt, consult an automatic-transmission specialist, but *do not* move the vehicle until you are absolutely certain it is safe to do so. To tow a car any distance, especially at high speed, with the four wheels on the road, will frequently ruin the automatic transmission. I heard of a case where two people died as a result of this oversight. The transmission disintegrated, pieces smashed through into the car, and the occupants were killed by the scalding-hot transmission fluid.

To avoid the possibility of danger, the car should be towed by lifting the rear wheels off the road. In the case of front-wheel drive, of course, the front wheels must be lifted. If for any reason, such as front-end damage, the car must be towed by the rear wheels, it is usually necessary to remove the driveshaft, which disconnects the transmission from the driving force of the rear wheels. Other alternatives are to put dolleys under the rear wheels or place the whole vehicle on a float.

Before attempting to push-start the engine on vehicles equipped with automatic transmission, consult your owner's manual carefully. Many automatics are so constructed that, no matter how fast the vehicle is pushed, the engine will not turn over. But, apart from being dangerous, pushing can ruin bumpers and other components, and it is wise to stay away from this brutal method of starting a temperamental engine.

The most common cause of starting failure is a dead battery, and a service truck is usually the safest and most economical approach. A set of battery-booster cables, which should be carried in the trunk at all times, can be hooked up to another car's battery to get you or a fellow motorist started in the event of a dead battery.

Most automatic-transmission-equipped vehicles tend to creep forward slightly when they are stopped with the transmission in gear. To remain stationary, it is necessary to apply slight brake pressure. The reason for this creeping action is that, even when idling, there is still a little pressure generated between the *driving* and *driven* turbines. However, excessive creeping is usually attributable to an engine that is idling considerably faster than the manufacturer's specifications. If, without touching the gas pedal, your vehicle insists on taking off by itself, have the engine idle speed checked immediately by a competent mechanic who will set it up according to factory specifications. Apart from the irritation of having to press hard on the brake pedal when waiting for a light to change, excessive idle speed overheats the oil in the transmission. Also, placing the car in gear when there is too much pressure between the driving turbine and the driven turbine can destroy certain parts in the transmission and other drive-line components, resulting in whopping repair bills.

Another safety tip: Make sure the automatic is not accidentally thrown into reverse when the car is moving forward. On some cars, this may wreck the transmission or throw the car into a dangerous skid. One of my cutomers had a close call when driving down the highway with his small son on the seat beside him. The little fellow pulled the shift lever into reverse, locking the rear wheels. The car slid broadside along the highway, but, fortunately, the road was wide and traffic was able to evade the skidding car.

The vast majority of domestic cars, and many imports, on the road today are equipped with automatic transmission. Whether offered as standard equipment or as an option, for the average driver I strongly recommend its use. Apart from the convenience of clutchless, automatic gear shifting in heavy traffic, when trading your car you will find, that, except for some sports cars, there is little demand for the standard—or, as it is called by some dealers, "handshake"—transmission.

The Driveshaft and Universal Joints

Up to this point, we have discussed how the combined efforts of the engine and transmission provide the power to offer satisfactory acceleration under all speed and load conditions. The next step is to transmit this power to the mechanism in the rear-axle assembly, then to the driving wheels. Depending on year and make of car, this is accomplished with one or more universal joints and a long steel driveshaft.

There are three types of driveshaft, all of which can be used with either standard or automatic transmission. One revolves inside a torque tube which resembles a long, thick pipe. One end of this torque tube is solidly bolted to the rear-axle assembly. The other end is attached to the rear of the transmission by means of a torque ball, which permits the torque tube to pivot at this connection. The reason for this type of connection is that the transmission is anchored to the frame, whereas the rear-axle assembly, and the rear section of the torque tube bolted to it, move up and down with every bump in the road. Thus, if, instead of a pivoting action, the torque tube were solidly anchored to the transmission, the up-and-down movement of the rear axle would snap the torque tube or shatter the rear of the transmission.

The driveshaft inside the torque tube has a spline attaching it to the rear-axle assembly. A universal joint connects the driveshaft to the output shaft which protrudes from the rear of the transmission.

Since the other two types of driveshaft are not enclosed in a torque tube, they are known as open driveshafts and are of one- or two-piece construction. The two-piece shaft, as well as having a universal joint at either end to attach it to the transmission and rear-end mechanism, has a joint in the center to connect the two pieces. In this case the center joint is supported by a bearing in a hanger attached to the undercarriage. This bearing and hanger do a mighty important job, and they should be inspected when the universal joints are being serviced. Vibrations at medium and high speeds, or a whining noise, are clues to defects in the center hanger or bearing.

The third type of driveshaft is a one-piece open driveshaft with two universal joints; it has been used on practically all makes of cars since the mid-sixties.

While in the past there have been several different kinds of universal joints, for many years the "cross and roller" type has been used on most cars. (*See Diagram* 32.) It comprises a cross and four

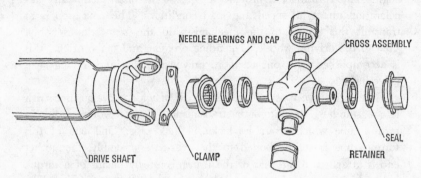

NEEDLE BEARINGS AND CAP   CROSS ASSEMBLY

SEAL

DRIVE SHAFT   CLAMP   RETAINER

Diagram 32. *Exploded view of cross and roller-type universal joint*

caps which are filled with needle bearings about $\frac{1}{10}$ inch thick. The job these small bearings do—transmitting the engine's power while allowing the driveshaft to flex up and down in response to road irregularities—is incredible. But when, due to normal wear, abuse, or lack of lubricant, these bearings start to fail, they can quickly turn to a rusty powder.

At high speed, the driveshaft, weighing about 20 pounds and revolving at the same speed as the engine, can rip away from the rear-axle assembly or transmission and either drop down on the road or grind a hole through the car's steel floor.

A worn universal joint can usually be detected by a high-pitched squeal when pulling away hard, or a clunking sound between acceleration and deceleration. If the joint is badly worn, the car will vibrate noticeably, and serious trouble lies ahead if repairs are not made immediately.

As the rear-axle assembly swings up and down, the distance between it and the transmission changes slightly. For this reason, some cars employ a universal joint so constructed that, in addition to transmitting power when the driveshaft is out of line, it allows backward and forward movement without undue strain on the other components of the drive line. Other cars use a slip-joint splined device to compensate for variations in distance between the transmission-output shaft and the rear-axle assembly.

The Rear-axle Assembly

The rear-axle assembly supports the weight of the rear section of the car, drives the rear wheels, transmits their force to the car's body, and allows the rear wheels to turn at different speeds when the car is going around corners.

We have seen how the engine's power is delivered to the rear of the driveshaft. One of the main functions of the rear-axle assembly is to change the direction of this driving force and turn it at right angles so it can twist the driving wheels to move the car. Here is how this is accomplished. By means of the rear universal joint, the rear of the driveshaft is connected to the *pinion* gear (a strong, short shaft with a gear on the end). The pinion gear meshes with the crown *gear*, (a large, round gear that rotates two axle shafts to which the driving wheels are attached).

As there is a difference in ratio between the driving and driven gears in the transmission, there is a difference in ratio between the rear-axle assembly gears. But, unlike the transmission, this ratio is built in at the factory and does not change. (*See Diagram* 33.)

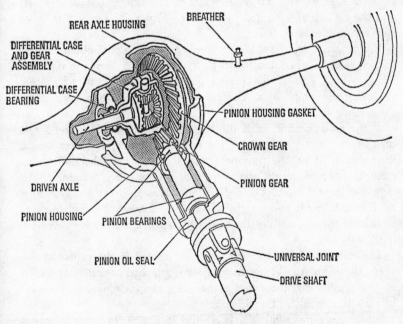

Diagram 33. *The rear-axle assembly*

The pinion is the *driving* gear, and the crown gear is the *driven* gear. There are many more teeth on the crown gear than on the pinion gear that drives it, and its diameter is considerably larger. This difference in number of teeth gives a typical gear ratio of about three-to-one, which simply means that for every three turns of the driveshaft, the rear axles and wheels turn just once.

The actual ratio varies from car to car and is determined by the manufacturer on the basis of engine horsepower, car weight, and type of operation. The lower the rear-axle ratio (say two and a half turns of the driveshaft to one of the wheels and axles) the higher the top speed of the vehicle. But a higher ratio (something like four turns of the driveshaft to one of the wheels and axles) gives more nimble acceleration for faster getaways. Optional rear-axle assemblies are available for the car buff who wants extra get-up-and-go and doesn't mind paying for it with increased gas consumption and a lower top speed.

The Differential

Rather than solidly attaching both rear driving wheels to a one-piece axle shaft, the left rear wheel is rotated by one axle shaft, and the right rear is turned by another. Why is it necessary to have two separate axle shafts?

If, for example, a vehicle is turning to the right, obviously the left, or outside, wheel must turn faster and farther than the right, or inside, wheel, just as the person on the end of a line of skaters "cracking the whip" must travel faster and farther than the one on the anchor end.

If the axles, and in turn the wheels they are driving, could not turn at different speeds when the car is cornering, the tires would drag and scuff on the pavement and the car would be difficult to control. Located inside the center of the rear-end assembly, an ingenious device called the *differential* allows the rear axles to turn at different speeds and, at the same time, deliver an equal amount of driving force to both of the rear wheels when the car is maneuvering.

The differential is a round metal case located in the center of the rear-axle assembly, and the crown gear is attached to and rotates with it. (Remember that the crown gear is driven by the pinion gear, which in turn is rotated by the driveshaft.)

While the differential is a fairly simple device, to attempt to describe it in detail would only lead to confusion. Basically, four small gears are in constant mesh inside the differential case. Two of these gears are held in place by a shaft, and the inner ends of both the rear-axle shafts are splined into the other two gears. When the vehicle is moving straight ahead on a smooth road, these four gears remain stationary, but the moment you turn left or right they go into action to compensate for the variation in speed of the driving wheels.

While the differential provides full traction from both rear wheels when cornering, it sometimes can present problems. For example, when pulling away on ice or snow, it can cause the driving wheel which has no traction to spin uselessly on a slippery surface, while the other wheel, which may be on clear pavement, remains stationary.

However, lack of traction when pulling away on a slippery surface has been largely overcome by a *limited-slip* differential that was introduced in the early sixties and is now offered as an optional extra. When the car is not cornering, the limited-slip mechanism engages *both* of the driving wheels, regardless of whether one or the other is resting on mud, ice, or snow, and traction is greatly increased. I especially recommend it because it can make the critical difference between bogging down on a slippery surface and sailing on down the road. In winter it is a terrific advantage on vehicles that are not equipped with snow tires.

But, remember, a car equipped with a limited-slip differential must not be put in gear when one of the driving wheels is jacked up, because the other one will turn and drive the car off the jack.

Sturdy bearings support the differential case and the pinion gear. Should these bearings become worn, they can throw the crown gear that is attached to the differential case, and the pinion gear, badly out of line. This is a serious failure and can usually be detected by a loud humming noise during acceleration or deceleration.

Just behind the rear universal joint, there is a large round seal that prevents the rear-axle lubricant from leaking out through the pinion-shaft housing. This seal should be checked occasionally for wear. If it leaks, the rear-axle lubricant can drain away, and all the internal mechanism in the assembly can be destroyed. Also, it is wise to check the bolts holding the pinion housing into the rear-axle housing. If these bolts are only slightly loose, the gasket between the two housings can chafe and drain out the lubricant.

The work of the rear-axle assembly is highly complex, and the unit is quite expensive to repair. Sound maintenance in this area can prevent whopping repair bills.

Rear-axle Assembly

In addition to determining its level, it is also sound practice to check the condition of the lubricant in the rear-axle assembly. Condensation can build up water in the housing, which can displace or emulsify the grease, resulting in serious damage.

While launching his boat one summer, a man I know had a costly experience that well illustrates this point. While backing his boat trailer down a launching ramp, he submerged the rear axle in water. After the boat was afloat, he pulled the car back onto dry land and thought no more about it. A few weeks later, the car developed a loud howl, and the owner pulled into a garage to find out why. A breather on the rear-axle assembly had allowed water to enter the housing during its brief immersion, and the water had entered the rear-axle assembly, damaging the crown and pinion gears.

(The breather is necessary to allow for expansion of the air and lubricant caused by the heat buildup on a long drive. The pressure has to escape, or it will force the lubricant through the rear-axle seals and the pinion seal.)

By the time the motorist had reached his launching ramp, considerable heat had built up in the rear end from the drive. When the car was suddenly plunged into cold water, the hot air inside the housing cooled and contracted. The consequent vacuum sucked in the water.

When launching a boat or driving through water, be sure the water is not deep enough to cover this breather. If the breather should be immersed, no harm will be done if the lubricant is immediately flushed out and replaced.

It is well to remember, too, that a mishap of this nature is not covered under warranty. It cost this man $150 to find this out.

Another reader of my column complained of a funny noise every time he turned left or right. He had replaced the rear-axle bearings, a broken rear spring, and the universal joints, but it hadn't helped. It turned out that he had broken some of the teeth on one of the four gears inside the differential case. When these gears are damaged the resulting noise may only be heard occasionally when the car is running on straight road. The reason for this is that they are barely in motion when the vehicle is on the straightaway. Under normal driving conditions these gears will last for the life of the car.

Odd-sized tires on the rear wheels make the gears work constantly even on a straightaway, and they are not designed for this purpose. Excessive revving of the engine when one rear wheel is spinning on ice can also damage these gears. Other damaging factors in the life of these gears include too much backlash in the drive line, and driving at high speed on rough or washboard roads.

A case-hardened shaft is pressed into the relatively soft cast-iron differential housing. If abused by savage acceleration, the shaft can wear loose in the housing. Once it is even slightly loose, it sets up a terrible pounding and soon elongates the hole, and the entire rear-end mechanism is a shambles.

The Axle Shafts

Many years ago I owned a 1929 Durant which was a chronic axle breaker. To cope with this problem, I carried a spare axle under the front seat at all times. I put six axles in that car in less than two years, and after all this practice I managed to whittle down the installation time to just twenty minutes.

I recall a friend who was belting down the highway in a 1937 luxury liner when the right rear axle snapped. This caused the right wheel to fall off, and the car dropped into the ditch and rolled over. Receiving only minor cuts and bruises, he chalked it up to experience and promptly had the axle replaced and the badly multilated body straightened out and painted. But this was not the end of his troubles. Only a week later while driving along the same highway, the left rear axle packed it up, and once again the car plunged into the ditch. This time he broke an arm, and the vehicle came to rest on its roof. Thoroughly disgruntled, he traded the car in immediately. However, he was quite apprehensive when he took delivery of his new chariot. The salesman had a hard time convincing him that the axles had been beefed up considerably and that the chances were all in his favor that they would remain intact.

Through the years, the manufacturers have built a lot of additional strength into the axle shafts used on our modern vehicles. While today's powerful, high-spirited engines subject the axle shafts to considerably more twisting force, seldom do we hear of them breaking.

A seal at the outer end of the axle shaft prevents the lubricant from leaking out of the rear-axle assembly. Occasionally this seal can fail and score the axle at the point where it is mated to the seal, drenching the rear-brake mechanism in rear-axle lubricant. When this occurs, the only cure is a new axle shaft.

As you have seen, the drive train consists of many complicated, expensive mechanisms. However, with common-sense driving habits and normal maintenance, you can easily drive for many years with no major repairs.

The Suspension System

One of the highlights of my life took place when I was ten years old and had my first car ride. My "rich" uncle took me to a picnic in his brand-new Model T Ford. He had bought it the previous day and was learning to drive on a trial-and-error basis. He did fairly well until we approached a steeply arched bridge at too great a speed. The rear of the car bounced up off the road as we abruptly jumped over the hump and began the descent on the other side. I was catapulted upward and my head hit the top of the car—hard.

Automotive engineers have done much to improve the suspension and riding qualities of the car since my eventful ride in that Model T Ford, and today the potholes have to be numerous and deep before we get a real shaking up from the road beneath us.

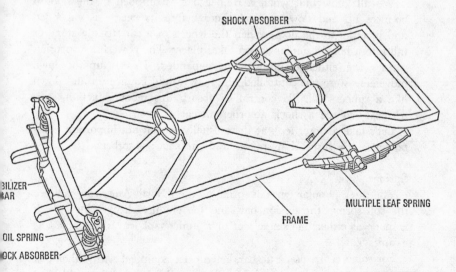

Diagram 34. *The suspension system*

What is suspension? (*See Diagram* 34.) The word means just what it implies. If the wheels and their supporting axles were attached rigidly to the body of the car, we would feel every ripple of the road, high speeds would be impossible, and the car would be unmanageable. The car body is therefore suspended and insulated, by a series of springs and rubber bushings, from the part of the car that contacts the road. Some cars (mostly imports) use hydraulic or pneumatic action for this purpose. The suspended section of the car is referred to as the "sprung weight"; and all parts of the car that are not suspended, such as the tires, wheels, and axles, are referred to as the "unsprung weight."

When the wheels of your car hit a depression in the surface of the road, the action of the powerful suspension springs forces the wheels down, but the body of the car, in response to its own forward momentum, tends to move forward at about the same level. The purpose of the suspension system is to permit the body to "float" over the bumps with minimum up-and-down bounce and to hold the road for smooth steering and stopping. When the wheel hits a bump instead of a hole, the spring action is reversed; the spring absorbs most of the upward action of the wheel, allowing the body to remain stable.

We all know that when a rubber ball is dropped to the floor it bounces up and down several times before its energy is expended and it settles to the floor. When the wheels of a car strike a stone or fall into a hole, a similar action takes place: The powerful suspension springs are either compressed or expanded. If this up-and-down movement were not controlled, the body would bounce up and down like a rubber ball. To control or absorb this rebound action, it is necessary to use a shock absorber on each wheel.

Let's take a closer look at these usually unseen but important components: the suspension springs and the shock absorbers.

Springs

The three popular types of spring used on North American cars are the coil spring, the torsion bar, and the elliptical leaf spring, which is made as either one single leaf or a number of leaves assembled as a unit.

For some years, domestic cars have been equipped with either coil springs or torsion bars on the front suspension, and coil or elliptical springs on the rear. Many vehicles have coil springs all around.

There is controversy about which of these springs is best for the rear suspension, but it has been my own experience that the coil springs in the rear offer a softer ride, while the multiple elliptical leaf spring is better for carrying heavy loads and providing stability at high speeds. Seldom do I hear complaints of a severe "snaking" sensation at high speed when cars are equipped with the multiple-leaf-type rear spring.

Regardless of the type used, normal use and age will eventually cause any spring to settle. Abuse or constant driving over rough roads speeds up this condition. The torsion-bar-type of spring is adjustable to compensate for normal sag. With the coil spring, while the car can be raised by installing shims under the coils or by placing rubber or metal blocks between them, this solution can break the spring. There is really no substitute for new coil springs when the old ones become tired.

The elliptical leaf spring can be re-arched, and sometimes an extra leaf can be added to restore the normal height of the car body. But it is essential that this be done by a reliable technician, otherwise the re-arched springs may settle back down again in six months or less, and the car owner's investment in repairs will be a dead loss.

It is dangerous to drive on weak or broken springs, particularly with the rear flat-leaf type. Just one broken flat-leaf spring is enough, but should both rear springs snap simultaneously, the rear-axle housing can twist, causing the back wheels to steer the car off the road or into oncoming traffic.

There are seldom grease fittings or recommended lubrication points on any of these springs, and occasionally nerve-wracking squeaks can develop in the multiple elliptical leaf spring. Most manufacturers use composition friction pads at the tips of the leaves to control squeaking and avoid the transfer of vibrations and road noise to the inside of the car. Should the car springs suddenly start to squeak, or the car develop a strange vibration or drumming noise, it is possible that these pads have worn through and the tips of the spring leaves are rubbing metal-to-metal. I have also cured "brake" squeals by replacing these insulator pads.

Rubber bushings (round rubber cylinders) are commonly used both to attach the springs and steering components to the car body and as a means of insulating the body from the "unsprung" section of the car. Normally, these bushings require no lubrication; but although they are unbelievably strong, they can wear through. The resulting contact of steel against steel can cause squeaks and vibrations. When this happens, replacement is the only cure. These bushings can also develop annoying squeaks when new. This can be a real headache to you or your mechanic. Although I have sometimes found that a shot of brake fluid aimed in the right direction will do the trick, in stubborn cases it may be necessary to dismantle the mechanism surrounding the bushing in order to lubricate and remove the squeak.

Track Bars and Trailing Links

Obviously, to propel the car the driving force of the rear driven wheels must be transmitted to the rest of the vehicle. With flat leaf springs this is accomplished by anchoring the rear-axle housing that supports the rear wheels to the center of the springs. In turn, the ends of the springs are attached to the undercarriage by spring bolts and flexible shackles.

Cars equipped with coil springs require additional components known as trailing links to transmit the driving force of the driven wheels. These trailing links are attached and pivoted to both the rear-axle housing and the undercarriage. Also, a pivoted track bar is sometimes fitted from the rear-axle housing on one side to the undercarriage on the other side to prevent excessive side-to-side motion of the car's body, while permitting up-and-down movement of the coil springs.

As mentioned in the *Drive Train* chapter, some older vehicles use a "torque tube" that firmly couples the rear-axle assembly to the transmission. With cars so equipped, the force of the driven wheels follows the torque tube to the transmission, which in turn transmits the force to the motor mounts that are anchored to the undercarriage.

Whether torque tube, leaf spring, or trailing links and track bar, these parts also play another important role. They hold the rear axle in proper alignment with the car's body and overcome the natural tendency of the rear-axle assembly to "wrap up" or twist as the car moves forward under acceleration.

Independent or Individual Suspension

I am frequently asked what is meant by "independent" wheel suspension. It simply means that the wheels are hinged and sprung individually and are free to move up and down independently on rough roads without drastically affecting the position of the other wheels.

Prior to the introduction of independent wheel suspension, both front wheels were mounted on one solid steel axle which extended across the front of the car from left to right. When one front wheel hit a bump or buried itself in a pothole, the car would tilt vertically,

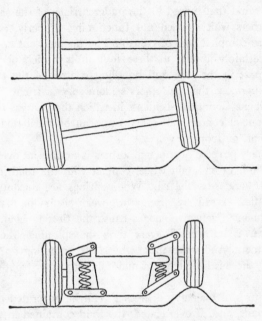

Diagram 35.   *Independent suspension*

affecting both riding quality and steering control. (*See Diagram* 35.) With rare exceptions, domestic cars do not use independent suspension on the rear wheels, but there are several imports that use it both fore and aft. Only trucks continue to use the solid-axle-type of front suspension, and even some of these, in the lighter class, now suspend front wheels independently.

Shock Absorbers

Most of us are familiar with the cylindrical silent-closing unit attached to many storm or screen doors. This unit prevents the door from slamming. The shock absorbers on a car work in much the same way. They are filled with a fluid, and, by the use of a series of internal valves, hydraulic pressure is used to create a damping action to restrict the bounce of the powerful suspension springs as they compress or expand on a rough road.

While there are several different designs of shocks, the most commonly used today are the hydraulic, double-action, telescopic variety usually referred to as "airplane" shocks.

Keep in mind that buried in the undercarriage of the car are four shock absorbers which, when not functioning properly, could quite readily cause complete loss of control. The maxim "out of sight, out of mind" certainly applies to these four units, which play such an important part in the ride and handling control of the car. It has been my experience that customers seldom suggest a checkup of the shock absorbers. Countless accidents in which the car was reported to have gone out of control and rolled over can be attributed to shocks that are weak or inoperative.

The primary purpose of shock absorbers is to prevent overflexing of the springs and to maintain wheel contact with the road in order to propel, steer, and stop the car. When springs are uncontrolled and allowed to flex excessively, premature wear occurs in many of the car's components. Defective shocks cause the tires to bounce off the road. Rubber is burned off every time the spinning wheel returns to the pavement. And when those wheels are pounding up and down on the road, there is little hope of maintaining proper front-end alignment.

Temperatures of over 275 degrees F. can be generated by friction on rough roads, and, if overheated, the fluid contained in the shocks will foam, considerably reducing efficiency. Unusual road conditions, such as a series of rolling bumps, can prove fatal when shock absorbers are badly worn. One car I examined had flipped over, killing the driver and passengers, because the owner—almost unbelievably—had removed the front shocks. He was driving to a nearby town to buy a set of economy shocks when he encountered a series of bumps that would have done no harm had there been shocks on the car. The car hit the first bump and bounced up; on the second, it bounced even higher; and the third bump proved fatal.

If the front end of the car bounces more than once after a sudden stop, it indicates that the shocks are weak or inoperative. A "bounce check" by hand when the car is parked is not too effective; the proper method is to examine the undercarriage and check for leaks, worn bushings, or loose supports. Look at the rubber stops under the springs. If they are glazed, the spring has been allowed to bounce too far by an inadequate shock absorber.

Replacing the Shock Absorbers

The shock absorbers that come as standard equipment on domestic cars (with few exceptions) are preset and cannot be adjusted. They are sealed units which cannot be dismantled and repaired, and it is not possible to replace fluid when it escapes due to seepage. The only cure for defective shocks is replacement.

Adjustable shocks that can be set for "Firm," "Normal," or "Soft" ride are available from some manufacturers and are usually sold by parts and accessory stores. These shocks can be helpful to a motorist who wants to experiment and establish the best setting for his own individual driving pattern.

There is another type of accessory shock absorber with a coil spring fitted around the outside of the shock's body to support the rear of the car and prevent the back from sagging too close to the ground when the car is laden down with baggage. Also available are "booster" coils that fit over the outside of regular shocks on most cars to take care of extra weight. These can usually be bought for a few dollars each. It must be remembered, however, that if these "booster" springs are not properly adjusted, they can rattle or cause the body of the car to ride high at the rear, throwing the car out of balance.

I sometimes recommend the pneumatic-hydraulic, airplane-type of rear shock absorber. I used these at the shop for many years and am of the opinion that they are the best all-around answer to the variety of demands placed on a car's suspension. The pneumatic-hydraulic shocks are not much bigger than standard equipment and are easily installed. A rubber sleeve connects the upper and lower sections of this shock, forming an air chamber. An ordinary tire valve is fitted in the floor or outside lower panel of the trunk. This valve is connected to the air chamber of the shock by a rubber hose. Another hose is joined to the air chambers of both shocks to ensure even pressure and functioning on both sides of the car.

After installation of these shocks, all that is necessary is to load the car with passengers and baggage, then drive to the nearest service station and inflate the shocks as you would a tire until the rear of the car body reaches the desired height. When the load is removed, they can be deflated in seconds, thus restoring the back end to its normal riding position.

A car-bug friend of mine who really likes to "belt" on the highway rolled into my shop one day with a brand-new powerful chariot equipped with coil-spring suspension front and rear. He was very disillusioned.

"This thing is a real dog at high speeds on the highway," he complained. "She pitches and rolls like an ocean liner when I make a fast maneuver." He then asked me if I had any suggestions.

We installed a set of pneumatic-hydraulic shocks on the rear and a set of the three-way adjustable type on the front. He went on his way, and after experimenting with various air pressures in the rear shocks and trying each of the three adjustments of the front shocks, he finally hit on just the right combination, and the suspension was "tuned" to his individual style of driving. But this little bit of research (and I guaranteed him nothing) cost him over $100, and not everyone can afford that kind of experimentation. However, sometimes an unsatisfactory riding condition can be cured by switching to another type of shock.

It must be remembered that the car industry spends millions of dollars on research, and careful consideration must be given before making a decision to alter anything that is standard equipment in the suspension.

The term "heavy duty" does not necessarily mean that the shocks are larger or of better quality or will last longer. While more expensive, better quality shocks are available, they may still be classified as "normal" or "heavy duty" shocks. The difference between heavy duty and normal shocks is the valving used internally and not the actual size of the shock. A stiffer-acting, heavy duty shock reduces bounce on rough roads, but the ride is less flexible, and road shock is more noticeable to passengers. That same stiff-riding shock equipped with another type of internal valving makes the ride "normal" and more flexible.

The manufacturers know what type of shock performs best on a rough road and what type is best on a smooth road. But since they also realize that most cars are driven on both, they attempt to reach a compromise that does the job under all road conditions. If your typical road conditions are rougher than normal, the addition of heavy duty shocks may give you a more controlled ride. But understand that a more controlled ride is a firmer ride; more road shock will be felt inside the car. The kind of ride you get is determined not only by shock absorbers. The springs and tires also absorb road roughness. The shock absorber is there to control the compression and rebound action of the springs as they sort out the bumps and potholes. New shocks will not necessarily perfect the ride if the springs are shot and the tires are improperly inflated.

There is a common misconception that new shocks will raise the height of a car which is sagging too close to the road. Regular standard-equipment shocks, either new or old, have absolutely nothing to do with suspending the body of the car in any position. When the car sits too close to the road, it is due to overloading, weak or broken springs, or some other defective part in the suspension system.

Loading

I am often asked how to cope with the rear end of a new car that practically drags on the ground when the car is heavily loaded. Sometimes people accuse the manufacturers of using too tender a suspension system, but actually it is difficult for the engineers who must design a vehicle to carry adequately the load usually hauled by a small truck and still offer a comfortable ride to the passengers. The car is expected to handle equally well whether it is carrying the driver alone or six people plus hundreds of pounds of luggage.

Most motorists insist on a soft-riding car and, when shopping around, will select the car that will give them the smoothest ride. Manufacturers are fully aware of this and attempt to design a car that will both ride well and at the same time carry a reasonable amount of weight. This "reasonable amount" is often exceeded by the motorist.

It is illegal to load a truck beyond its rated capacity, but I have never heard of a motorist being penalized for overloading his car. For those drivers (such as camping enthusiasts) who load the trunk with hundreds of pounds of luggage, carry six passengers and a dog, sometimes use a cartop carrier and haul a trailer, it is essential to reinforce the rear suspension in some manner. It is extremely dangerous for the rear of the car to sag close to the ground. Rear springs can break and road wheels can split apart, and such other expensive parts as ball studs, pins and bushings, and tires can all suffer premature wear.

When the rear of the car sags, the headlights are tilted upward (blinding oncoming motorists), steering is dangerously affected due to loss of front-end alignment, and braking action becomes sluggish. I have seen the front wheels leave the ground when the rear wheels of an overloaded car hauling a trailer dipped into a deep pothole. Gas tanks can be ripped open by being dragged over loose gravel on rural roads, and the driveshaft can be bent.

Some manufacturers offer as optional equipment an automatic load-leveling device to cope with varying loads, or heavy-duty "packages."

A word of warning while we're on the subject of loading: Be careful how you load the inside of the car. Some time ago a news item read in part: "Man crushed to death in cab of truck as load of steel shifts forward." This kind of accident happens too often in trucks, and a lot of people overlook the fact that the same thing can happen in a car.

I recently investigated an accident in which a man lost his life because of a load of canned goods on his rear seat. He was going downhill at approximately 40 mph on wet, glare ice. The car was equipped with shoulder-type safety harness which was not in use, and on the rear seat, directly behind the bucket seat in which he was sitting, was stacked 56 pounds of canned goods. Traveling at 40 mph, it could develop a forward thrust of about 3000 pounds. This force slammed him forward against the steering wheel as his car collided with another, which had skidded broadside on the hill.

Never travel with loose objects on the rear parcel shelf of the car. Stones and rock samples which children often collect can be very dangerous in a collision when they hurtle forward into the heads of driver and passengers. Even children's toys have been known to cause the death of the driver or passengers in head-on crashes. In panic stops alone, without a collision, loose objects will fly forward with enough force to knock the occupants unconscious.

Stabilizer Bar

Often when a car corners at high speed, there is an uncomfortable sway to the side away from the direction of the turn. This sway is caused by centrifugal force and the "give" in suspension systems. The stabilizer bar is designed to reduce this sway. (*See Diagram* 34.)

Composed of a spring steel bar attached to the front and sometimes both ends of the "sprung" section of the car, the stabilizer bar is in turn connected to the "unsprung" section of the car. As the car's body rolls to the right on a left turn, the stabilizer bar transfers part of the rolling thrust to the left side of the car, considerably reducing the rolling or swaying action.

These bars require very little servicing, but a jingling, rattling sound can sometimes be caused by worn rubber bushings in the connecting links of the stabilizer unit. Occasionally a stabilizer bar will snap in two, and a mechanic will attempt to weld it. A brand-new bar is the only answer, as a welded one will soon snap again near the weld. Not all domestic cars come equipped with this assembly; it is found more often on the heavier or luxury cars. I have sometimes cured side sway and other steering problems at high speeds by installing a stabilizer unit on a car that was not so equipped at the factory.

Frames

We are all familiar with the structural steel of a high-rise office building, which provides a base on which to hang walls, ceilings, and floors. The car frame is much the same; it is the foundation and supports all the component parts of the car.

Until the late fifties, most domestic-car frames consisted of a solid mass of heavy, thick steel members either riveted or welded together and running the full length of the car. Now, many cars are equipped with the all-welded "unit" body construction, and the whole body is so constructed as to form the frame. The lower, or floor, section of the body replaces the conventional frame, and there is considerable reinforcement of the sheet metal while the engine and unsprung components are mounted.

Another design has a partially solid steel frame attached to the unit body, both front and rear, to provide rigid support for the engine and suspension system.

I have discussed the advantages of the different types of frame with several automotive engineers, and it seems to be a matter of individual opinion as to which type is best. Some swear the conventional solid frame is better, while others are equally emphatic that the "unit" type is superior and maintain that in a collision the "unit" construction collapses like a concertina and absorbs more of the energy of impact, protecting the passengers from some of the sudden forward thrust.

Unless damaged in a serious collision, frames will usually last the life of the car, but abuse can cause metal fatigue and lead to disintegration. An example of this came to my attention when one of my mechanics bought a five-year-old luxury car with a solid-steel frame. All went well until he drove on a washboard road at high speed, at which point the front end seemed to flex and rattle, and the car began to wander. "It feels like the steering linkage is made of stretched rubber bands," was the way he explained it. We checked it out and discovered a dozen small cracks in the frame area supporting the steering linkage and engine. The engine had to be removed to allow reinforcement and repairs to the frame.

On another occasion we towed in an old car and found that the power-steering ram had torn away from the frame. Examination showed that the frame, which was too thin, had been constantly flexed by the pressure of the ram. Finally, a piece of metal had torn away.

One time we had an old car in the garage for a brake adjustment. As my mechanic started to jack up the front wheels, another of the boys walked past the car and yelped, "Hey, that car's bending in the middle." I walked around to the side and, sure enough, the body had started to buckle in the center. Rust had eaten huge holes in the floor and supporting steel members of the "unit" frame. It was beyond repair, and the unhappy owner sold the remains to a wrecker.

All points of stress on the frame, particularly steering-linkage connections, should be examined periodically for minute cracks. Repairs and necessary reinforcements should be done only by a qualified frame specialist, since rough welding by an amateur could literally let you down.

Steering Alignment

Most drivers shy away from talk about their steering "geometry." After all, a discussion about "caster," "negative camber," "positive camber," and "toe-in" is enough to give anybody cold feet. However, once the hocus-pocus language is removed, the car's steering is fairly easy to understand.

Before we talk too much about steering alignment, let's look at the suspension components upon which the car rolls, and which are designed for adjustment to various angles to keep the front wheels in proper contact with the pavement, whether driving in a straight line or cornering.

When you move the steering wheel, the turning motion is transmitted by a shaft to the "steering gearbox," where the gearing ratio is such that your efforts at the wheel do not have to be too strenuous to change the direction of the car.

The steering energy from the steering gearbox is transmitted by a series of linkage parts (such as the sector shaft, the pitman arm, the center link, the idler arm, tie rods, the tie-rod ends, and ball joints).

This series of linkage parts is attached to the steering arms which control the front wheels. (*See Diagram 36.*)

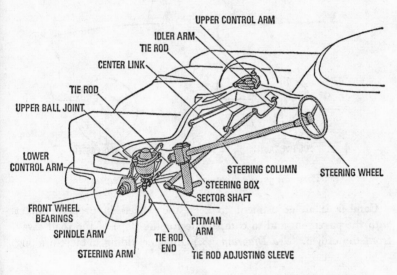

Diagram 36. *The steering mechanism*

Many of these parts can be adjusted to various angles for alignment purposes. But steering adjustment on a modern car is very exacting and must be carried out under scientifically controlled conditions. When I started in the garage business, alignment machines were practically unheard of in an independent garage.

Wheel Alignment

Today's scientific approach to wheel alignment calls for skilled technicians and sophisticated equipment. Caster, camber, and toe-in are now exact measurements. The front wheels are adjusted to lean out at the top and point inward at the front. The former adjustment is called camber; the latter, toe-in. Both adjustments are so minute that they are invisible to the naked eye.

Caster allows easy steering and road stability. The forward sweep of the front forks of a bicycle create caster in the bicycle wheel. The same is true, to a lesser degree, in the front wheels of a car. (*See Diagram* 37.)

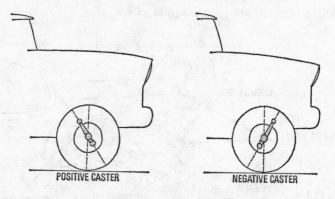

POSITIVE CASTER   NEGATIVE CASTER

Diagram 37. *Positive and negative wheel casters*

Camber is an adjustment to keep the wheels in proper contact with the pavement and to compensate for the slope of the road away from the crown. (*See Diagram* 38.) Imagine riding a bicycle along

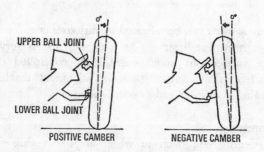

UPPER BALL JOINT

LOWER BALL JOINT

POSITIVE CAMBER   NEGATIVE CAMBER

Diagram 38. *Positive and negative camber*

the side of a hill. To keep your balance you must keep the bike in a vertical position and at an angle to the hillside. This means that the tires are running on only one side of the tread. Camber on the car simply means tilting the wheel to an angle specified by the manufacturer to maintain full-tread contact with the pavement.

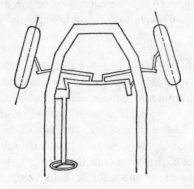

Diagram 39. *Wheel toe-in*

"Toe-in" is the most important steering adjustment of all. (*See Diagram* 39.) It avoids a scrubbing action as the tire rotates; if improperly set, it can result in erratic steering and scuff off the tire tread in only a few hundred miles. Tie rods are responsible for this adjustment, and if they are accidentally bent they can cause an excessive degree of toe-in or toe-out. This has the effect of pushing the tire down the road sideways, and the tread is literally ripped off.

Poor alignment in a car causes wheel fight, tire equal on corners, sloppy steering, and uneven tread wear on the tires.

Steering Linkage

Steering troubles, of course, are not confined to alignment. All of the individual parts in the steering assembly are subject to wear and damage. Ball joints, which replaced the kingpins used on earlier cars, are particularly hazardous when worn. Kingpins, too, would wear in time, but posed no threat comparable to worn ball joints. When a ball joint wears out, it can pop right out of its socket, resulting in instant loss of steering.

Worn tie-rod ends are equally dangerous in this day of the extended lubrication interval. I shudder to think what could happen to a ball joint or tie-rod end which has deteriorated due to constant road pounding or damage to the seals. One thing is certain: With faulty seals, these parts will not function properly for thirty thousand miles or more without lubrication. (See also the *Lubrication* chapter.)

I put my own car on a hoist every two or three thousand miles to inspect for possible damage to steering linkage and other components.

Steering Bolts

It is sometimes taken for granted that any bolt of the right size and thread can be used anyplace in the car's steering mechanism. But this is far from true. For example, the tensile strength of an ordinary low-carbon, ¾-inch bolt would be around 74,000 pounds per square inch. The same size bolt formulated from chrome-nickel-alloy steel would be in the area of 150,000 pounds per square inch. Obviously, the size of the bolt is not the only criterion of its strength.

The tensile strength of the assorted bolts used on our automobiles varies according to use. For instance, a mild steel bolt is more than sufficient to attach the oil pan to the engine. But bolts used to attach components that are subjected to millions of cycles of vibration, such as steering components, are formulated from better-quality steel.

Mild steel bolts can stretch and loosen when used in stress areas of the steering mechanism. We can stretch an elastic band and it will return to its original length, but once a bolt is stretched beyond its elastic point, it remains stretched and eventually works loose. The component it is supporting can drop away, resulting in complete loss of steering control.

Radial lines stamped on the head of a bolt indicate its quality—the more lines the greater the strength. When replacing any bolt, the use of one of lesser tensile strength than that recommended by the manufacturer could prove disastrous.

The Steering Box

The steering box can also be a source of trouble. Occasionally this box will work loose from vibration, causing the car to shimmy wildly after hitting even a minor bump. Should this happen, touch your brakes firmly but gently until the shimmy stops—then drive to a garage. If inspection shows the bolts to be undamaged, the cure is simple: Tighten the bolts.

Some troubles in the steering box can be quite puzzling. I remember one car that was brought into my garage around Christmastime. The driver complained that on some mornings he simply could not turn his steering wheel—even enough to turn off the driveway. Other mornings, he said, the steering was extremely stiff until he had driven a few miles.

He was afraid of total loss of control and had taken his car to a local repair shop several times. The last time, when his steering wheel had refused to budge at all, he'd had it towed back. A mechanic raised the car on a hoist, lubricated everything in sight, lowered it to the ground, and—presto—instant steering.

But the motorist's relief was short-lived. The very next morning his steering wheel was again as stiff as a boot. By this time he was extremely worried, so he brought the car into my garage.

While he was telling us his tale of woe, his car sat in the second bay of the garage. I walked over, turned the steering wheel, and, to my surprise, it worked perfectly. When I asked the owner to tell me more about when the trouble cropped up, he said it seemed to be worse on cold mornings. Thinking for a moment, he said he remembered that there had been a warm spell the week before, and he had had no trouble.

This was a major clue, and when we found the actual cause of the trouble, it turned out to be one of those million-to-one chances. A rubber hose designed to bleed water away from the cowl grille under the windshield had broken and was allowing water to drip down onto the steering column. A missing rubber plug in a hole in the steering column allowed water to enter and trickle down into the steering-box housing. When the temperature dropped below freezing, the gears inside the steering box became encased in ice and refused to budge. The "miraculous" cure when the mechanic greased everything in sight was really caused by the warmth in the shop, which allowed the car to thaw out.

We removed the steering box, cleaned out all the moisture, lubricated the entire assembly, put the plug back in tightly, and replaced the drain hose from the cowl grille. The motorist went on his way and had no more trouble with his steering.

Power Steering

The power-steering unit has been pretty well perfected and stands up well, but, like any other "power" unit, it can go wrong and require minor or major repairs.

Since the power unit does most of the work, I advise motorists (particularly ladies) who are trying power steering for the first time to practice on a parking lot or quiet street until they are familiar with its sensitivity.

On heavy cars, power steering is almost a must for women drivers; it is also an advantage for men who do a lot of maneuvering on parking lots and drive mostly in the city. It is also helpful in handling blowouts at high speed, or recovering the pavement after you have inadvertently driven onto the shoulder. However, particular caution must be exercised with light cars. A woman I know was driving at high speed in a compact equipped with power steering, and she rolled the car over by oversteering in a high wind.

There are two kinds of power steering, both actuated by hydraulic fluid pressurized by a pump driven by the engine. One system is fully self-contained, and the hyraulic pressure is employed inside the steering box. In the other type, hydraulic pressure is applied directly to the steering linkage by an external power unit.

Power-steering Belts

Provided the level of fluid is kept up and the unit is not abused, both types of power steering are fairly trouble free. But it is important to make sure that the rubber belt that drives the power-steering pump is properly adjusted and in serviceable condition. In the event of belt failure, all power-steering-equipped vehicles can be controlled manually. Once the power assist is lost, however, the steering becomes stiff and sluggish, and handling is more difficult than it is in a vehicle equipped with standard steering.

In order to get the feel of sudden power-steering loss, drive slowly along a quiet street, put the car in neutral, shut off the engine, and go through a series of steering maneuvers.

Some time ago I investigated an accident caused by a power-steering-belt failure. While making a right turn, the belt split, the driver panicked, and the car swung wide and collided with an oncoming vehicle.

It is surprising how durable these belts are. As well as being constantly flexed and stretched, and operating in extreme hot and cold temperatures, they must transmit several horsepower from the engine to the power-steering pump when the car is turned sharply. But, like other moving parts, they eventually wear and must be adjusted or replaced.

If you hear a squeal or if the steering wheel tends to shimmy or quiver when turning sharply, have the power-steering belt checked immediately. A squeal only when the wheel is turned to the extreme left or right usually indicates that the steering mechanism is being forced beyond its limit. Forcing the steering doesn't really help you to turn more sharply; in fact, it can cause dangerous metal fatigue of several steering components. Even with power steering, it is wise to have the car moving slightly while cutting hard in and out of tight parking spots.

To prevent failure, be sure the power-steering belt is included in a twice-yearly safety check.

Wheels

Wheels are fastened by a number of bolts which screw into the hub, or by studs which protrude out from the hub and require nuts as fasteners. These nuts or bolts are sometimes lefthand- and sometimes righthand-threaded, and care must be exercised when installing them to avoid cross-threading.

Left- and righthand threads can lead to considerable confusion; some motorists find this out the hard way when attempting to change their first flat tire. Keep this in mind: A righthand-threaded nut or bolt is tightened by turning it to the right, or clockwise, and loosened by turning it to the left, or counterclockwise. A lefthand-threaded fastener is just the reverse: It must be turned to the left, or counterclockwise, to be tightened. The next important thing to remember is that on vehicles that employ lefthand threads, these threads are used *only* on the wheels on the left, or driver's, side of the car.

Where lefthand-threaded nuts or bolts are used, there is usually a large "L" stamped into the end of the stud to which the nut is attached or, in the case of a bolt, on the outside end of the bolt. The fasteners used on the *right*-side wheels are marked with an "R."

No markings are used on cars where the wheel fasteners are *all* of righthand thread. Why are lefthand-threaded wheel fasteners used on some cars? There is less chance that the fasteners will work loose, it is claimed, if they are tightened in the same direction as the wheel rotates. However, whether left- or righthand-threaded, I can't recall any wheel fasteners that worked loose if they were tightened properly in the first place. If at all in doubt about the type of fasteners used on your particular car, I strongly advise you to ask your service-station attendant to explain the tire-changing procedure. Incidentally, with rare exceptions, such as the left front wheel bearing adjusting nut on a few vehicles, and the steering-adjusting mechanism, the nuts, bolts, and other threaded connections used throughout the car are of conventional righthand thread. They are tightened by twisting them to the right, or clockwise. There is also a right way and a wrong way to install the wheel nuts.

I am all in favor of the do-it-yourself driver who has some working knowledge of his car and does a number of minor jobs himself. But a little knowledge can sometimes be dangerous.

Some time ago, a car drove into my shop, and the customer complained of a rough, erratic sensation which became worse as the speed of the car increased. He was quite convinced that the front end was badly out of alignment. I road-tested the car, and it certainly was a weird sensation. It felt like the "cakewalk" they used to feature at the oldtime midways. We removed the hub caps and found that all the wheel nuts had been put on backwards. The customer sheepishly admitted that he had rotated the wheels and didn't know the nuts could go on two ways.

These nuts are tapered to a cone shape on one end in order to center the road wheel to the hub. If these nuts are screwed on with the flat side facing the hub or brake drum, the wheel can be off center, causing a jackrabbit action each time the wheel rotates. It is impossible to tighten a wheel properly under these circumstances, and the wheel will move and chafe. In a short time the holes in the wheel become elongated, and the studs in the hub are ruined. The wheel could fall right off if it is not caught in time.

This mistake cost my customer two new front road wheels and all new studs in both front hubs.

Highways today are vastly improved over the cart tracks we once drove on. But even so, the car occasionally encounters a deep pothole, and wheels can be bent. Obstructions in the road, or high curbs, can also take their toll. Minor bends can usually be straightened; when a wheel is badly bent, however, it should be replaced. If the metal has been bent beyond its elastic point, hairline cracks will develop, and they will become worse as the wheel is pulled back into shape.

A wheel should only be straightened by skilled technicians who can determine if repairs will be safe. I have encountered the odd road wheel that tends to flex slightly with each revolution, resulting in a noise between the mating area of the wheel cover (hubcap) and wheel. This is more apt to occur with a heavily loaded vehicle traveling at low speed. To prove whether or not this is the culprit, and to pinpoint the exact wheel, remove the wheel covers one at a time and road-test the car.

If it is discovered that one or more of the wheels are causing the noise, they should be carefully examined for minute fatigue cracks. Defective wheels have been known to split and cause sudden tire failure.

Offbeat Noises

Here are some other possible causes of mysterious noises that seem to tie in with the movement of the wheels: stones trapped inside the wheel covers; foreign matter, such as pebbles or metal particles, inside the brake drums; wheels not properly tightened to the mounting hubs; improperly adjusted or worn front- or rear-wheel bearings; brake shoes dragging against the drums.

The wheels may appear to be firmly attached to the hub when, in fact, they are not, since excessive loading or abuse, such as savage high-speed cornering or operating with slightly loose wheels, can stretch and chafe the wheel's mounting holes. If the metal is worn in this area, the nuts or bolts may be torqued down to the recommended pressure, but the wheels will not necessarily be solidly attached to the hubs. A rumbling sound when the vehicle is moving usually warns of this danger.

Wheel Hubs and Bearings

The wheel hub supports the brake drum or brake disk. The front-wheel hubs rotate on ball or tapered roller bearings (known as front-wheel bearings) which are held in place by a nut. With proper maintenance and inspection, there is little that can go wrong with the hub. However, it is important that the bearings be cleaned and repacked with grease periodically and, if necessary, that the grease seals be replaced at the same time. When they are being repacked, it is important that the bearings be washed down to the bare metal to allow proper inspection for possible wear.

If these bearings are not sufficiently tightened, the whole wheel assembly will vibrate and shake. This can loosen the bearing cup in the hub, and there is no cure but replacement of the hub—an expensive component. It is also possible for the bearing to fly apart, allowing a wheel to fall off. The adjustment of front-wheel bearings should be done by an experienced mechanic, or at least by someone who knows factory specifications for adjustment.

If overtightened, the front-wheel bearings will overheat and tear themselves apart. Again, a wheel can fly from the car. These bearings require very little torque, and to overtighten them can be the kiss of death. But it does happen; I've heard of these bearings being tightened as much as possible with a large wrench.

The rear-wheel hub is often formed by a flanged section of the axle to which the wheel is bolted or mounted with studs. On some older cars the hub is mounted onto a tapered axle shaft by a nut and prevented from slipping by a flat steel key.

The flanged hub requires little or no maintenance. The same applies to the tapered axle hub, provided the single retaining nut does not work loose—which can lead to serious damage or loss of a wheel.

The rear axles are supported by bearings mounted behind the wheel hubs. On domestic cars these bearings do not require repacking, but it is sometimes recommended that they be removed and inspected when the rear drums are removed for other service such as brake work. They will not last forever, and excessive wear is usually announced by a gravelly rumbling noise, which increases with wheel speed. Another indication of wear is rear-axle lubricant leaking onto the brake mechanism. A simple check for wear in these bearings can be made by examining the rear wheels for excessive in-and-out or up-and-down play.

The Tires

How a Tire Is Constructed

While the durability and performance of present-day tires are truly amazing, no other car components are more taken for granted.

In the mid-twenties I learned about the importance of tires the hard way—when my older brother took me on a 200-mile trip in his used 1924 Star (the same car that once stranded us with mysterious ignition trouble). We finally reached our destination, and even got back, but not before we had repaired and inflated with a hand pump no less than fourteen flat tires. Rather than the simple one-piece wheels used today, the tires were then mounted on a split rim that was bolted onto a wire or wooden wheel, and it was necessary to split and collapse the rim before the tire could be removed from it. Even after removing the rim from the wheel, invariably the mechanism that held the split rim in a locked position was seized with rust, and making it operate was a major challenge.

We eventually broke the hand pump, ran out of tires and patching kits, and rode home on the rim of one wheel—about 10 mph.

But that was back in the twenties, and at that time the best material they had come up with to reinforce the tire's carcass was cotton. In the late 1930s, the North American tire industry started using *rayon* cord as a reinforcing agent in passenger-car tires. During World War II, *nylon* cord, which, pound for pound, is stronger than steel, appeared on the scene. Shortly after the war the use of nylon in passenger tires became popular due to its superior characteristics. In the early sixties, *polyester* cord was introduced, and at this writing, *fiber glass* is the latest tire-reinforcing entry.

Nylon performs well at high speeds and is incredibly strong, but under certain conditions it tends to give a rough ride. Rayon and polyester, while not quite as strong as nylon, provide excellent riding qualities, and their general performance is good.

At present, fiber glass, which is by far the strongest of all the reinforcing materials, is used in some tires to strengthen the crown of the tire carcass.

Another major breakthrough by the tire industry was the development of the tubeless tire, which became standard equipment on most domestic cars in the mid-fifties. The addition of a soft-rubber inner liner as part of the first ply in the tubeless tire minimizes the danger of sudden blowouts. Rather than collapsing, as tube-type tires frequently did when pierced, the tubeless tire seldom goes instantly flat. The tire also runs cooler without an inner tube, which in itself is a major advantage.

Few of us are aware of the extensive research and countless millions of dollars spent by the tire industry to perfect and mass-produce today's modern tires.

The major ingredients used in a tire are rubber, fabric, chemicals, and metal. At the base of the tire is a *bead,* which is made of several strands of high-tensile steel encased in rubber. It is this sturdy bead that holds the tire snugly onto the rim of the road wheel.

The tire's carcass is composed of two or more layers of stranded nylon, rayon, or polyester impregnated in rubber. Known as *plies,* these tough layers of rubberized fabric constitute the tire's basic strength. When the carcass is being formed, the plies and the cord inside the plies are positioned to run from bead to bead at an acute angle. Because of this angle, they are known as *bias* plies. (*See Diagram* 40.)

Bonded to the outside of the carcass is the tread rubber and the sidewall rubber. With some tires, fiber-glass or steel belts are placed

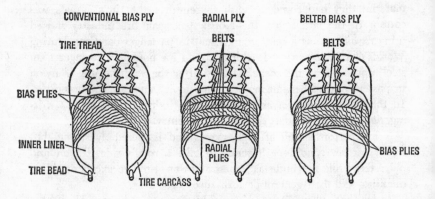

Diagram 40. *Tire-carcass construction*

circumferentially between the carcass and the tread rubber to provide additional strength.

While the outside layer of rubber is bonded together in a single piece at the time it is bonded to the carcass, the rubber in the tread area is much thicker than that used on the sidewalls. The tread rubber is specially formulated to resist road wear and provide traction to propel and stop the vehicle. The sidewall rubber is compounded of abrasion-resistant rubber to minimize wear resulting from such things as curb scuffing, and also to protect the plies that form the carcass underneath.

Mistakes have been made, some new cars were under-tired, and there have been bad production runs of tires which gave a black eye to everyone involved in the business, but I believe these mistakes have been recognized and phased out by the entire rubber industry.

I have visited the factories of the leading tire manufacturers in Europe and North America, and I am convinced that not only are they capable of producing a reliable product, but they are doing everything possible to do so.

At one laboratory in the United States I saw a tire rated for 85 mph spun without load or contact to demonstrate the effect of centrifugal force at high speeds. This test was conducted in a cell lined with steel boiler plate, and we left the room to watch the test on a TV monitor in the lab. Dials were turned on the control panel, and the wheel began to rotate, its speed measured by a speedometer on the panel. When it hit about 200 mph, the body of the tire started to balloon out and reached enormous proportions as it finally disintegrated at 331 mph.

When we returned to the cell, I could see why it had been lined in boiler plate. The tire had blown into a thousand pieces.

In another laboratory I witnessed several overloaded and under-inflated tires being tested to establish exactly how much punishment a tire can stand. And they don't stop until the tire is destroyed. Smoke was pouring out of these overburdened tires. It is incredible how many hours they will run under these conditions before they disintegrate. Then, after they do fail, they are cut into dozens of pieces, and a meticulous post mortem is performed to locate stress points and weaknesses.

To point out the disastrous effects of underinflation, they inflated a tire to only 20 pounds pressure and proceeded to spin it at 120 mph (normal pressure at this speed would be about 32 pounds). High-speed cameras were used to take photographs of the deformed shape of the tire as it rotated. In the photographs I could see that the tire's tread section that was pressed under load against the test wheel did not go back into round for approximately half a revolution of the tire.

I saw another machine, a two-story-high press, force a steel plunger into the tread of a tire while instruments measured the force required to cause a fracture.

At the Daytona International Speedway in Florida, a professional driver bombed me around the track in a high-performance stock sports car at 140 mph—the fastest I have ever traveled by car. On another occasion, I visited a multimillion-dollar proving ground in Texas, where in one year 400,000,000 test miles were recorded without the the loss of a single life. A crack test driver drove me around a track capable of handling speeds of up to 200 mph. I saw tires being tested at fantastic speeds on asphalt, cement, gravel, sand, and cobblestone surfaces. During these tests in the blazing sun, with the temperature hovering around the 100-degree mark, tires were subjected to the tortures of Hades—there's no other way to describe it.

Remember, the tires that enable professional drivers to push their cars toward the speed of sound are designed and produced by the same factories that make the tires for our cars. These same plants make the tires for the ultimate punishment of jet-aircraft landings. While such tires cost thousands of dollars, we expect to buy a whole set of tires for a fraction of the cost of one aircraft tire.

As well as withstanding the burning temperatures of equatorial deserts and the subzero cold of our nothern areas, modern tires are almost impervious to the chemicals we throw on our roads, and they can bear normal beating from stones, potholes, curbs, and the brutality of some drivers. Apart from providing a comfortable ride and adhesion to propel and to stop a car, the tires play a vital role in a vehicle's handling characteristics. Today's tire goes farther, lasts longer, and costs less than the tires we used to buy.

At one time when buying a set of tires, about the only styling decision we had to make was whether we wanted black or white walls, but now there are almost as many styles as there are cars—white walls, red walls, blue walls, one stripe and two stripes in high or low profile, and many more to come. The fashionable is being added to the functional, and deciding on the right type of tire for your particular needs is a major challenge for all but the experts (and some of them don't know all the answers).

The following letter is one of a countless number I have received from my column readers regarding tires:

"My car needs new tires, but today's assortment of sizes, shapes, qualities, and prices confuses me. My present tires are size 775×14, and while I don't exactly know what these numbers mean, at least it gives me some idea of what size tire I am getting.

"Today, on some tires the size 775×14 has been changed to F78–14. Would you explain what 775×14 and F78–14 mean?

"Are there any advantages to the bias-belted tires? Regardless of what I select, what assurance is there that it is a safe tire and suitable for my type of driving?

"I do about 10,000 miles per year, half of which is in the city. On the highway I drive at the maximum speed limit, and frequently the car is heavily loaded."

Regarding safety, it is now mandatory that all passenger tires in Canada and the U.S.A. meet minimum safety standards. Whether a tire sells for $15 or $50, it is required by law to come up to the minimum requirements.

This does not mean that a $15 tire offers the same tread mileage and all-around durability as a premium tire—far from it. The cheap tire, while it meets minimum standards, will not compare with the extra protection and lasting qualities of a more expensive tire.

For example, in the late sixties the bias-belted tire was introduced. Fitted between the rubber-tread area and the bias-ply carcass of this tire are two extra belts. (*See Diagram* 40.) While this type of tire is fairly expensive, the car makers were sufficiently impressed to make it standard equipment on most of the 1970 models. The additional strength of the two extra belts minimizes tread and sidewall distortion as the tire rolls against the road. The stretching and scrubbing action of the tread as it grinds on the road is one of the major causes of tread wear.

In addition to meeting minimum standards, it is also mandatory that the following information be shown on the sidewalls of all new tires:

DOT—which indicates that the tire will meet or surpass the minimum standards. (Other marks you may find, such as SAE, V-1, RMA, mean the same thing, but the accepted code now is DOT);

Composition of the material used in the construction of the inside carcass—nylon, rayon, polyester, fiber glass, etc.;

The maximum load-carrying capacity of the tire in pounds;

The maximum permissible inflation pressure;

Name of the manufacturer;

Size of tire—if a conventional tire size were 775×14, the equivalent size in a "bias belted" tire would be F78–14;

Tube or tubeless type of tire;

The word "radial" if the tire is of radial-ply design;

The number of plies used in the carcass and the number of plies in the undertread area, if they are different.

Regarding tire sizes, "775×14" simply means that the width of the tire from the extreme outside edge of both sidewalls measures 7.75 inches. The "14" means that it will fit only a 14-inch wheel. The width of a 600×13 tire would be 6 inches, and it would fit a 13-inch wheel. (*See Diagram* 41.)

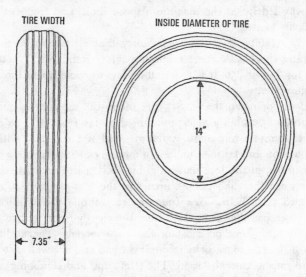

Diagram 41. *The meaning of tire sizes*

To further complicate things, in addition to the F78 series already mentioned, there are a 70 series and a 60 series. Since these three tires are obviously squat, they are referred to as low-profile tires. (*See Diagram* 42.)

The numbers in the three series indicate their height-to-width ratio.

For example, the height of a 78-series tire is roughly 78 percent of the inflated width from sidewall to sidewall.

Before switching to a low-profile variety in vehicles equipped with conventional tires, be sure there is sufficient clearance in the wheel wells and steering radius to permit the use of wider tires.

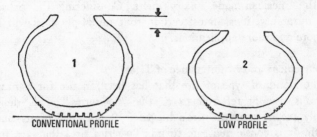

Diagram 42. *Conventional and low-profile tires*

Radial-ply Tire

There is yet another design—the *radial-ply* tire. Developed in Europe and reputed to be one of the safest and most durable, the radial-ply tire has attained favorable recognition in this country in recent years and is now being produced here.

The major advantages of the radial-ply tire are its more flexible sidewalls, which allow more tread to remain flat on the road, thus providing a greater grip when cornering, improved over-all traction, and easier handling due to a more rigid tread.

Firm belting built into the circumference of the tire between the tread area and the carcass prevents tread squirm, which minimizes friction, thus reducing heat buildup. The stiffness of the tread also prolongs tire life and allows the tire to roll with less resistance, which aids fuel economy.

On the minus side, on some vehicles road shock is more noticeable at lower speeds, and tire noise is more apparent in the same range. However, in due course it is quite possible that these disadvantages can be more or less "tuned out" by modification to the suspension system.

Another vast difference in the radial-ply tire is that the cord in the plies runs radially from bead to bead, or on a 90-degree angle to the tread, as compared to the diagonally placed cords in the conventional bias-ply tire, or the bias-belted tire. (*See Diagram* 40.)

Due to the entirely different handling characteristics of radial-ply tires, it is quite dangerous to mix them with tires of a different construction. This warning also applies to the use of conventional snow tires. Should you decide to buy radial-ply tires, it is essential that the car be fitted with a full set. Just one odd tire can disturb the stability of the car.

Several imports are equipped with radial-ply tires, and on the 1970 models they appeared as standard equipment on at least two

North American-made luxury liners. Considering the extra safety and durability, it is almost certain that radial-ply tires will be used in more and more applications.

Replacement and Maintenance of Tires

The standard type of tire that has been in use for a number of years is usually referred to as the "80 series." This designation simply means that the tire's height is 80 percent of its maximum width. It is considered safe to mix 80-series tires that are made by different manufacturers.

There is a difference of opinion as to whether or not it is advisable to mix the 78 bias-belted series with the standard 80 series, but in my book it is wise to at least mate them in pairs on the front or rear wheels of the car.

With the superwide-tread 70 and 60 series, while it is permissible to mount them in pairs on the front or rear wheels, for maximum efficiency complete sets should be installed. These tires are fairly expensive, and when you are spending this kind of money, it is wise to go all the way and do the job properly.

Maintaining recommended tire pressure, based on gross weight of vehicle (weight of vehicle plus passengers and luggage), is vitally important. For instance, a 775×14 or F78–14 tire's maximum load capacity is 1500 pounds when inflated to 32 pounds air pressure. The same size tire when inflated to 24 pounds will carry a maximum load of only 1270 pounds.

Heat is a tire's greatest enemy, and underinflation, coupled with sustained high speed, generates fantastic temperatures. A tire can operate in temperatures up to 250 degrees F. (water boils at 212 F.), but beyond this point it may disintegrate.

If the tires on your car are job-rated to suit maximum load, if the air pressure is properly adjusted, and if you remain within posted speed limits, then, regardless of the price of your tires, there should be no major problem. Remember, however: To drive at maximum recommended pressure with a light load can lead to a very harsh ride, and the suspension components suffer.

To drive with tires that have only $\frac{1}{16}$ inch, or less, of tread depth is inviting disaster.

Tread wear indicators which are molded into the bottom of tread grooves are now incorporated into new tire designs. When tires are worn to a point where only $\frac{1}{16}$ inch of tread depth remains, the indicators show up as a smooth band across the face of a tire. There are generally six or eight such bands which, when exposed, indicate that the tire is worn to the point where it should be replaced.

Actually, the job of tire engineers is not all that simple. In many ways a tire must be a compromise. Tread and carcass material, while ideal on the turnpike, may not be satisfactory at lower speeds. A thick carcass and thick treads with deep tread pattern offer far more miles of service, but generate more heat at sustained high speed. The manufacturers consider all these facts and endeavor to come up with the best of both worlds.

The production of tires is far from being completely automated. Each individual tire is put together by a skilled technician, and just the slightest error on his part, or a minor flaw in the machine he is operating, can result in a defective tire.

Ply Ratings

Since it was once generally considered that the more plies the greater the tire's strength, at one time up to six plies were used in the construction of many passenger-car tires. For several years, the average passenger-car tire was of four-ply construction. Many people were confused and thought the quality had been reduced when, in the early sixties, most domestic tire makers started producing two-ply tires which were classified as "four-ply rating."

The term "four-ply rating" indicates that, while the tire has only two plies, it has the same strength as a four-ply tire. Two plies can offer an advantage over four plies, and if we look inside the tire we soon see why. A tire's biggest enemy is heat; the same heat that vulcanized it in a mold can also destroy it. Excessive high-speed driving and underinflation are causes of tire overheating, but it is rarely appreciated that heat is also generated by friction between the various plies in the tire. By building a tire with two instead of four plies, part of the potential for friction is eliminated. At the same time, by using as much cord to make two plies as was formerly used to make four, the tire has the same strength. In addition, it is claimed that the two-ply tire provides a better ride and a small improvement in fuel economy.

The term "ply rating," which has been used to identify a given-size tire with its load and inflation limits, is now being replaced by the tire industry. In its place is a new term, "Load Range," which is followed by a letter: A.B.C.D., etc. A tire marked "Load Range B" has the same load and inflation limits as a tire of the same size marked "four-ply rating."

The switch in terminology should eliminate confusion over ply ratings.

Wheel Balancing

There are two ways to balance wheels. One is known as *static* balance (done when the wheel is off the car and stationary), and the other is called *dynamic* balance, which I much prefer.

With dynamic balancing, the tire and road-wheel assembly are spun by a machine up to 100 mph or more to simulate actual driving conditions. The exact point of imbalance is located, and the number of lead weights required to bring the assembly into perfect balance is indicated.

Balancing wheel assemblies is a tricky business, and it is essential that the technician who performs this task be thoroughly trained and familiar with the capabilities of the particular make of balancing machine he is using. As with most sophisticated testing equipment, it is only as reliable as the man who operates it.

To be certain that a wheel is balanced both statically (when still) and dynamically (when rotating), it may be necessary to divide the lead weights and position them on the inside and outside of the wheel. The tire and wheel makers strive to turn out a balanced product, but just a slight variation can result in an unbalanced tire and wheel assembly.

Occasionally a new tire can be out of round and cause peculiar, hard-to-pinpoint vibrations. Or perhaps the bead may not be seated properly on the rim, or the wheel could be bent. These conditions can be detected by raising the wheels slightly and constantly measuring the distance between the tire tread and the floor as the wheel is slowly rotated. Similar observations should be made by lining up the center of the tread with a mark on the floor and checking this from a head-on angle during rotation. Deviations from the normal pattern indicate points to be further inspected.

Seldom will wheel balancing prove a cure when vibrations are caused by one or more bent wheels or out-of-round tires. Tire manufacturers will usually replace a badly out-of-round tire under warranty.

Occasionally the brake drum is the source of the imbalance. Wheels, brake drums, and tires are usually balanced at the factory, but if you request optional tires on a new car, be sure you ask to have them balanced.

A balancing job is incomplete unless all wheels have been balanced.

Frequently the rear wheels are overlooked, yet they are just as important as the front wheels. Vibrations caused by the rear wheels can be transmitted to any part of the vehicle and are often mistaken for front-wheel imbalance or other more expensive items such as bent driveshaft, worn universal joints, and wheel bearings.

Centrifugal force can balloon just a 1-ounce imbalanced condition to a 12-pound hammering action at 60 mph. Chronic imbalance causes a tire to hop off the road with each revolution of the wheel, which is not only dangerous and causes unpleasant vibrations but results in premature wear in the whole suspension system, including tire treads.

In most instances, annoying vibrations have their beginnings in the tire and wheel assemblies. To avoid possible danger and unnecessary expense, accept that telltale vibration as a warning and head for an experienced wheel-balancing craftsman.

I cannot overemphasize the importance of locating a reliable man to do the job. I have seen too many instances where vibrations that persisted right after the wheels were balanced were blamed on other components that were mighty expensive to repair, when in fact one or more wheels were still badly out of balance. Remember this before authorizing major surgery to overcome an offbeat vibration.

Aquaplaning

Recently I heard about a man who lost control of his car while driving too fast in heavy rain with almost bald tires. Suddenly, he was a victim of aquaplaning—a water-wedge that builds up between the tread of a worn tire and the road at high speeds and robs the driver of control.

In the laboratory of a major tire manufacturer I have seen a most dramatic—and frightening—demonstration of aquaplaning. I was shown a bald tire operating under a normal load of 800 pounds running against a water-soaked test drum rotating at 60 mph. In spite of the weight, yet because of the speed, the tire had lifted off the surface of the drum—as it would have lifted from the road. The wheel soon slowed to the point where a technician was able to put his hand on the wheel and stop it. This means that a car could be traveling at 60 mph on a wet highway with the front wheels raised off the surface, and the wheels could be almost stationary. The wedge of water building up between the tire and the road lifts the tire away completely and there is no adhesion left. A tire with deep tread can cut through this wedge and displace the water through the channels between the treads; it will not aquaplane under average wet weather conditions. But under adverse conditions where water is exceptionally deep, even a brand-new tire can aquaplane.

The rear tires do not aquaplane, because the front tires clear enough of the water in passing to allow the rear tires to keep contact with the road. It doesn't take much imagination to realize the danger of having power in the driving wheels if the driver has little or no control over the car's direction.

The phenomenon of aquaplaning has undoubtedly accounted for many mysterious traffic accidents that have occurred on wet highways. It should impress upon motorists that the danger of skidding is not limited to icy, snowy roads.

Apart from aquaplaning, one of the most dangerous times for skids is during the first few minutes of a downpour, when the roads have been dry and blistering hot. The rain, along with the normal oil slick and droppings from tailpipes, forms a greasy substance on the pavement, making skids or loss of control as likely as they would be on ice. During one recent summer I saw three cars slide off the road under such conditions.

Someday, it is hoped, tires, cars, and roads too, will be engineered to make skids a thing of the past. In the meantime, it is up to the driver to keep good tires on his car and drive with respect for the elements.

Although we can recognize tire failure as the cause of fatal accidents, it amazes me that so many people neglect their tires, pound them over rocky paths, and screech around corners without ever checking their condition. They also insist on squeezing every last mile out of the treads, despite the warnings of experts that something like 90 percent of tire failures happen in the last 10 percent of the tire's life.

Today, as an accident investigator, I see the depressing spectacle of people who tried to save a few dollars by driving on bald or otherwise neglected tires.

Snow Tires

Since standard tires are usually quieter and handle better at high speeds, I do not recommend installing snow tires until they are really necessary. However, in heavy snow they are a decided asset, and to be caught in a blinding snowstorm without them can prove disastrous.

The best way to buy snow tires is to get them complete with wheel.

Wheels are not too expensive, and all you have to do is switch them when it is snow-tire time, in the same way you would change any tire. Occasionally, too, removing a tire from a wheel can harm the seal in a tubeless tire, which will result in a slow leak. Furthermore, a tire that is mounted on another wheel must be checked for balance. If the tire and wheel assemblies are balanced the first time they are mounted, it is quite possible that they will not need balancing the second year they are used.

For those who holiday in the south when the north lies buried in snow, it is obviously safer to start out with snow tires and remove them after passing through the frigid zones. This means packing conventional tires, and after loading luggage, sometimes there is no room for them. If I were heading south during the winter and had to decide between one or the other, I would take my chances with conventional tires.

The excessive heat generated on hot pavement at sustained high speeds can prove damaging to snow tires. Also, regular tires are quieter and less inclined to cause an uncomfortable weaving, or snaking, sensation that sometimes occurs at high speeds.

Tire Studs

From personal experience driving with steel tire studs, I would endorse them without reservation as an ideal aid to traction when driving on ice. One February while driving on the highway, I suddenly ran into freezing rain, and within minutes the highway was covered with wet glare ice. On one grade, the rear wheels of dozens of cars were spinning uselessly as their drivers tried desperately to gain traction. Although I was slowed by the cars straddling the road and sliding into the ditch, my car climbed past them with no effort. By the time I had reached the top of the hill, I had collected a load of unhappy drivers headed for a night at a nearby motel.

Tests by Cornell University show that stopping distance is reduced by about 30 percent when the two rear tires are studded, and studded tires on four wheels will lower stopping distances by up to 50 percent. For the utmost in safety, all four tires should be studded. In Europe, where these devices were introduced, many motorists insist they be fitted to each tire. As well as providing driving and stopping traction, they will prevent a vehicle from sliding off the crown of the road or drifting out of control in a strong wind. Snow tires without steel studs provide little or no extra traction on glare ice.

At the time of writing, studded tires are permitted in the winter throughout Canada, with the exception of Ontario, where they were banned on April 30, 1971.

The Highways Department in Ontario reports that tests have shown that in areas where roads are quickly cleared of ice and snow by use of plows, sand, and salt, the steel studs tend to grind off the traffic marking lines and to wear ruts in the driving surface. These ruts fill with water which in mild weather can cause aquaplaning (explained on page 191) or in freezing conditions can turn to solid ice. This ban on studs applies even to visitors from neighboring provinces and states.

Whether further tests and accident statistics after a few seasons of driving without studded tires will bring a change in the legislation remains to be seen.

In the United States, studded tires are banned at present in Minnesota, Missouri, Louisiana, and Utah. Stiff penalties can be imposed on those who ignore the ban. I heard of a motorist who was caught using studded tires in one of these States. He was ordered to buy conventional tires immediately. I doubt that you would be able to question price while buying tires under these circumstances. I have been told that offenders can be fined up to a thousand dollars, and they can also be jailed for a year. However—again, at the time I am writing—provided they are not fitted with steel studs, it is quite legal to drive in any of the Southern States with snow tires.

But keep in mind that the laws existing today can suddenly change, and to avoid problems it is wise, when planning long trips in Canada and the United States, to belong to a recognized motoring club. Before leaving on a trip, these clubs will map out the best possible route to follow, as well as point out the existing speed limits and various other laws, some of which are mighty confusing and can vary considerably as you travel from one State or Province to another.

When removing studded tires in the spring, it is important to mark clearly the direction of rotation of each tire. When remounting in the fall, they must go back on the same side of the car from which they were removed—do not rotate them from the left side to the right side, or vice versa. If all four wheels are fitted with studded snow tires, the fronts can be switched to the rear, provided they are positioned on the same side of the car. Studs seat into the tread at an acute angle (much as a corn broom develops a bias in one direction), and if the tires are remounted to rotate in the opposite direction, they will reverse their position. This can enlarge the hole to which they are fitted, resulting in tread damage and loss of studs. Before storing tires, they should be thoroughly dried and placed in a dry area away from the direct rays of the sun.

Studs in Used Tires

I am sometimes asked if studs can be installed in used snow tires. While I have seen it done, I don't recommend it. Before studs can be installed, the holes must be free of stones, salt, and other foreign matter, and it could take up to an hour to do this preliminary cleaning. If the holes aren't clean before the studs go in, the tire could be damaged and leaks could result. If something prevents the stud from going all the way in, the stud could protrude more than the recommended limit of $\frac{1}{16}$ inch beyond the tread of the tire.

Shorter studs are available to compensate for normal tread wear, but a tire seldom wears evenly. A stud installed in a worn spot will protrude farther than one installed on a part of the tire that is not as badly worn. To remain within the recommended protrusion, it would then be necessary to use a variety of lengths of studs.

For these reasons, studs should be installed when buying snow tires. Special equipment is used to install them, which makes it impractical for the driver to install them himself.

At 100 mph, each stud exerts a pull of about 5 pounds. It is not wise to drive at excessive speeds with studs. But if the studs have been properly installed and the car is not accelerated or stopped too abruptly, the losing of studs should not be a problem. It takes about 100 miles of driving before new studs are seated properly.

Wheel Rotation

For various reasons, tires on one side of the car do not wear in the same places as do the tires on the other side. Similarly, the tires on the front take on different patterns of wear than do the tires on the back. For this reason, the tires should take a turn running in all positions, including a turn at resting as a spare.

There are several suggested rotation patterns. Here is a well-known one (*Note:* the left side of the car is the driver's side): spare tire to right rear, right rear to left front, left front to left rear, left rear to right front, and right front to spare. This method of rotation was suggested years ago, but obviously it does not apply today to the many vehicles fitted with snow tires. Also, during the summer some people use a snow tire for the spare. Then, since it is not safe to use winter tires in hot weather, only the four running wheels can be rotated.

Radial tires, however, should not be switched from one side of the car to the other. Makers advise that radials be changed only between back and front wheels on the same side. If you are using the spare during rotation, mark the wheel that goes into the trunk with information about which corner of the vehicle it was on and the direction in which it was rotating. During the next rotation it should be returned to the same side of the car. If, because of a flat tire, the spare has to be used in a position where it will rotate in the wrong direction, repair the flat tire promptly and return the spare to the trunk.

While it is recommended that the tires be switched about every 5000 miles, few people bother to do so. But tire life is definitely prolonged if it is done at least every 10,000 miles. For those interested in maximum safety, the tires should be removed from the wheels periodically and inspected for internal damage. Most tire failures begin as a result of internal ruptures.

Rather than rotation, think in terms of safety. Once the tread pattern is less than $\frac{1}{16}$ inch deep, the tire should be replaced. To minimize the danger of aquaplaning, it is vitally important that the front tires have good deep-tread patterns. If some of the tires are worn more than others, mount the best tires on the front wheels. If the spare is a snow tire and the four running tires are in good condition, rotate them in this manner: right front tire to left rear, left rear to right front, left front to right rear, and right rear to left front.

It is not necessary to align the front end each time the tires are rotated, provided of course that it was properly aligned before the tires were switched. To avoid annoying vibrations, especially when the tires have been removed from the wheels, it is wise to check each tire for balance upon completion of the job.

Rim or Road Wheel Size

Problems can arise from having the wrong rim width for the tire in use. Too wide a rim causes abnormal tread wear and a harsh ride. When the rim is too narrow, the tread bulges in the center, wearing that part down faster and causing the sidewalls to flex too much. The ride is softer, but lateral stability is reduced.

Flats

When a tire is being repaired, I do not favor the use of external plugs which are forced in from the outside of the hole and expand inside. They will stop the leak, but they could also leave you with a seriously damaged tire. Sometimes a puncture is caused by a nail being driven through the tread. A bent nail can scuff and weaken the carcass from inside. If the hole is simply filled with a plug, the tire could be ready to fail at any time.

A punctured tire should be removed from the wheel and inspected internally. If there is no other damage, it is all right to repair the hole. Rather than plugs, I recommend the use of a hot vulcanized patch.

Patches and plugs can sometimes throw a wheel out of balance; it is therefore wise to have the balance checked after having a flat fixed. Removal of the tire can also throw it out of balance if the tire and rim are not marked in one spot to assure that the tire goes back on in exactly the same position.

A leak in a tubeless tire is sometimes caused by a defective rim or a poor fit where the tire presses against the wheel. As a last resort, you can put a tube in a tubeless tire, but the use of a tube tends to make the tire run a little hotter.

While frequently overlooked, the rubber in the valve-stem assembly can disintegrate and allow the air to escape. Salt and moisture can corrode the inside valve core, especially if the mechanism has not been protected by a valve cap. Valve caps should never be left off the rubber valve assembly.

Cars are often equipped with wheel disks instead of the plainer hubcap. Very often the design of these disks makes it impossible to reach the tire valve with an air hose, and extensions are sold to screw onto the original valve and reach out past the disk. Other valve extensions are available which lock the disk to the wheel to make theft all but impossible. Their modest cost provides good insurance against a loss that can run into a hundred dollars on an expensive car.

Retreads

In the days when speed limits were much lower, retreads perhaps were a sound investment. Today they may be suitable at lower speeds, but I do not recommend them for expressway travel. When installing new rubber on my car, I settle for nothing less than brand-new tires. The plies and sidewall rubber of a retread have already been subjected to millions of cycles of flexing and pounding as the original tread was worn away. Retreads may be justified on large, expensive truck tires, but motorists who use retreads should probably avoid high-speed travel.

Inflation

Engineers tell me that 25 percent of tire replacements would not be necessary if people would only maintain proper air pressure. Find out the recommended pressure for your tires and make a practice of checking the pressure about once a month. Most important of all is remembering to adjust the tires to suit load and speed conditions.

Underinflation and overinflation account for a great deal of trouble in tires. Underinflation wears down the outer portion of the tread faster than the center and also causes excessive flexing of the cord, which generates too much heat. This leads to flex fatigue of the plies and separation of the carcass from the rubber tread.

Overinflation is hard on the suspension, causing a harsh ride, and tends to wear down the center of the tread faster than the outer portion.

Actually, it would be a lot simpler if we thought of tire pressures as an adjustment of pressure to suit load, rather than only as inflating tires. More pressure is needed when the car is heavily loaded, whereas with only the driver, obviously pressure can be lower. It is surprising how often people add to the burden with cartop carriers, heavily laden trunks, six passengers, and a house trailer, without stopping to adjust the tire pressure. One of the handiest accessories to keep in the glove compartment is a tire-pressure gauge. They are available at most parts stores at modest cost.

On my own car, which weighs just over a ton and a half, I use 28 pounds all around. This is a little more than recommended, and I do pick up a little extra road shock, but the car handles better. On the other hand, when starting out on a camping trip with a loaded trunk and all the children plus a trailer, I adjust the rear tires to 32 pounds. (If I forget to bring the pressure back to 28 pounds when the car is unloaded, a harsh ride reminds me.)

When properly maintained, the tires on which we ride today are safe and incredibly durable, but I can think of no other components that are so taken for granted and so neglected until we are faced with sudden failure. Research continues. Right this minute new materials are being tested in the laboratory and on the proving grounds. The result of this research will produce tires with capabilities as yet unknown.

The Brakes

One of the greatest steps forward in creating the highly mechanized world in which we live today was the invention of the wheel. However, the birth of the wheel led to an immediate problem—how to control its speed and stop it from rolling.

At first, wedges were placed in front of the wheel. Later came the introduction of friction in the form of a crude rubbing block. Leverage was added to increase the force of the friction.

With the advent of the car came the use of the brake drum, usually installed on the rear wheels only. Then came brakes on all four wheels, and the improvement was so great that manufacturers installed a red triangle on the rear of such vehicles to warn the motorist behind of the superior stopping power.

Then followed another revolutionary advancement—the hydraulic brake. The steel cables in the old system were replaced by pipes filled with brake fluid. When the brake is applied in the hydraulic system, a plunger in the master cyclinder builds up pressure that is transmitted to the brake shoes, which are then forced against the brake drum. Introduced shortly after four-wheel brakes, the hydraulic system allowed the driver to stop his car faster and with less effort and did away with erratic pulling problems. By 1939, hydraulic brakes were standard equipment on all domestic cars. (*See Diagram* 43.)

Brakes continued to improve. Through research and testing, engineers have made brakes almost foolproof. For this reason, they are sometimes overlooked in general maintenance. I've often been asked by mortorists to do a good, cheap brake job. Their reasons varied, but usually it was because they were planning to turn the car in soon, or because they just didn't think it was necessary to do a proper job.

There is no such thing as a good, cheap brake job. Either pay for the best materials available and allow time for a *good* job, which is

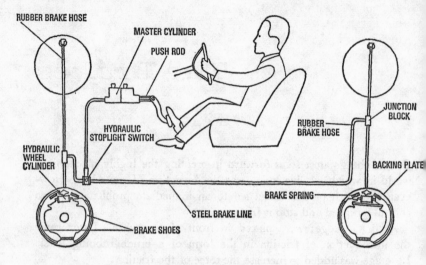

Diagram 43. *The hydraulic-brake system*

guaranteed, or trade your car in right away and let the dealer take care of the brake work. A cheap brake job has about as much value as a $10 brain operation—and can be just as dangerous. Remember, your brakes are all that stand between you and thousands of pounds of runaway metal when you are on collision course with another vehicle or a concrete wall.

I remember one woman whose brake trouble and accompanying tale of woe tops anything I've heard in the way of inefficiency and mechanical bungling in all the years I've been associated with the repair business.

The woman had taken her car into a local garage at regular intervals for servicing and minor repairs, but nobody had ever suggested a general safety checkup. One day, as she was driving down a busy street, she hit the brake pedal—but the car kept going! She shut off the key, and in due course the car came to a halt. Only luck saved her from crashing into any of the dozens of other cars on the road. After a short wait, the brakes came back to normal, but they failed again after she had driven another mile.

Thoroughly frightened, she had the car towed to a garage. She was told that they would have to reline the brakes, turn the drums, bleed the lines, and repack the front-wheel bearings to the tune of

$60 (plus $6 for towing and $2 for fluid). This, they said, would cure the ailment. No mention was made of the master cylinder, which usually causes failures of this nature.

A week later, the lady was doing 25 mph on another busy road when the brakes failed again. The car was towed back to the garage (another $6), and this time she was told that new steel hydraulic brakes lines were needed. On this occasion they extended a 20 percent discount, and the net bill was $33 plus $2 for fluid. The man who delivered her car to the house told her that he "didn't think the brakes were all that good yet," and took the car back to the shop for further diagnosis. The car was returned again, but after a few days' driving, she still felt the brakes were too spongy. She again took the car to the garage and asked them to road-test the brakes. The garage assured her that everything was just dandy: "No problems there, ma'm. Safe as new." (There was no bill this time.)

Still not convinced that all was well, she returned to the garage a week later and once again was told the brakes were 100 percent efficient. The following morning, she backed out of her driveway and put her foot on the brake pedal, only to have it fall limply to the floor.

The car was towed back to the shop (tow charges on the house this trip), and finally the master cylinder and power-brake assemblies were rebuilt. The net cost was only $15.31, but once again she was charged $2 for brake fluid.

The brakes then seemed to be all right, and she slowly regained confidence—after considerable briefing by friends on the use of the handbrake, shutting off the key, and gearing down (even, as a last resort, putting the automatic transmission in reverse).

When the woman told me her story she asked if there was anything else that could go wrong and was very discouraged when I had to say, "Yes, ma'm, there are four-wheel cylinders, any one of which could spring a leak and drain the fluid from the system." She decided to have those wheel cylinders overhauled right away—at another shop.

All of which goes to prove the wisdom of doing a *complete* brake job when working on the system.

Brake Fluid

Although frequently forgotten, the fluid used in the hydraulic brake system is its lifeblood. If you stop to think that roughly one pint of fluid is responsible for stopping a machine traveling 88 feet per second at 60 mph, you will realize how important it is to pay more attention to checking and topping up the master cylinder and making sure that the quality of this vital fluid has not deteriorated.

Hydraulic-brake systems and brake fluid have improved considerably over the years. However, these improvements have been accompanied by conditions that place more and more strain on the brakes and fluid. Heat and condensation (just plain water) are the greatest enemies of brake fluid. Our ever-increasing speed limits, crowded roads (creating the necessity for more panic stops), heavier cars, smaller wheels (which increase rpm), solid-wheel design, power brakes—all add up to heat ranges never before experienced in the braking system.

Let's say you are on your way to the office, on the highway, and you have to make a fast stop at 70 mph. The heat buildup, due to friction between the brake linings and the drums, begins to raise the temperature of the system. As you enter town, you stop for several traffic lights and slam on the brakes every time someone cuts you off. This increases the temperature even more. Finally, you drive down a long, steep hill in heavy traffic with your foot almost constantly on the brake. All of this can cause a fantastic temperature rise and make the brake fluid boil. The fluid then turns to vapor, and the brakes fail completely.

This phenomenon makes it difficult to prove whether a motorist is right or wrong when he claims that his brakes completely failed and caused an accident. By the time the brakes are inspected afterward, the fluid has cooled, restoring normal hydraulic pressure, and the brakes work perfectly.

The fluid is also affected by condensation. Just a small quantity of water decreases its boiling point and builds deposits of muck and sludge which can lead to brake failure.

Researchers are aware of the ever-increasing heat problem and have been working on it in their labs. They have now come up with fluids that can withstand a lot of punishment. Heavy-duty brake fluids are now available with a rating of 500 degrees F. or better before boiling, and they will not congeal at temperatures as low as minus 60 degrees. Low-boiling-point brake fluids have been outlawed in most areas of North America.

Brake fluid must be handled with great care to keep it perfectly clean. In this respect, cars are far less tolerant than people. We are sometimes concerned when we see children eating candy held in dirty hands, but there is seldom any ill effect. If the brake fluid were contaminated with one tenth the dirt the average child swallows in a week, the brakes would be sure to fail. The hydraulic-brake system is so sensitive that even slight traces of air mixed with the fluid must be removed to avoid a spongy pedal and seriously decreased braking power. This is the reason why brake lines must be bled (the brake fluid replaced).

No matter how careful we may be, mistakes can happen. I recall an apprentice who bled the lines on four cars which had just been given brake jobs. The following day he discovered that, in error, he had used pure antifreeze instead of brake fluid. The color of the antifreeze and the brake fluid was the same, and both came in five-gallon cans painted yellow and red. He had simply taken the wrong can. The cars were hastily recalled and the mistake corrected.

While I certainly don't recommend substituting antifreeze for brake fluid, the component parts of the cooling and brake systems are made of much the same materials, and it is doubtful that the error would have caused immediate failure unless the temperature had suddenly dropped. Since pure antifreeze congeals at lower temperatures, there might have been four brake failures.

Lubricating oils, on the other hand, will cause almost instant failure if put into the brake system. Accept nothing but heavy-duty brake fluid from a reputable manufacturer. If a can is not clearly marked BRAKE FLUID, throw it away and buy a new one.

The Master Cylinder

No part of the car is more hazardous than a faulty master cylinder. Our brakes and our lives depend on it. The master cylinder does not always give warning when it's about to fail. It is possible to make a perfect stop at one intersection, and fail completely at the next. Once a leak develops in this unit, the few ounces of fluid in the reservoir can drain out quickly, resulting in total loss of brakes. True, all cars are equipped with a parking brake, but when the service brake fails, motorists often panic and forget to use it. When they do remember, too often it is out of adjustment or seized up.

In normal operation, the fluid level in the master cylinder will occasionally drop a little, and fresh fluid should be added. When adding fluid, extreme care must be taken to ensure that no dirt gets into the system.

It has been my experience, however, that most dirt in the master cylinder, or in any other area of the hydraulic system, develops inside. Condensation within the system leads to chemical change of the fluid, and a thick sludge is formed that can be removed only by dismantling the unit.

Ask your service-station attendant to include a check of the master-cylinder fluid level when checking under the hood. There is a rubber cover at the rear of these cylinders which will fill with fluid if the unit is leaking. If the fluid runs out when the cover is squeezed with the fingers, the master cylinder should be repaired immediately.

But a master cyclinder doesn't have to be leaking externally to be defective. Here is a test every motorist can make. While parked, press your foot on the brake pedal for a minute or two, using the same pressure you would for a normal stop. Don't press too hard. If, as you push, the pedal slowly drops to the floor, it indicates serious wear in what is called the primary cup, or perhaps there is foreign matter scoring the cylinder bore. Either of these conditions can cause brake failure.

Buried out of sight in the master cylinder are a group of rubber cups, springs, and a check valve and piston operating in a cylinder about one inch in diameter. The primary cup is about the size of a twenty-five-cent piece and weighs about one-quarter ounce. The disintegration of this tiny part causes many sudden brake failures. How many times a week do you apply your brakes? Even normal driving causes wear on this tiny part, and sooner or later it is bound to wear to the point of failure.

All too often the internal condition of the master cylinder is overlooked. The fluid level may be checked and occasionally somebody remembers to look for an external leak. But in too many instances the entire unit is not overhauled until after it has failed— provided the car and driver still exist.

The master cylinder *cannot* last the life of the car. It wears, just as tires wear. But worn tire treads are visible, whereas wear inside the master cylinder remains unseen. The cylinder must be removed and dismantled to find the wear. I have seen worn brake linings replaced as many as six times while the master cylinder remains untouched—even when it shows signs of leaking.

Under normal driving conditions, I recommend that the master cylinder be overhauled or replaced every second time the owner has the brakes relined. When the vehicle has been subjected to extremely severe braking conditions, it may be wise to replace it along with the first reline.

Other points that may cause failure are the breather passage and the pushrod. A breather passage is provided in the master-cylinder filler cap, or cover. Should this breathing system become plugged, pressure may build up in the hydraulic system, causing the brakes to drag, overheat, and finally fail. The pushrod connects the master cylinder and the brake pedal. It is essential that this rod be adjusted to manufacturers' specifications to allow sufficient clearance between the brake pedal and the master cylinder when the brakes are not in use. Otherwise, even when your foot is not on the pedal, the brakes will drag.

Dual Master Cylinders

Prior to 1967, the hydraulic system in most cars was comparable to the water system in your town. Each house along the street is linked to the water main, and if the water main breaks, there is no water pressure in any of the houses.

Until 1967, the same thing occurred in the hydraulic system of your car. A single leak meant brake failure on all four wheels. Now, suppose the town supplied two water mains and that the bathroom was served by one main, while the other fed the kitchen. A leak in one main would be less of a problem. If the kitchen were cut off, at least there would be water in the bathroom. That kind of insurance is unlikely for a town water supply, but, since 1967, all domestic cars have been equipped with a split, or dual, master cylinder. (*See Diagram* 44.)

The idea, though not exactly new, is a boon to safe driving. I have sometimes heard this new system referred to as "dual" brakes, but the term is misleading. The system is not really dual, but *divided,* and there is no additional stopping power. The engineers have divided the master cylinder into two separate chambers, one to exert pressure on the front brakes, and the other to work the rear brakes. If the front hydraulic system fails, the rear system is still able to stop the car, or vice versa. But if one system fails, it will take longer to stop the car, since you have only part of the usual braking power. There is a warning light on the dashboard to tell you when either the front or the rear system has failed.

But such benefits carry their own dangers and responsibilities; they should not be allowed to lull the motorist into a false sense of security.

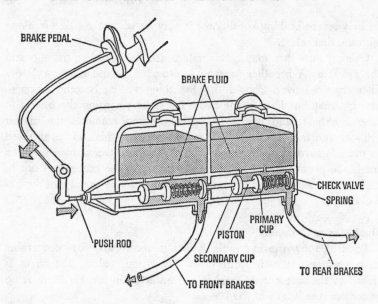

Diagram 44. *Dual, or divided, master cylinder*

Meticulous service and periodic inspection are still important requirements. Things can go wrong which may not affect the warning device; sometimes the warning-light bulb burns out. The bulb can be checked when starting the car. When operating properly, it flashes on momentarily as the ignition key is turned on.

Another point to remember is that the brake pedal may feel fine as long as one of the systems is working, at least for normal stops at low speeds. Your foot may no longer tell you anything, and a failure in half the system could go undetected. This is especially true if it is the rear brake system that is at fault. Only about 35 percent of the stopping power is directed to the rear wheels, while roughly 65 percent goes to the front. A loss of brakes in the front will generally be noticeable, as it takes considerably longer to stop the car, whereas the loss of 35 percent in the rear brakes is clearly less noticeable. There is only one way to be sure even with the extra safety of a divided system and its warning lights—check those brakes regularly!

Wheel Cylinders

In addition to the master cylinder, and in need of just as much attention, are the wheel cylinders. (*See Diagram* 45.) Smaller, simpler

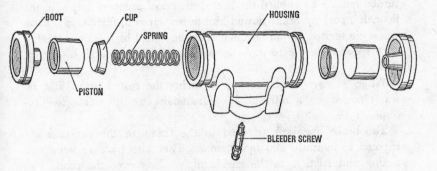

Diagram 45. *Exploded view of wheel cylinder*

units located at each wheel, these cylinders transfer the master-cylinder pressure to the brake shoes and drums. Inside most of these cylinders are two pistons, two rubber cups, and a spring. A defect in any one of the wheel cylinders can cause total brake failure just as fast as a worn master cylinder—and in the same way—by draining all the fluid from the system. When the brakes are being relined, the wheel cylinders should be dismantled, cleaned, inspected, and at least new rubber cups installed. The pistons should also be lubricated with brake fluid or brake-cylinder lubricant to prevent seizure. While on the first reline, you may get by without doing the wheel cylinders, for the modest cost of installing new cups, it's cheap life insurance.

Brake Lines

Roughly 30 feet of steel and rubber brake line is used to link up the master cylinder with the wheel cylinders. Just one tiny hole any-where in this network of tubing—which is exposed to the worst pun-ishment our roads can dish up, together with such other hazards as dripping battery acid—means instant brake failure.

It baffles me that while rusted, corroded brake lines are probably one of the most frequent causes of brake failure on cars over three years of age, seldom does the owner or serviceman think to check them. Deteriorated brake lines can blow open under hydraulic pressure without a second's warning. When this happens, the brake fluid gushes out and the service brake is useless.

This actually happened to a friend of mine who was driving his four-year-old V-8 convertible downhill when a traffic light ahead turned red. As he applied the brake, the pedal dropped limply to the floor. His parking brake slowed him somewhat and, fortunately, there was a big service station on the corner; he aimed his car onto the lot. At a speed of about 10 mph he sailed safely into a large display of tires.

While $8 covered the cost of replacing the rusted brake line, he was charged an additional $25 for repairs to the damaged tire-display rack.

The brake lines are attached to the frame of the car and are exposed to moisture and flying stones. They also have to withstand flexing and friction as the car bounces along over the road. I've replaced thousands of feet of this line, and I've seen lines corroded to one tenth their original thickness. Often these lines break as they are being removed.

On older cars, before starting a visual check of the lines, it's wise to press down on the brake pedal with many times the pressure needed to make a panic stop. In about one out of twenty tests of this nature, a line will burst. If your car is aging and the brake lines have not been checked recently, make the same check while your car is parked in the driveway. You may be lucky and blow a line while the car is standing still, rather than when you are speeding toward disaster. I recommend checking these lines at least once a year on cars over two years old.

Because the suspension components move up and down and from side to side on rough roads, rubber hoses are installed at some stress points in the brake system. While not as vulnerable, rubber hoses can still present a hazard, especially if they are old and tired. Care must also be taken when replacing flexible hoses. If the replacement is too long, it may rub against wheels, tires, or undercarriage, which can wear a hole through it. When it is too short, there may not be enough play to allow for the motion of the car, and it can snap. Replacement hoses must be exactly the same length as the originals, and positioned in such a way that they do not come in contact with the rotating wheels or other moving components.

Hydraulic-brake Switches

There are two types of stop-light switches. The first type is a mechanical unit that works much like the light switches in your home. When the brake pedal is pressed down, it actuates an arm or button that closes a circuit, allowing the electricity to flow to the lights.

The other type is a hydraulically operated switch mounted integrally in the brake lines, which is tripped by pressure of the brake fluid when the brakes are applied. This type of switch is also an integral part of the hydraulic system, and it, too, can fail and drain out all the hydraulic fluid. The base of this switch is made of metal, and a plastic insert, containing part of the switching mechanism, is fitted tightly inside. To provide a leakproof seal, the metal of the base of the switch is pressed around the outside edge of the plastic insert. When the brakes are applied, terrific pressure is exerted on the whole mechanism. In time, the metal base can be eaten away by corrosion and the plastic section forced out by the hydraulic pressure. The brake fluid then pours out, resulting in instant loss of brakes. I have seen dozens of such failures.

When your brakes are being serviced, request a thorough inspection of this switch. Replacement costs only a few dollars. Like other components, both types of switches can become defective and fail to operate the brake lights.

Brake Linings

The hydraulic system is not the part of the brake system that actually stops the car; it provides the pressure to move the braking mechanism. The actual braking is done by a set of brake shoes which are forced against the inside of the revolving brake drum which turns with the wheel. Since the brake shoes do not rotate, they drag against the drum to stop the wheel from turning. The brake lining is the sole of the brake shoe.

The brake lining is made of asbestos molded together with a variety of other compounds to meet specific braking requirements. When overheated, the material tends to glaze, thereby losing some of its frictional characteristics. This condition, called *fade*, leads to a loss of braking potential. Brakes designed for severe, high-speed service often employ linings with a metallic content to reduce fade.

There is much discussion of the relative merits of bonding and riveting as a means of fastening linings to brake shoes. In the early days of bonded linings, adhesives were not always reliable and sometimes allowed the lining to fall away. This defect has been overcome, and I have heard no instances of this happening for many years. On today's automobiles the bonded brake lining is just as reliable as the riveted kind although most manufacturers use riveted linings on their heavier trucks and buses. Since the manufacturers use both kinds, it may be assumed that both are suitable. Regardless of the type of brake lining you use, have them checked regularly.

A problem sometimes experienced by the outdoor enthusiast is the overloading of brakes by pulling trailers and other extra burdens that the brakes were not designed to stop. Brake drums worn out-of-round by frequent high-speed panic stops can cause brake fade, as can drums that have been turned or machined to too large a diameter.

The quality of brake linings varies. Linings are somewhat like children's shoes. How often have you seen a small boy dragging his foot along the pavement to stop his tricycle or wagon? This is essentially what we ask the brake shoes to do inside the drum when stopping the car. If you buy cheap shoes for a child, he will wear them out dragging them along the pavement long before he outgrows them. The same thing happens to brake linings. As with children's shoes, the best quality is usually the least expensive in the long run. You are obviously going to get more from a top-quality brake lining than from an inferior variety—and, unlike children, brakes don't outgrow their shoes!

With brake linings you get exactly what you pay for—or don't pay for. The friction needed to stop a car generates a fantastic amount of heat. Inferior linings are less resistant to heat and quickly lose their frictional properties.

Brake Drums

For efficient, safe braking, the drum against which the lining or sole of the brake shoe presses must be smooth, round, and parallel to the surface of the brake shoe. In time, the action of braking can wear the drum out-of-round and make it egg-shaped or bellmouthed. When the sole of the brake shoe no longer touches the drums evenly or fully the result is poor braking, pulling, squeals, or a spongy pedal. (*See Diagram* 46.) Panic stops are certainly not the only cause. Time and constant friction eventually wear down the inside of the drum. Even if the drum has not been scored by frequent panic stops or worn-out brake linings, it may still need machining to bring it back into true.

When a drum is machined, a small amount of metal is cut off to make the surface smooth and round again. It also makes the in-

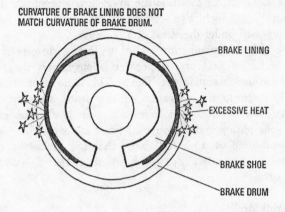

CURVATURE OF BRAKE LINING DOES NOT
MATCH CURVATURE OF BRAKE DRUM.

BRAKE LINING

EXCESSIVE HEAT

BRAKE SHOE

BRAKE DRUM

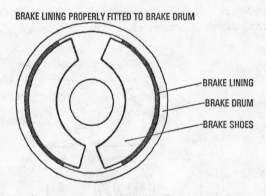

BRAKE LINING PROPERLY FITTED TO BRAKE DRUM

BRAKE LINING

BRAKE DRUM

BRAKE SHOES

Diagram 46. *Effect of undersized brake linings mated to oversized brake drums*

side diameter of the drum larger. There are three remedies available: the first is to use oversized brake linings to make up the difference; this is the best way whenever possible. The second, when rivets are used to hold the linings to the shoes, is to insert a thin liner, called a *shim*, between the lining and the brake shoe to compensate for the metal removed from the drum. The third way is to grind off the brake lining to match the arc of the oversized drum. By this method the arc of the brake-shoe lining can be made to fit the arc of the machined drum, although it does plane away part of the lining, thereby reducing its life.

Clearly, whenever possible, the first solution is the best. It is dangerous, however, to machine the average passenger-car drum beyond about $^{60}\!/_{1000}$ inch. I've seen drums machined to a point where they disintegrated under the stress of a fast stop.

Many people complain that after the brake drums have been turned, the brakes pull or the pedal is spongy, and they are told that it takes time to seat in the linings. This is not true. If the shoe is properly fitted to the curvature of the drum, no working in is necessary. (How often do you have to work in the brakes of a new car?) If your garage hands you back your car with the claim that "brakes need time to work in," insist that the brakes be made to fit—and work—properly. Your car needs shoes that fit comfortably, just as you do.

Self-adjusting Brakes

For some years, self-adjusting brakes have been standard equipment on many North American cars. (*See Diagram* 47.) There were

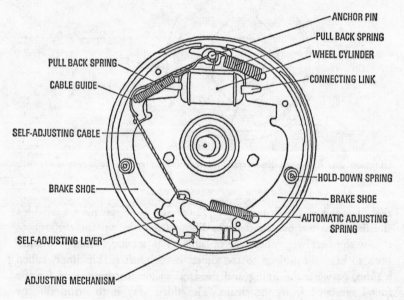

Diagram 47. *Self-adjusting brake mechanism*

problems when they were first introduced, but today they are almost trouble-free. The mechanism is quite simple; it consists of a type of ratchet assembly that automatically turns out the adjusting screws to compensate for gradual wear on the brake linings. But on most cars the mechanism is actuated only when the brakes are applied as the car is backing up. If you feel that your brake pedal is not as high as it should be, it might just be that with your type of driving pattern you don't back up often enough to operate the mechanism. If this is the case, try backing up on a parking lot or a quiet street and applying the brakes several times. The brake pedal may then come up to its proper height.

While self-adjusting brakes provide an extra safety margin by keeping the brakes adjusted to the top of the pedal travel, they still present one possible problem. Some motorists forget to remove the wheel to check the condition of the brake linings when the brakes seem to be operating perfectly and the pedal is high. Usually, they wait until they hear a scraping noise as the brakes are applied, and only then do they head for a garage to find out the cause. By this time, it is too late, and the scraping noise turns out to be bare brake shoes scoring the brake drums. Sometimes the drums can be repaired by machining, but if they are too badly worn they will probably need to be replaced, and new brake drums can cost up to $50 each, and sometimes more.

Don't wait to hear that expensive scraping noise before checking the condition of your linings. On a new car, have a lining inspection at 8000 miles. While it is highly improbable that the brakes will need attention at this low mileage, I've seen cars with 8000 miles (or less) which required lining replacement due to adverse driving conditions. It costs little to check linings, and it may prevent your having to buy new brake drums or, even worse, the possibility of complete brake failure.

Brake Springs

Excessive heat, usually generated by the friction of panic stops, is the biggest enemy of brakes. This danger applies to brake springs, too. Heat can cause them to lose all their tension and leave them as limp as spaghetti. When this happens, the springs do not pull the brake shoes back properly when the brakes are not being used. This, in turn, causes the linings to rub against the drum, wearing themselves down and overheating.

In addition to losing their springiness, these springs can snap. When they do, the pieces fall between the brake shoe and drum, and irreparable harm can be done. Deterioration of the spring assemblies which hold the brake shoes down can result in a similar problem. The heads which hold them to the backing plate can rust off. Then the hold-down springs fall between drum and lining, and the entire shoe assembly flaps around loosely, rubbing against the side of the brake drum. If you hear a scraping sound, have the wheel removed right away.

Power Brakes

Power brakes were designed to reduce the amount of pressure the driver needs to press the brake pedal in order to stop the car. (*See Diagram* 48). Another advantage is that the distance the pedal must

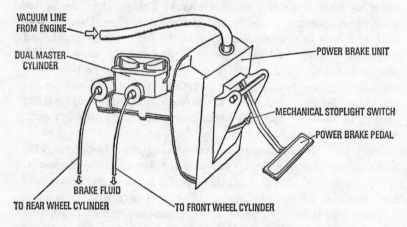

Diagram 48. *Power-brake assembly*

travel for full pressure is reduced, and the pedal need not be as high. This makes it easier to move the foot from accelerator to brake. Power brakes are a real boon on intermediate-sized and heavier cars.

They also take some getting used to. If you buy a new car with power brakes and have never used them before, take the car onto a quiet street, and—at low speed—experiment with the brakes until you know how they react. It is a natural reflex to slam on the brakes when you have to stop in a hurry. Doing this with power brakes will lock the wheels and can cause a nasty skid on a wet or icy road. On a dry road surface, slamming on the brakes when you don't know what to expect can throw the occupants against the windshield or dashboard.

Power brakes use engine vacuum to help apply the pressure, giving more braking power with less effort. There is a factor in the use of this engine vacuum that can cause brake failure. It is possible on some cars for the brake fluid to be drawn through the power booster into the engine by way of a rubber vacuum hose. The resultant brake failure could be sudden and deadly. If brake fluid is mysteriously disappearing from your master cylinder, have the garage check for fluid in the bottom of the power unit. If there is any fluid, have the master cylinder and possibly the power unit overhauled or replaced.

Disk Brakes

With disk brakes, the drum is replaced by a plate, or disk, with a pad (corresponding to the shoe) on either side. When the brakes are applied, the pads are squeezed by a hydraulic caliper against the sides of the disk to stop the wheel from turning. This system is comparable to the blocks that press, pincer fashion, against the wheel rims of some bicycles. (*See Diagram* 49.)

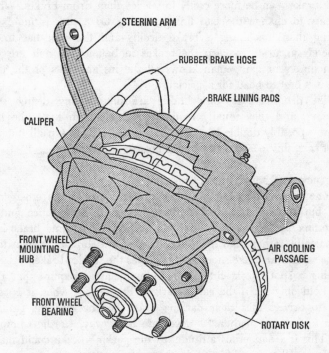

Diagram 49. *Disk-brake assembly*

In recent years there has been an increase in the use of disk brakes on domestic cars (available on front wheels only), and they are certainly advantageous in certain specific situations, especially in high-speed panic stops. The biggest advantage of a disk brake is that pedal fade is rare, since the disk is exposed to the air stream, and overheating to the point of fade is not prevalent. (On the other hand, high-quality drums, some with cooling fins to help dissipate the heat, offer somewhat the same advantage.) The disk brake is also self-cleaning and, after being driven through puddles, scrapes off water that could severely reduce the efficiency of standard drum brakes. However, when the car is being driven under wet conditions, the disk brake is exposed to the elements—not to mention road salt—and corrosion can become a problem. The brake drum, by its very shape, affords some protection. Be sure when you have disk brakes serviced that the pistons in the hydraulically operated calipers are carefully checked and overhauled if there is any evidence of corrosion or seizure.

Disk brakes can be more costly to service than drum brakes. While it is easy to change the pad linings, truing up a disk is more demanding than machining a brake drum—and the disk has to be completely accurate to keep the brakes in balance. If you are not certain that your garageman knows all the ins and outs of the disk brake, it is best to head for a specialist.

Unlike drum brakes, disk brakes are not to any degree self-energizing, and they usually require extremely high hydraulic line pressure—possibly double that of conventional brakes. On all but the lightest cars, this means that a power booster is necessary.

Emergency, Parking, or Hand Brake

At one time the second brake was referred to as the emergency brake, but through the years it has declined in importance and is now commonly known as the parking brake. The parking brake is a mechanically, rather than hydraulically, operated braking system that uses the same rear-brake shoes and drums as the service brake.

During a spot check, the police in many areas require that this brake hold only when the car is parked. Frequently, when it is suggested to drivers that their parking brake be checked, the garageman is told not to bother. "I never use it anyway," is the common reply. This is a dangerous attitude, as the parking brake could mean the difference between life and death.

There are several reasons why the parking brake should be applied every time you park the car. First, if the parking-brake mechanism remains idle for only a short time, it can seize up and become inoperative. Second, if you are parked with a standard transmission in low gear, and the motorist parked behind smacks into your bumper in his effort to get out of a tight parking spot, a tooth can be ripped off one of the transmission gears by the sudden impact. With an automatic transmission, placing the gearshift lever in the "Park" position without engaging the parking brake, puts undue strain on the parking pin inside the transmission. If you are parked on a steep hill, the parking pin can shear off under the strain and cause a runaway car. If the pin does not break, the whole weight of the car bearing down on the mechanism may make it impossible to pull the gearshift handle out of "Park" without first pushing the car uphill to remove the pressure. To avoid the possibility of a runaway car when parked on a hill, always turn your wheels toward the near curb.

Many motorists feel that the parking brake would not help in an emergency. But if the parking brake is operating freely and is correctly adjusted, its use can usually lock both rear wheels at speeds of up to 30 mph. Beyond this, it will still enable the car to stop, if only gradually.

If a panic stop is necessary, pull the brake handle sharply (push with your foot if the car has the extra foot pedal) with all your strength. With the rear wheels locked, the car may be hard to handle, but this is far better than crashing full force. If the car uses a drum at the rear of the transmission as a parking brake, it will be especially hard to cope with in a panic stop, but it's still better than to continue out of control.

Choose a quiet street and practice using the parking brake in imaginary panic stops. Find out exactly how it behaves—and how you react to it. Train yourself to remember to use it in an emergency.

Never leave the parking brake on after a panic stop unless absolutely necessary. If the overheated drums cool while the brake is on, they could be warped, resulting in out-of-round rear-brake drums.

Grease Seals

Grease seals retain the grease within the wheels and also prevent the entry of contaminants. Defective grease seals are often ignored when a brake job is done, despite the fact that they can be dangerous, particularly on the front wheels, where most of the stopping power is applied. Grease will melt when the temperature is high enough, as it can be after a couple of panic stops. If the melted grease spills out around a faulty seal, you're in trouble. A small amount of grease on the brake lining congeals and a wheel can lock, refusing to release even when you lift your foot from the pedal. The result is a vicious skid. On the other hand, when the lining is saturated in grease, it will reduce friction on that wheel, causing erratic brake action. If there is any sign of a leak in the seals, replace them. They cost only a dollar or so.

Riding the Brake Pedal

Although the automatic transmission has taken a lot of the effort out of city driving, in many instances it is directly responsible for the development of a bad driving habit. Some motorists feel that since there is no clutch to keep the left foot busy, they have to find a job for that foot. "Why should it just go along for the ride when it can be put to work on the brake pedal?" Much easier to feed the gas with the right and stop with the left.

Well, so far so good. On the surface there doesn't seem to be much wrong with the switch. Experts tell us that with normal reflexes it takes three quarters of a second to switch the right foot from the gas pedal to the brake, which at 60 mph amounts to 66 feet. Using the left foot can reduce this time and the stopping distance.

But some motorists leave their foot resting lightly on the brake pedal at all times. Even the slightest pressure on the pedal can cause the brake shoes to drag against the drum. The excessive heat generated can boil the brake fluid and wear thousands of miles off the linings.

I know a man who ground out a set of brake linings in 8000 miles and ruined all four brake drums by riding the brake pedal. Four new drums alone cost him over $100—and that's a lot of money to spend after driving only 8000 miles. If the left foot is to be used to stop the car, keep that foot *off* the brake pedal until you really mean to use the brakes.

Erratic Brakes

I recall a man who bought a new car with standard drum brakes. All went well for about a month, then the brakes developed a habit of grabbing violently in the morning. Sometimes they pulled left, sometimes right. There was no predicting what they were likely to do. After a mile or so, with a few routine stops, the grabbing disappeared and the brakes seemed normal. He had the wheels removed and the brakes checked, but there seemed to be nothing to cause the trouble. He asked me what might be the cause.

This is quite a common problem. The grabbing is frequently caused by moisture on the linings and is usually at its worst on rainy or foggy mornings. Brake linings absorb moisture like a sponge, and while a lot of moisture will make the linings slip ineffectually, slight dampness increases the friction, much as grease does, and normal stopping pressure can be enough to lock the wheels.

When pulling to the right or left occurs under these conditions, it is because one set of linings is damper than the other. On damp days it is wise to test the brakes as you start out at a low speed. If they are supersensitive or pulling to one side, apply a little brake pressure while driving slowly for the first hundred feet or so. This will usually generate enough heat to dry the linings out and restore proper braking.

Another dangerous cause of erratic brake action is driving through deep puddles. Water can splash onto the brake mechanism and cause the completely opposite effect from grabbing—an almost total loss of brakes. Drive very slowly through deep puddles, and test your brakes immediately afterward. If they don't work, apply slight brake pressure until they do.

If water is not the cause of erratic brake action, they will continue to act up even after they have had a chance to dry. If the car tends to pull to the left or right, and then seems to even itself out after a second or two, it's usually either a restricted front-brake hose on the opposite side to the pull, or the sluggish action of a partially seized wheel cylinder. If a flexible hose leading to one of the front-wheel cylinders swells up internally, it restricts the flow of fluid to that wheel and results in violent pulling. Since hydraulic brakes are self-equalizing, flow to both sides must be equal.

Scored brake drums, or drums with different diameters, will also cause erratic stopping. This is why it's not wise to machine just one brake drum. Each time a drum is machined it loses some of its strength and can stretch under braking pressure and cause pulling when paired with a standard drum. This is particularly true of the front wheels.

Similarly, an unmatched set of brake linings with varying friction characteristics can cause a pull and, incidentally, result in a particularly baffling diagnostic problem. I had one customer who came in complaining of pulling brakes. We carried out every conceivable test but could find nothing wrong. There were no grease leaks, brake-fluid leaks, wet shoes, or warped drums. All brake lines and hoses were functioning properly. We were scratching our heads and contemplating starting from the beginning when Emil noticed that the color of the shoes on the left side was slightly different from the color of those on the right. The owner divulged that he had just done a lining job himself with shoes he picked up at a wrecker's. The shoes were the right size and in good condition, but the linings on each side were of different manufacture and different composition, and they had entirely different friction characteristics.

Loose steering mechanism, worn or badly adjusted front-wheel bearings, a loose backing plate, improper installation or adjustment of brake components—all of these factors can contribute to erratic braking action.

If this list seems a bit technical, it at least points out the advisability of selecting a technician who is well-versed in the problems that can crop up in the braking system. It also illustrates how impossible it is to estimate the cost of a brake overhaul until the system is dismantled and thoroughly inspected.

I have sometimes noticed people who will demand a complete and thorough brake job but ignore the condition of their tires. In the final analysis, it is the friction between the tire and the road that stops the car. In wet weather, even a perfect brake system is not completely effective and can throw you into a skid when the tires' tread pattern is dangerously thin. The brakes can stop the wheels, but only the tires can stop the car.

The Lubrication System

One word crops up more than any other in this book. That word is "lubrication." At the risk of being repetitious, I have stressed the importance of lubrication to every part of the car. Proper lubrication is necessary to the very life of the car and, occasionally, to the lives of its passengers.

Too often, motorists regard lubricants as a "dash of oil or a blob of grease to do away with squeaks." Yet the list of parts that can wear out prematurely or fail when not properly lubricated is astonishing. We all know that we have to put oil in the engine and grease the chassis, but how many of us think about lubrication for the transmission, drive line, rear end, wheel bearings, speedometer cable, door locks and striker plates, window mechanisms, accelerator and automatic-transmission control linkage, brake cables, brake mechanism, door hinges, hood latches, and even the thick rubber weatherstripping on the door and trunk lid, and internal lubrication of the water-pump sealing gland? But, all these parts require lubrication, and if they don't get it they can cause trouble.

The part of the car we are most accustomed to lubricating is the engine. We all know that sometime the oil has to be changed, but it is difficult to know exactly when. However, without proper lubrication the engine can destroy itself in minutes. (*See Diagram* 50.) Some motorists have had the misfortune to lose their oil while driving on the highway and find their engines completely burned out within a mile or two.

A friend of mine from Detroit once drove his car into my shop to have us check a knock that had developed during his trip to Toronto. A stickler for maintenance, his car had been thoroughly serviced before the trip—including an oil change and a new filter. He was therefore shocked when I told him the engine was practically burned out because his oil level was down to less than a quart.

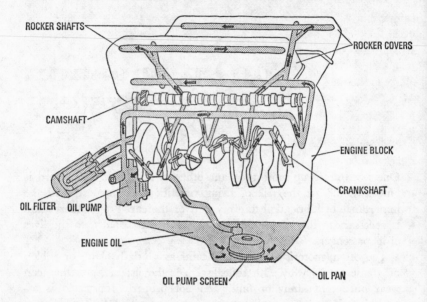

Diagram 50. *Engine lubrication system*

Apparently, when the oil was changed in Detroit, a new oil-pan drain-plug gasket had been installed. The inside diameter of the gasket was an eighth of an inch too large and was allowing the oil to drip out. This cost my friend $400 for a rebuilt engine.

A customer of mine owned a new convertible. The speedometer showed 3000 miles when she set out for a holiday. On the return trip she had to drive across a rough bush road and struck a stone which loosened the oil-pan drain-plug assembly. Eight miles down the highway the engine seized and the car ground to a halt. We towed the car into the shop and rebuilt the motor at a cost of over $600.

Oil Changing

We sometimes overlook the multiple task charged to the engine oil. In addition to providing lubrication or actually separating all the moving parts with a thin, slippery film, the oil must clean, protect against rust and corrosion, and assist in cooling the engine. Oil also provides the final seal between the pistons, piston rings, and cylinder walls, ensuring good compression.

With today's extended lubrication periods, many a motorist assumes that all he has to do is take the car in for an oil change every 4000 miles or so, regardless of his driving pattern. It must be remembered, however, that the change interval recommended by the manufacturer may only apply when the car is operated under favorable conditions.

But what constitutes favorable conditions? It has been my experience that most cars are not driven under these conditions. If all cars were highway driven at maximum speed limits with little stop-and-go city driving, 4000-mile oil changes would usually be more than enough. On the other hand, a motorist who makes only short city runs in cold weather could ruin the engine by waiting up to 4000 miles before changing the oil. Under these circumstances, the owner's manual usually recommends changing the oil more frequently.

Condensation and combustion produce water and acids, and corrosive acid action can be as damaging to the engine as frictional wear. For each gallon of fuel burned during combustion, nearly one gallon of water is produced. Most of this water is expelled through the exhaust, but some finds its way into the oil. This contamination is much more pronounced during short city trips at lower speeds, particularly in cold weather. So, in frigid areas, you can imagine what an awful beating the engine oil takes in a month of stop-and-go, low-speed city driving. Under such conditions, if the oil is not changed frequently, premature engine wear could result.

Since water is heavier than oil, should the two be mixed, the oil will rise to the top. But when oil and water are forced under pressure through the engine's moving parts, they soon emulsify and the water is permanently held in suspension. This mixture, together with the products of combustion, forms corrosive acids, gums, varnish, and sludge. If this condition is allowed to continue, the resulting contamination can cause the piston rings to stick in their grooves, and can coat the inside of the oil-feed passages, restricting or completely plugging the flow of lubricant. Two of the most vulnerable areas are the oil-pump screen and the passages supplying oil to the valve mechanism. In extreme instances, I have seen the oil-pump screen so solidly coated with sludge that the pump couldn't draw lubricant through it. In modern cars the valve mechanism is usually the first area to fail as a result of plugged oil-feed passages—a good reason to remove the rocker covers and check the valve mechanism for adequate oil supply when the engine is being tuned.

To minimize the danger of excessive accumulations of water in the engine, either drive the car regularly on long, high-speed runs which heat the oil sufficiently to vaporize the water and exhaust it through the engine's breather system, or change the oil more frequently.

Many motorists don't read the owner's manual, and those that do usually skim through it. But manuals can be quite complicated and must be read carefully. For example, take the recommended oil-change period in one car manual. On page 28 it reads: "Every three months (not to exceed 4000 miles) . . . drain and refill crankcase. When a car is driven more than 2000 miles per month, the oil should be changed at least every 4000 miles. The oil should be changed more frequently under adverse conditions of operation, such as less than 10 miles per trip."

Then, on page 39, the same manual returns to the subject: "The optimum engine-oil-change period will vary widely, depending on the type of operation, weather conditions, and other operating variables. For instance, during short-trip driving in cold weather or driving on dusty roads, oil changes should be made as frequently as every 500 miles.

"Cross-country driving with good oils will permit 4000 miles of operation between changes. As a general rule, however, it is recommended that the engine oil be changed approximately every three months (not to exceed 4000 miles). We suggest you consult with your dealer to determine the oil-change period required to meet your special driving conditions."

Simple, isn't it? As you can see, you should read your owner's manual thoroughly—regardless of what kind of car you own. No manual gives you a set of standards or service intervals to which you can absolutely adhere. Your own special operating conditions will be the deciding factor on oil-change intervals. Cars that are subjected to constant stop-start operation may still require the traditional thousand-mile oil change.

Contrary to common beliefs, oils do not wear out after continuous use. They are, however, unable to do their job when they become heavily contaminated with carbon, water, lead salts, and other products developed in the combustion chamber. The oil itself can also oxidize, particularly when hot, to form troublesome acids and varnish.

Reputable refineries produce oils capable of resisting oxidation and the formation of acids, just as they produce oils resistant to the foaming that can reduce lubricant effectiveness and interference with the operation of oil pumps and hydraulic valve lifters.

I have visited oil fields in Pennsylvania and have seen the crude oil pumped from the wells and then on to the refineries. In the laboratories I saw the engineers working with test tubes and other forms of equipment. Experiments were being conducted on a battery of engines running under various speed and load conditions. I found myself comparing what I saw with medical research. More and more, medication is replacing major surgery. Through improved refining techniques and the use of additives, the petroleum industry has perfected lubricants to the point where it is seldom necessary to remove the oil pan from modern engines for major surgery. In North America the petroleum industry spends millions annually on research to meet the ever-increasing demands of modern high-speed, powerful, high-compression engines.

Nonetheless, some contamination must occur, especially when the car is driven under adverse conditions. To a degree, the detergent-dispersant additives in modern oils play much the same role as the detergents used in our household washing machines. As the heavy-duty lubricant circulates throughout the engine, it cleanses and minimizes the formation of foreign deposits. Contaminants that are not recovered by the oil filter are held in suspension by the detergent-dispersant additives, and drained out when the oil is changed. Since most cars today use detergent oils, there will be little chance of excessive contamination if the oil is changed when necessary. It must be remembered, however, that while the oil itself will not wear out, the additives will become overloaded, and the detergent-dispersant will eventually lose its ability to clean and suspend contaminants.

The appearance of the oil does not always indicate its condition. Detergent oils generally develop a darkish, or sometimes grayish, shade after a few hundred miles of use. The reason for this is well explained in an operating manual issued by one of the "Big Three" auto makers, which reads: "The color of Service MS (high-detergent) oil does not indicate its condition, since it normally becomes dark after a few hundred miles of driving. This is because the detergent content envelops and holds in suspension extremely fine, but harmless, soot (soft carbon) and lead particles. The oil-filter element does not remove this harmless material, but it does remove larger, harmful particles such as road dust, metal chips, and hard carbon."

One of the major oil refiners points out that it should be remembered that these additives (detergents) can be used up. They can be depleted if the oil is used too long a time for the existing conditions. This means that the oil can no longer keep the contaminants suspended in a harmless state. Deposits and/or sludge should then be expected.

Crankcase Ventilation

Harmful fumes normally accumulate to some degree in the engine crankcase. To dispose of them on most cars built prior to the mid-sixties, fresh air is brought in through a vent on top of the engine (usually the oil-filler cap) and is exhausted through a breather tube at the rear of the motor. (*See Diagram* 51.)

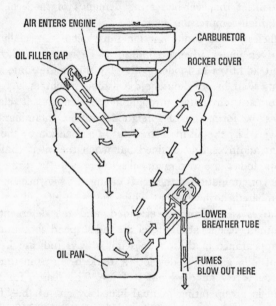

Diagram 51. *Open crankcase ventilation*

Should either the top air-intake vent or the lower breather tube become plugged with road dirt or crankcase sludge, the oil soon becomes contaminated. Also, pressure builds up inside the crankcase, forcing the engine's lubricant out of such areas as the front and rear crankshaft seals, the oil-filler-cap tube, and the oil-dipstick hole.

A clue to proper operation of this ventilation system is light smoke flowing from the end of the lower breather tube as the engine idles. The older the engine and the higher the mileage, the greater the volume of smoke. Heavy smoke pouring from the breather tube indicates badly worn piston rings and/or damaged pistons. Adequate ventilation is vitally important to the life of the engine.

Positive Crankcase Ventilation (P.C.V.)

In about 1963, many car makers discontinued the draft-tube method of ventilation and introduced what is known as the Positive Crankcase Ventilation System (P.C.V.). This system was primarily developed to prevent crankcase fumes from polluting the air, but other benefits such as better gas mileage and longer engine life are reported.

With this system, the fumes are drawn from the crankcase by means of the vacuum from the engine's intake manifold and are burned along with the fuel/air mixture in the combustion chamber. (*See Diagram* 52.)

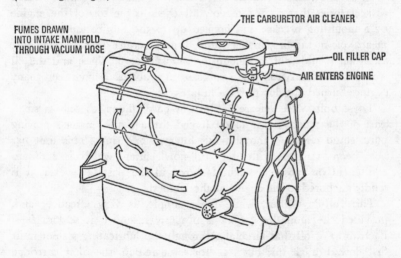

Diagram 52. *Positive crankcase ventilation*

On most cars, the key to this improved method of crankcase ventilation is a small metal device known as the P.C.V. valve. The internal mechanism of this valve is designed to control the vacuum flow at various engine speeds.

Foreign matter from the fumes passing through this unit can cause the internal valving arrangement to stick, preventing the fumes from being drawn from the crankcase. When this occurs, the crankcase becomes pressurized, resulting in serious loss of engine lubricant, and the oil becomes contaminated with damaging by-products of combustion.

A surprising number of motorists are unaware of this valve's existence; if it is not called to their attention by a mechanic, they ignore it completely. But servicing this valve and various other components incorporated in the P.C.V. system, as spelled out in the owner's manual, is imperative. Failure to do so could rapidly ruin the engine. To combat air pollution, all vehicles sold in the United States and Canada are now equipped with Positive Crankcase Ventilation systems. I recommend that the crankcase-ventilation system be checked and serviced as necessary during each oil change.

Oil Filters

Years ago when oil filters first came into being, they were offered as accessories that were somehow attached to the top of the engine by a mounting bracket and hooked up to the lubrication system by means of metal or flexible oil-feed and return lines. Frequently, vibration would split the mounting brackets or oil lines, and the oil would be drained from the crankcase in minutes. I have seen many engines burned out due to these failures.

These units were referred to as "by-pass" filters, as only a small part of the total volume of oil forced through the engine's moving parts could circulate through this filter at one time. This unit has now been replaced with the "full-flow" filter, which is standard equipment on most cars manufactured in the past few years; it is solidly anchored to the engine at the factory.

This full-flow filter, while fairly simple, is very effective, and, provided the mounting gasket is properly installed, it seldom fails. Each drop of oil that circulates through the lubricating system must first flow through this filter. If, for some reason, the filter cartridge becomes plugged, a by-pass valve automatically opens, thus assuring an uninterrupted oil supply.

Even with this improved unit, in time the filter becomes contaminated, ceases to do its job, and must be replaced. A good rule of thumb borne out in many owner's manuals is to replace the filter cartridge with every second oil change. However, under adverse driving conditions, it may be advisable to replace it with every oil change. Read your manual and, if in doubt, consult your serviceman.

As an example of the importance of oil filters, in my Navy days we used to keep the oil clean in our diesel engines by passing it through a series of filters and then whirling it around in a centrifuge, much like a milk separator, to remove all the solid foreign matter. While the oil remained remarkably clean, we still discarded it periodically because of possible acid contamination. Even if the oil appears clean, there is still danger of acid contamination.

Oil Classifications

We sometimes fail to realize that the crude oil we obtain from the ground in Texas, Pennsylvania, Western Canada, and other localities, provides us with far more than just oil. From the original crude oil, the petroleum companies refine gasoline, kerosene, fuel oil, diesel fuel, propane, other petroleum gases, various grades of lubricating oil, asphalt, wax, and many other by-products.

Crude-oil composition varies according to its source and requires considerable refinement, blending, and the addition of additives to function properly as a fuel or lubricant. When oil is blended with certain metallic "soaps," it becomes the grease which is used to lubricate various parts of the car. In some instances, synthetic greases are manufactured by mixing metallic soaps with nonpetroleum fluids.

In order for motorists to choose the proper lubricant for an engine, the American Petroleum Institute long ago formulated a "Classification of Internal Combustion Engine Service" for oils. For gasoline-type engines, these classifications are: ML, MM, and MS. ML or "Motor Light," is an oil designed for light duty in engines operating under light loads and favorable conditions. These oils were used extensively in pre-World War II cars, but are obsolete today. MM, or "Motor Medium," is a nondetergent oil for engines in normal operation at occasional high speeds and subject only to normal amounts of dust, but are generally not recommended for modern cars, particularly those with hydraulic valve lifters. (See *Engine* chapter.) MS, or "Motor Severe," is recommended for most late-model cars and will effectively lubricate and protect engines that are used for a lot of stop-and-go driving, are operated at high speeds with heavy loads, and are subjected to hot and dusty conditions.

Motor Severe oils are of a highly detergent-dispersant nature and have an abundance of additives to guard against wear, acid formation, oxidation, sludging, and foaming. For cars today, the importance of Motor Severe oil is obvious when you consider that there is a cushion of lubricant only about $\frac{1}{1000}$ inch, less than the thickness of a human hair, separating the bearing surfaces of the connecting rods and the crankshaft. Even more critical are hydraulic valve lifters, which have a clearance of around $\frac{2}{10}$ of $\frac{1}{1000}$ inch. Nothing can be allowed to interfere with this critical lubrication lest serious damage result. Regardless of these close tolerances, properly lubricated engines can last for 100,000 miles or more.

Your best assurance of obtaining top quality motor oil is to purchase an oil carrying the designation "MS," and one which has passed the Automobile Manufacturers "MS sequence tests." These are often referred to as "MS sequence tested" oils. In most cases, this can be accomplished by purchasing the oil company's "top of the line" product.

However, motorists who drive older cars or collectors' items which have used the non-high-detergent oils should exercise extreme caution and consult their serviceman before switching suddenly to these high-detergent lubricants. The deposits in the older motors can be loosened, causing excessive oil consumption, plugged oil-pump screens, and other undesirable conditions.

Viscosity (SAE Grades)—Oil Weight

In addition to the A.P.I. classifications of ML, MM, and MS, the oil's viscosity is also classified. The standards, devised by the Society of Automotive Engineers, relate to the oil's thickness under certain temperature conditions. A viscous oil leaves a heavier oil film on engine parts than a less viscous oil. This is an important advantage for two reasons: It will not allow working parts to come together and wear, and it will offer a tight seal to escaping compression—technically called "blow-by"—at the piston rings. However, if the oil is too viscous, it will not allow the engine to turn over at low temperatures, and it may fail to get in between closely fitting components in sufficient quantity to guard against wear or heat buildup.

The ideal oil is one whose viscosity is tailored to the temperature-operating range of the engine, one that will function correctly when the engine is either hot or cold.

Viscosity is measured by an oil's ability to flow through a hole of precise dimensions at a particular temperature. The faster the oil flows, the lower its viscosity and SAE number. Thus, a low-viscosity oil suitable for extremely cold conditions of starting would have a much lower number than an oil suitable for warm-weather starting. Oils that conform to the Society's low-temperature requirements have the suffix "W" tagged onto their viscosity number.

Oil loses viscosity as its temperature increases, and when an oil of extremely low-viscosity rating is used for low-temperature starting, there is some loss of body at higher temperatures and a consequent reduction in lubricating properties. For this reason, it was the practice for many years to change the type of oil according to the season— using, perhaps, an SAE 10W in the winter, and an SAE 30 in the summer.

Multiviscosity oils, such as 10W30, have become popular because they offer the required cold-starting characteristics as well as high-temperature protection. As an example, an SAE 10W30 oil meets SAE requirements for a 10W oil at 0 degrees F., while still meeting the requirements for an SAE 30 oil at 210 degrees F.

The car manufacturers specify in the owner's manual the kind of oil which should be used in their cars according to the lowest anticipated operating temperature.

Other Types of Lubricants

The oil used for gear lubrication is of a special nature and performs just as tough a task as the lubricants used in the engine. It must flow easily at low temperatures to enter between the gear teeth, and it must be able to move back in promptly as it is wiped or squeezed out. Excessive viscosity will impair the oil's ability to flow between the teeth at low temperatures, and serious wear will result. Gear lubricants are available in several SAE grades. Those most commonly used in cars are specially formulated to flow properly at low temperatures and still provide adequate lubrication at the higher operating temperatures. Lubricants of this type are used in standard transmissions and rear-axle differential assemblies.

By and large, lubrication of gear assemblies is quite easy, provided an oil of the correct type and viscosity is employed. Specially designed gears, called hypoid-type gears, are found in nearly all rear axles today. These gears apply considerable pressure and tearing force to the lubricant and require E.P. (Extreme Pressure) gear oils. Special additives are used in these gear oils to plate the mating-gear teeth surfaces in order to prevent wear, scoring, and welding of the gear teeth.

The lubricant in standard transmissions should be checked twice a year or as often as recommended in the owner's manual. The manufacturer usually recommends that the lubricant level be checked more frequently when the car is used under severe driving conditions. When necessary, the oil level should be topped up with the lubricant recommended by the car maker. If you ever see oil on the driveway and it seems to have come from the transmission, check the level immediately.

Owner's manuals usually suggest checking the rear-axle differential lubricant level twice a year, but no harm will be done by checking more frequently. The manual will specify the procedure and the correct type of lubricant. Remember, the car should be in a level position while making this check.

Limited slip differentials (discussed in the *Drive Train* chapter) also require a special lubricant. The mechanism contained in these units operates in a fluid bath in a manner similar to the clutches in the automatic transmission. The wrong lubricant will cause an annoying chatter and can result in serious damage.

Greasing Points

Even heavier than the oils used in gear assemblies, lubricating grease is used to lubricate the chassis, wheel bearings, universal joints, and other component parts. Greases, being thicker than oils, do not flow but cling firmly to bearing surfaces.

Most modern water pumps are lubricated at the factory and do not require further greasing. Liquid additives are available to lubricate the internal sealing gland and prevent coolant leaks. Their importance is discussed in the *Cooling System* chapter.

Universal joints should be inspected externally at least twice a year. Some manuals state that they never need lubrication under normal conditions, but specify intervals for their disassembly and repacking when driven under severe conditions such as constant high-speed driving on rough roads, or when towing trailers.

As pointed out in the *Drive Train* chapter, failure of a universal joint can cause the driveshaft to drop to the road or carve its way through the steel floor of the car. For my money, it's a good idea to dismantle, inspect, clean, and repack universal joints at intervals of about 20,000 miles.

A grease is also used to lubricate various chassis points, including the all-important ball joints. Unfortunately, in this day of the extended lubrication period, with specified lubrication intervals ranging up to 36,000 miles, many motorists neglect their cars completely for such periods. A ball joint without lubricant can fail completely, resulting in a loss of steering. In my accident-investigation business, I have seen the results of as many as three accidents in one month which resulted from steering-ball-joint disintegration while the car was in motion.

I have my own thoughts on chassis lubrication. I recently called a few of my pals in the garage business and found that they also have their own ideas about when and how a car should be given a chassis lubrication. A lot of maintenance-conscious people insist on a grease job every 2000 or 3000 miles.

The manufacturers have improved the front-suspension components and, under normal circumstances, they don't often require greasing. The ball studs and tie-rod ends are now sealed to keep out moisture, but this makes it very important to have a good man behind the grease gun.

If the man operating the grease gun applies too much pressure when the joints are lubricated for the first time, the seals can blow open, allowing lubricant loss and moisture and dirt to enter. I hate to think of what could happen to a car that was neglected for up to 36,000 miles after the seals had burst.

Front-wheel bearings also require lubrication with a special formulation of grease which must withstand extremes of temperature. Here, again, the manufacturers have extended the service interval. One typical owner's handbook states: "Front-wheel bearings should be cleaned and repacked whenever brake linings are inspected or replaced, or the brake drums are resurfaced." The same manual suggests that brake linings be inspected every 20,000 miles.

The bearing lubricant will normally stand up for 20,000 miles or more, but this seems to me a long time to wait before at least checking them in view of the modest cost of repacking the bearings. It is understandable how a certain measure of confusion arises from such extended service periods.

A prime example was provided by a reader who recently stormed into my office with a box full of worn parts which had just been replaced on his V-8 sedan—to the tune of $156. He had bought the car used with 17,000 miles on the clock. Before taking delivery, he asked the dealer if anything needed servicing immediately. The dealer assured him that he had bought a good car, with brake linings "just like new," and that the car had been completely serviced.

The customer was one of the few people who reads his manual thoroughly, and he did—from cover to cover. He read the section on checking drums and brake linings, but since he had just been assured by the dealer that everything was O.K. and the brake linings were like new, he reasonably assumed that he could leave servicing of the front-wheel bearings for another 10,000 miles or so.

While driving on a major highway a few weeks later, he felt a severe vibration similar to that caused by a flat tire. He stopped and checked, but the tires seemed fine. He next pulled into a service station and reported the vibration to an attendant, who, after a cursory examination of the tires, said: "Well, the car is still running, so you might as well keep on driving." The next morning he started out to have the car checked by the dealer, but it moved barely five feet and then refused to budge. The car was towed to the garage, where it was found that the right front wheel was ready to fall off.

The wheel bearings had seized and torn off the end of the brake-drum hub, which in turn ripped a deep groove in the steering knuckle and bent the brake shoes. Paying out the required $156 was painful enough, but his greatest concern was that he could have been killed on the highway and another car would have been reported as having "mysteriously gone out of control."

Have those front-wheel bearings checked every 10,000 miles. Whether they seem to need it or not is beside the point—for the few dollars involved.

And if you decide to do the job yourself, don't be like the young driver I know who had just bought his first car (used) and decided to repack his own front-wheel bearings. He had always used kitchen fat to lubricate the bearings on his bicycle, a trick he had learned from his older brother.

Thinking it would serve the same purpose on his car, he used bacon fat on his wheel bearings. While heading for Cleveland at high speed, the fat melted, the bearings ran dry, turned blue with heat, and seized. A wheel fell off as he was about to cross a railway crossing, and he ground to a halt in the middle of the tracks. With the help of passing motorists, he managed to get the car off the tracks before a train came along.

When repacking your own bearings, be sure to use the correct high-temperature lubricant. Your manual or local garage can tell you what to use.

The manual tells you when to grease the car. To protect the warranty, it is essential to do so at least at those intervals. It is well to remember that lubrication intervals vary considerably from model to model and from manufacturer to manufacturer. One may specify 6000 miles, another, 36,000 miles. Regardless of when a grease job is called for, it is a good idea to put the car on a hoist every 2000 miles. Consider it more as a safety check than a grease job, and if a spot of lubricant is required, this is a good time to take care of it.

Under normal driving conditions, the car may well do the mileage recommended by the manufacturer before chassis lubrication. But if your type of driving runs to rough washboard roads, exposure to salt and water and extremes of temperature, I recommend checking frequently and, if necessary, greasing more often. A grease job and safety check cost only a few dollars and can save hundreds on repairs —plus minimizing the danger of sudden mechanical failure.

For the most part, the owner's handbook is the best guide to the lubrication of your car. It specifies the correct lubricants and, if not misinterpreted, points the way to proper lubrication. However, cars of different makes have different lubrication requirements. This can even be true of two cars of identical model, make, and year, if one incorporates modifications and if the lubrication requirements are changed in midyear. Be sure you have the manual for *your* car. Read it, study it, think about it, and make the necessary allowances for your own special driving conditions.

Other Lubrication Points

We have covered lubrication of the major components and trickier parts of the car. There are still a dozen or so other places that should be checked and/or lubricated at least twice a year.

One is the steering box. Keep the housing filled to the bottom of the filler-plug hole so that the lubricant covers the internal mechanism.

The automatic transmission in some cars does not require a change of lubricant for the life of the car, in normal service. However, others require draining, refilling, and servicing of the screen or filter at specified intervals. The frequency of fluid change should be determined from the manual with due allowance for operating conditions.

The draining procedure varies according to make of car; in many instances it is not simply a matter of removing a drain plug and letting the oil pour out. If your transmission needs to be drained, be sure it is done by a competent serviceman according to the manufacturer's recommendations.

Servicing the speedometer cable is possibly one of the last things thought about by motorist or repair shop. The speedometer cable is not self-lubricating and should be removed once a year, preferably just before winter, and coated with a special lubricant.

The complete assembly is composed of an outer flexible casing in which an inner laminated wire cable spins to operate the mechanism in the speedometer head. This cable works hard and is incredibly strong. About five feet long and about as thick as a wooden match, it turns over at between 800 and 1500 rpm when the car is traveling at 60 mph. When a loud, rasping noise is heard in the area of the instrument panel, or when the needle begins to jump up and down the dial, a dry cable or wear in the speedometer head is indicated.

You can remove some cables by simply reaching under the dash and unscrewing from the speedometer head. In others, part of the instrument panel has to be removed. When replacing a broken inner cable, especially on difficult installations, it is a good idea to check the speedometer head as well. If it is jamming, the new cable will soon break. Apply lubricant to the cable sparingly. Too much can result in the speedometer figures being spattered with grease.

Windshield-wiper mechanisms also require lubrication. Electric wipers sometimes have to be dismantled for this purpose. Vacuum-type wipers sometimes stall because of lack of lubricant, and a temporary cure may sometimes be found by removing the vacuum hose and pumping oil up into the wiper motor.

In cold weather it is a good idea to wipe flexible cables on heater controls with a little penetrating oil. Enough oil will usually get through to prevent seizure. If possible, squirt a little oil into the ends of the cables.

Another must for cold weather is the application of lubricant to the external door and trunk-lock cylinders. I will never forget being called at my garage by a nervous young fellow who wanted me to come and unlock his car doors. His key wouldn't work because there was ice in the cylinders. I hurried over and found him in a great state of agitation, standing on the sidewalk and shivering with cold. It turned out that he was getting married and was due at the church in half an hour. Working with a piece of coat hanger, I was able to catch the inside door handle and open up the car for the trembling groom. For a wedding present I gave him a can of lock-cylinder lubricant.

Another winter worry is frozen door and trunk-lid weatherstripping. If it is not lubricated, it can freeze solid on cold damp days, especially after the car has been washed. If a door or trunk lid is forced open, the weatherstripping rips apart, allowing salt, water, and a cool breeze to get through.

The weatherstripping on some cars can cost as much as $25 per door. To avoid this expense, coat the weatherstripping with ethylene glycol (ordinary radiator antifreeze) mixed half and half with water, or specially formulated spray-bomb preparations. Make it a winter-time practice to follow this procedure periodically to avoid frozen doors.

If the car has fender skirts, lubricate the release mechanism occasionally. They may stick when you most want to remove them—such as when trying to change a tire. In the winter, a lot of people leave them off entirely to guard against their freezing into place.

The hood latch is also a must for frequent lubrication, not so much to guard against jamming as against improper latching and the danger of its flying open when traveling at high speed.

A variety of other unseen points need an occasional dab of grease or oil in order to operate effectively. These include door-lock striker plates, door-check arms and locks, tailgate hinges on station wagons, door-latch rotors, trunk-lid latches, parking-brake cables and mechanism, license-plate-access-door hinges over the rear gasoline filler cap on cars so equipped, and anywhere else you can find a hinge, striker plate, or lock. Even the radio antenna appreciates an occasional drop of oil between the sections.

Above all, regardless of how long it takes, it is imperative to read and understand your car's manual. A lot of people make notes to jog their memories as to when their car requires lubrication. If your car is under warranty by the manufacturer and you service your car as recommended in the handbook, you will have the assurance of knowing that your warranty will remain intact throughout the warranty period. Proper lubrication is an essential part of required warranty services.

The Body

The car's biggest single enemy is rust. This corrosive action works night and day to devour the sculptured metal panels and shiny trim which give our modern chariots their eye appeal. Corrosion caused by industrial smog is also taking an increasing toll. Steel is not the only metal that falls prey to the process of oxidation. Copper, chrome (one of the hardest metals), and aluminum will corrode, too. Not even stainless steel is immune.

Rusting is a complex chemical process that takes place wherever metal and oxygen are in contact with each other. When water and certain chemicals are also present, the process is accentuated. Industrial impurities, such as sulphur dioxide, combine with water to form acids (sulphuric acid, in this case) and greatly speed up the process of corrosion. The only way to protect the metal of the car body from this complex corrosive activity is to isolate it completely from water and its damaging allies.

I've been through automobile plants in Europe and North America and have seen that the manufacturers are making an all-out effort to protect the cars from rust. They submerge the bodies in vats of chemicals and rust-resistant primer-surfacer; they use galvanized panels increasingly; they apply layers of underbody coating—all to ward off the moisture and chemicals that add up to corrosion. Finally, they finish the car with a coat of paint—but not simply to give it a colorful appearance. That paint also provides a protective armor for the outside of the car body.

But we must still face the fact that, in time, cars will rust away, especially in areas where they are driven in snow and where salt is used on the roads to melt it. Even cars that winter near the sunny beaches of the south are threatened by salt carried in from the ocean by every breeze. I have seen cars that have never encountered snow affected by salt action in two or three years.

Salt speeds up the rusting process, and in areas where it is used on the roads, damage is sure to follow. In Toronto, my home town, about fifty million pounds of salt are dumped on the roads every winter. It is estimated that in extreme cases this can cost a motorist up to $150 annually in repairs and extra depreciation resulting from corrosion.

Some time ago a friend of mine decided to trade in his low-mileage, mechanically sound five-year-old car for a new model. He was shocked when the dealer explained the the body was beyond repair, and the car was therefore not worth anything on trade. The body was blighted with the worst case of rust I have ever seen. Gaping holes had been eaten through doors, fenders, trunk lid, hood, and rocker panels. There were holes in the floor big enough for a child to fall through. The only cure would have been to install new body panels throughout, a job that would have cost more than the car was worth. His luxury liner went to the wrecker at the tender age of five years.

Many of us criticize the use of salt on the roads and highways because we have learned from experience that it is a major cause of corrosion. I'm sure people would agree, however, that the saving in human life by keeping the roads free of snow and ice justifies its use.

Some people suggest neutralizing the salt by the addition of chemicals. Research has been undertaken in the United States and Canada into the use of additives to reduce salt's corrosive potential, and some success has been recorded. However, these additives are expensive and do nothing to combat the other causes of body blight.

A better approach is to treat the car, not the salt. While manufacturers have done much to protect their products against rust, there is mounting evidence that even more can be done. According to corrosion experts, cars can be effectively rustproofed for many years, using materials and methods already in existence.

Whether or not car manufacturers can make use of these techniques is questionable. Their thinking must be influenced by dollar considerations, and they will not lightly add the cost of complete internal rustproofing to the price of a car. If they did, many motorists would accuse them of profiteering. Besides, there are technical problems. If the rustproofing agents are applied before the car is put together, it is difficult to obtain proper welds during assembly. Moreover, the rustproofing material melts away in the excessive heat generated during spot welding.

Various companies in the United States and Canada offer internal rustproofing with up to a ten-year guarantee. The effectiveness of their treatment is attributable to the materials they use and the way they use them. The material they use is a nonflammable compound which does not hold or trap moisture. It will not crack or peel, remains pliable down to 40 degrees below zero, and can withstand temperatures as high as 275 degrees above zero. Its creeping action ensures protection even in inaccessible areas of the car. It is vastly superior to conventional underbody coatings, which will peel and crack, forming pockets that hold saline solutions in close contact with the body, enabling them to do their worst.

The technique calls for drilling holes from inside or underneath the body to gain access to the inside of double body panels, doors, and other areas where moisture collects. Most corrosion starts from inside, where there is the greatest need for rustproofing. Tubes of various shapes are used to spray the sealant into areas that would not otherwise be accessible. The high pressure used for spraying and the creeping action of the sealant ensure complete coverage. Plastic plugs are then used to seal the holes. Even undercar parts, such as steel brake lines, are given a coat of the sealant and, where necessary, tail-light housings, headlamp pots, and pieces of chrome trim are removed in order to reach hidden areas and ensure maximum protection.

I have seen vehicles up to five years old which, thanks to this treatment, were still completely free of rust. I, for one, am sold on the idea. So, too, are many operators of large truck fleets in North America. I know of several large utility companies that rustproof their vehicles by this process and keep them operating in the worst that weather, ocean, and industry can dish up.

If you have a new car, I recommend that you invest in this protection before driving anywhere. Experts tell me that exposure to salt and rain for just one day can start the rusting process. On the other hand, even older cars can benefit and gain a new lease on life, provided corrosion hasn't already done too much harm.

The deadliest time for salt action is right after a snowstorm, when tons of salt are dumped on our city streets. If practical, and where public transportation is available, avoid driving the car during or right after a blizzard. In addition to the damage from salt, you can avoid the mechanical damage caused by skidding wheels and revving the motor as you try to avoid becoming bogged down. And, of course, there is always the increased danger of a collision.

If you must take the car out in such weather, get it to a car laundry as soon as possible afterward and have the undercarriage washed down with power hoses. The salt on the painted top surfaces is not nearly as dangerous as the salt that accumulates inside the fenders, rocker panels, and other areas of the car.

Wash the car frequently. I know it hurts to pay for a car wash when slush on the roads guarantees it will soon get dirty again, but every effort should be made to keep the car free of salt.

Many car owners who keep their cars in a warm garage are shocked when they find rust developing rapidly. The fact is that a warm salt solution corrodes much more quickly than a frozen one, and a warm, moist garage simply speeds up the process.

In addition to rust, other strange things can happen when salt finds a permanent home on your car. Recently I heard of a motorist who had a very odd experience after a weekend holiday in the country. On the way home, he drove into a service station to gas up and have his oil checked. When the attendant opened the hood he stared down into the engine compartment and then asked the motorist to get out and have a look. The motorist looked under the hood and was astounded the see that the rubber had been stripped off his heater hoses, several rubber grommets were missing from the firewall, and the insulation was missing from the battery cables. "Sabotage!" he deducted. "But whodunit? And why?"

While he tried to figure out why anybody should try to wreck his car, the country-raised service-station attendants put their heads together and came up with the answer. The culprit was a porcupine. It seems that a porcupine will eat almost anything with salt on it, and I imagine everything under the hood of the car was liberally coated with salt from the previous winter. I have even heard of holes being chewed in tires by these animals. This is one more reason to make certain all the salt is washed from your car during the winter and before you head out to porcupine country in the summer.

Most cars have special vents cut into the bottom of door panels, rocker panels, and other points to allow water to escape. If these vents become plugged, water and salt accumulations act much like a big rust-producing poultice.

Some years ago, a customer drove into my garage and asked me to road-test his two-year-old car.

"I think the baffles in my gas tank have worked loose," he said. "Every time I turn a corner I hear a loud sloshing noise, and I think it's my gasoline slopping around in the tank."

I took the car for a drive, and sure enough, there was a noticeable gurgling sound coming from the rear every time we took a corner. Examination showed that the drain holes at the bottom of a rear quarter panel were plugged solid with mud. I drove a screwdriver into the drain holes, and about three gallons of water poured out.

Check these vents after driving over muddy or sandy roads, and ask to have them flushed out when you get your car washed.

Some cars have wells for the spare tire in the bottom of the trunk, and if water seeps into the trunk these wells can fill. This, too, will rust the metal, and during a cold spell it can lock the spare wheel in a solid block of ice. It's wise to remove the spare occasionally and check for water. Usually there is a plug in the well which can be removed to drain the water.

If corrosion has eaten a hole in the bottom of your trunk, deadly exhaust fumes can creep through and enter the passenger section of your car.

Body Repairs

As hard as we may try to protect the finish of our chariots, sooner or later such things as scratches, broken grilles, and bent fenders will result as the natural outcome of the contest between cars named after a growing number of predators. Cars today masquerade as marauders, barracudas, wildcats, cougars, mustangs, stingrays, and various birds of prey.

Restoring the lines of our curvaceous modern cars requires a skilled technician with the artistic flair of a sculptor. Don't go to a fly-by-night body shop that offers to repair the body and paint it for a ridiculously low price.

An unscrupulous bodyman can fake your bodywork with plastic, plaster, and paper, and by the time you see the car again the crime has been covered with a few coats of primer-surfacer and a finish coat of paint. It might look good, too, but shortly you'll find the patchwork is cracking, peeling, and falling to the pavement.

Your best bet is to select a reputable bodyman who promises to give you what you pay for. Whether he uses metal, solder, or plastic is beside the point. All have their place. But how he uses them is very important.

Body Plastic

While many motorists feel that solder alone should be used as a body filler and frown upon the use of plastic, there are times when plastic serves a very useful purpose. Heat must be used to apply solder, and the heat from a welding torch can warp a long body panel to such a degree that it would take hours of work to straighten it again. Where a long panel is badly dented, it is often better to beat the metal back to approximately the original contours of the panel, and fill it with plastic. Plastic body fillers are now available that will stand up a lot longer than the metal they are used to repair.

Used in the right places, plastic can reduce the repair cost, and when we consider that about 50 percent of the money we spend on car repairs today goes into bodywork, price as well as quality of workmanship is important.

Metal panels are available to repair fender sections, quarter panels, rocker panels, and other body sections of the car, and it is often preferable to use them. But if your bodyman suggests plastic, in some instances it can be a perfectly good choice if properly installed. There are several makes of cars on the road today whose original bodies are formed partly or entirely of fiber glass.

Fender and other parts made of fiber glass are available to replace original steel sections. When produced by reputable suppliers, such parts can do a good, economical job.

Plastic will not conduct electricity, and problems can arise if a light assembly mounted in a plastic replacement panel is not properly grounded. The electrical parts of the car depend on the metal of the car body or the chassis to provide part of their circuit. If they are attached only to plastic, a ground wire will have to be added to connect them properly to a metal section of the body.

Plastic fillers may crack or chip if used in areas that are subjected to extreme flexing. When used over rusty areas that are full of small holes, metal should first be welded into place to support the plastic. Otherwise, a sheet of fiber glass an inch or so larger than the area to be covered should be installed to seal the holes and prevent moisture from attacking the metal supporting it from the inside. If neither of these precautions is followed, rusting action can gradually loosen the plastic and it will drop away. Even the smallest hole will allow moisture to enter and prevent proper bonding.

Plastic technology has made many advances, and plastic is assured of a continuing role in both building and repairing cars. As I see it, the biggest problem when using plastic for repairs is faced by the bodyman. As he grinds away to restore the original contours, clouds of choking dust are raised, filling his eyes, ears, and nose. But the use of sanding machines with vacuum attachments tends to minimize the volume of dust.

Bumpers

Being of robust construction, bumpers can usually be straightened and rechromed after they have been damaged. In fact, in most areas an exchange service is available where a bumper can be traded for a guaranteed reconditioned unit.

Other parts, such as moldings and headlamp or tail-light rims, usually cannot be straightened and rechromed. With rare exceptions, the cost would exceed that of a replacement unit.

If a bumper or other piece of chrome decoration is badly rusted, very fine steel wool and an approved chromium cleaner helps to restore the sparkle. Another approach is to rub briskly with a wet soap pad—usually small pads of fine steel wool impregnated with an effective detergent. Then apply a protective coat of wax or clear lacquer.

In extreme cases, such as where the bumper is dented and pieces of chrome have actually stripped off, the damaged area can be filled with body plastic or other filler, sanded smooth, and sprayed with an aerosol paint bomb. Some aluminum enamels have a brilliant shine and can go a long way toward restoring the original appearance of a bumper.

Paint

When the dents have been straightened out, a protective coat of paint is needed to restore the original glossy finish. But I often wonder if cars today shine as much as some of those dazzling machines I used to see in my youth.

An old friend of mine, who has operated a body and paint shop for forty years, tells me that they shone more in the old days. He points out that even before the twenties, it was possible to get a glasslike shine on cars, but it took as long as two weeks to do the job, and usually the paint wouldn't last more than six months. That kind of paint job called for all the skill and patience that only the old-time craftsmen tutored on coachwork could provide. In those days, they laboriously hand-brushed several coats of colored rubbing varnish onto the car. Each coat was rubbed down until every trace of brush mark or imperfection had vanished. Finally they brushed on a coat of clear, high-gloss varnish. The resulting shine outdid any mirror—for a few months. Today, we expect a lot longer life from a paint job than from six months to a year.

In 1923, synthetic lacquers appeared on the scene, and the spray gun began to take over from the brush of the old carriage painters. By 1930, synthetic enamels were also available, and the transition to modern painting materials and techniques was well on its way. Shortly after the war, the addition of aluminum particles to automobile finishes was introduced, producing the popular "metallic" colors used so effectively on many cars today.

There is a considerable difference between lacquer and enamel finishes. Lacquer dries by evaporation of its solvent thinners within about ten minutes after application. This minimizes the problem of dust particles becoming imbedded in the wet finish. However, much time-consuming rubbing and polishing is necessary with lacquer in order to attain the maximum smooth glasslike finish of which it is capable. For many years, a number of manufacturers have chosen this finish for their prestige cars.

Enamel dries largely by evaporation, but also by the chemical reactions induced by oxidation. It is possible to "force-dry" enamel in the spray booth in about an hour by using heat lamps that produce temperatures of from 140 to 200 degrees F. But at room temperature, the car may have to sit overnight before the finish hardens sufficiently to be exposed to the elements. The prolonged drying time required by enamel increases the hazard of its being marred by dust floating around in the paint shop. However, enamels dry to a relatively high luster and do not require polishing to bring out their maximum sheen.

Before the introduction of "acrylic" finishes (which I shall explain shortly), enamels were considered the most durable of the two finishes, and the bulk of production cars were sprayed at the factory with enamel.

One of the most revolutionary milestones in the automotive painting industry was the development in the late fifties of "acrylic" lacquers and enamels. They are based on plastic materials similar to those used to manufacture bulletproof canopies for aircraft. Since 1958, acrylic finishes have gained in popularity, and today all domestic cars roll off the assembly line coated with these more durable synthetic finishes.

The application procedures for acrylic lacquers and enamels are quite different both at the factory and in the body-repair shop. At the factory a car that has been sprayed with acrylic lacquer is baked at some 200 degrees F. It is then given a second baking at about 285 degrees F. This results in a melting and reflowing of the surface of the lacquer, which minimizes scratches, gives excellent surface leveling, and provides a rich, glasslike gloss. Obviously, rubber, glass, and other body components cannot tolerate these extreme temperatures, and this baking procedure must be completed prior to their installation.

Acrylic enamels applied at the factory are baked on at temperatures ranging up to 350 degrees F., and no rubbing or polishing is necessary to bring out their maximum sparkle.

Millions of dollars were spent on the development of acrylic finishes, and more millions have been invested by car manufacturers in assembly-line conversions in order to apply these improved finishes. When acrylic finishes were first introduced, the application techniques led to considerable confusion for the body-repair shops. However, practical experience and technical advice provided by the paint manufacturers has helped provide the necessary know-how, and the problems experienced by the refinishing shops are diminishing.

Originally, because of the extremely high temperatures required to apply acrylic enamels, it was not possible for body shops to use them for either complete refinishes or repairing damaged sections of cars that were coated at the factory with acrylic enamels. In 1967, however, leading paint manufacturers produced an acrylic enamel that could be applied by the body shops.

Acrylic lacquers can be applied at room temperature and have the same drying speed as ordinary lacquers, but rubbing in necessary to bring out its full brilliance. Acrylic finishes have a high gloss and resist weathering for long periods; they hold greater amounts of aluminum particles, which produce brighter, more pleasing metallic colors; and they shed dirt more readily and dry more cleanly after exposure to heavy rain.

To avoid the rubbing and polishing operation required by acrylic lacquers, some body shops will use a standard enamel of matching color to refinish damaged panels on cars that are coated with an acrylic paint. The match may be perfect at first, but since the acrylic finish has better lasting qualities, a difference will eventually show up. Also, the switching of enamels and lacquers used prior to the development of the acrylics can lead to mismatched colors a few months after application.

For best results, when spraying sections of a car finished in acrylic lacquer, it is wise to use acrylic lacquer, which, because of its superior lasting qualities, is also recommended for use on cars finished with acrylic enamel.

Motorists are often shocked to discover that the newly painted panels on their older car do not match the rest of the body. Regardless of durability, all finishes are eventually affected by exposure to the elements, and it is not possible to achieve a perfect match with a color that has faded. In time, the newly painted panel will also fade, and may come very close to matching the older finish on the rest of the car.

Some people hold the mistaken belief that the more coats of paint applied to a car, the better. Since different paints behave differently, there is no set number of coats that will apply to all of them. But regardless of the type of paint used, too many coats are as bad as too few. Having a different expansion rate than metal, paint cannot expand and contract as much in response to temperature variations when it is applied too liberally. The result is cracks and blemishes. In fact, modern paints usually go on very thinly, and rely on good surface preparation for their smoothness and lasting qualities.

This, in a sense, compares with the careful work of my friend when he varnished, rubbed, and varnished those chariots back in the twenties. Those were the days when a good car painter would take brush in hand and settle down to do a perfect job of striping a car. The contrasting stripes along fenders and around louvers gave many an old car that classic appearance that still quickens the pulse of the vintage-car fancier. My friend is the only man I know who still does this demanding, highly skilled work. His shop is often host to Rolls Royces, Bentleys, or restored classic cars whose owners put perfection ahead of price.

Striping is staging a comeback, though, and in the last few years many cars have been adorned with the classic stripes of red on black, blue on white, or other contrasting colors. While they add to the appearance of the car, these stripes are not the work of craftsmen. They are applied either by spraying through special masks which are available in roll form, or they are decals that are stuck onto the car's body.

A number of people, when having a fender repaired, decide to have the whole car refinished at the same time, and a few months later they are outraged to discover rust showing through the "new" paint job. Unless the rust comes through where the body shop did the repairs, we can hardly expect them to assume responsibility. The rust was probably there—lurking beneath the surface of the old paint— before refinishing. Unless you are willing to go to the expense of having the entire body repaired and rustproofed, don't expect too much.

It is well to remember that on a car that has been internally rustproofed, the application of heat when straightening a damaged section of the body may melt the rustproofing and cause it to drop away. The newly repaired section should be checked internally and rustproofed again if necessary.

The technology of the painting industry changes so quickly that it is difficult to stay abreast of it. Constant research is being conducted, and innovations as yet unheard of could suddenly be developed, throwing into a state of obsolescence all our present methods of refinishing and protecting the body of the car.

Door Slamming

Recently, I received a complaint from one of my readers that made me feel like the "Dear Abby" of the automotive world.

His wife's girl friend, a hefty girl at that, had a nerve-shattering habit of slamming the door in such a way that it seemed the whole car was being hit by a cannon. This led to perpetual arguments with his wife—she forbidding him to mention it, and he plotting all sorts of fiendish ways to get even. In desperation, he wrote and asked me to say something in my column.

While I suppose some people slam doors to ensure that the lock is safely caught, it is not necessary if the mechanism is lubricated and properly adjusted. Slamming can break the glass as well as jar the owner's nerves. It is also damaging to window and door-lock mechanisms and can lead to annoying rattles. The striker mechanism, which is responsible for holding the door in the closed position, can be worn or loosened, allowing the door to fly open when the car rounds a curve or hits a bump.

Periodic lubrication and adjustment of door locks and window-winding mechanisms is essential to avoid expensive repairs. When windows are hard to roll up or down, take the car to a body shop and have them checked. Forcing a stiff window can break the costly mechanism. The mechanism can also be damaged by forcing a window frozen in place by cold weather, and the window's weather-stripping is likely to be torn in the process.

It often helps to open a window a bit while closing the door. This reduces the air pressure that builds up momentarily inside the car, and makes a hard tug and a slam unnecessary.

Rattles

For letting you in on this secret, I may be branded a traitor by my fellow garagemen, but if you want to know the garageman's night-mare—it's rattles.

One sure way to upset your favorite garageman is to drop in some Monday morning and casually mention that while you have no *real* problem, there seems to be a slight rattle that you are sure will take only a minute to fix. Then stand back for the reaction. He will possibly turn quite pale, or if he's a quick thinker he may suddenly remember that he has to take his wife to the hospital to have a baby, or perhaps that he just happened to overlook a funeral. Don't accept these excuses. Insist on a road test immediately. He will finally give up and reluctantly slide behind the wheel.

One of my customers used to come in regularly with an old limousine. He was loaded with money, but I never saw it in large quantities. To make matters worse, he was hard of hearing, and invariably we would end up bellowing at each other. Usually I gave up and wrote him notes. His pet beef was rattles. While he could scarcely hear a word I said, he could detect rattles that I'll swear were nonexistent. The wheels could be falling off, but this wouldn't bother him. Once, when road-testing his car, I discovered his steering box was making a horrible rattling sound. It was about ready to drop off, but he couldn't hear it. One of my mechanics tightened the steering and removed half a dozen bad rattles.

Our friend was back again in ten minutes stating that we had done nothing to remove the rattle. I went on another road test, taking a mechanic with me. We couldn't hear a sound, but the customer could, and told us so in no uncertain terms. We took the car back to the shop and worked on it another hour, but the owner could *still* hear the rattle. I finally sent him on his way, no charge, suggesting that this might be an excellent time to trade.

Another customer, a completely different personality, came in complaining that his car developed a strange rattle at high speeds. We tested the car on the highway, but neither of us could hear a rattle. He then belted the car around a cloverleaf at 70 mph. Why the tires didn't curl under, I'll never know. Finally, I was told to take the wheel and drive up to 70 mph, while he turned himself upside down and buried his head under the dash in an attempt to locate the rattle. The first time I had a chance to take my eyes off the road, I found to my horror that he was lying limp on the floor, completely blacked out. A passing motorist gave me a hand in relieving the sudden rush of blood to his head, and in a few minutes he was all set to continue the test. I told him I wasn't feeling well and talked him into driving me back to the shop.

Yes, sir—rattles can prove to be quite a problem, but the important thing for a garageman to remember is that from the dozens of rattles *he* might hear, he must locate and eliminate the one the *customer* hears—if, indeed, it can be heard on a wavelength they both receive.

Glass

The difference between the two kinds of safety glass used on our cars is not widely understood. One type is a single piece of tempered glass, the other consists of two sheets of glass bonded, or laminated, to a center core of clear plastic.

Some people feel they cannot be harmed by these improved types of glass and think they are "breakproof," "shatterproof," and "cutproof." But nothing could be farther from the truth. Both types are vastly superior to the thick plate glass used prior to 1927, which used to shatter into swordlike shards with jagged edges. I have been told that two thirds of all auto injuries prior to that time were caused by broken glass. The new types are safer, but they are still glass and, as we all know, glass can be dangerous.

Safety experts feel that laminated glass is the safest material for automobile windshields, and the law requires that all new cars in North America be so equipped. The laminated glass yields and cracks more easily at the point of impact, and the plastic core stretches. At lower speeds this elastic action reduces injury by absorbing some of the shock. It also keeps the passenger inside the car. But at higher speeds the passenger's head may smash a hole through the window, and he is likely to be lacerated by a deadly collar of razor-sharp edges of glass which can prove fatal.

Tempered glass is treated to give it the ability to withstand heavy impact. It will stand more shock than laminated glass, but when it does break, the entire window shatters into thousands of tiny pieces. This means that a passenger colliding with a tempered-glass window will have to hit it quite heavily before it smashes, and the fact that it does shatter completely reduces the possibility of deep lacerations from jagged edges. On the other hand, the original impact can be sufficient to inflict serious or even fatal injuries, and, once the window is gone, the passenger may be ejected from the car. Tempered glass is used in the side and rear windows of all cars sold in North America.

More than any other factor, this proves the need to wear safety belts when riding in a car. The further the occupants can be kept away from the windows, the better.

I have heard of rare instances where tempered glass has shattered without apparent cause. A glass manufacturer told me that this can sometimes be caused by the presence of small particles of foreign matter accidentally mingling with the molten glass. Another remote possibility is when there is insufficient clearance between the glass and the frame to which it is fitted. Expansion from the heat of the sun forces it so hard against the metal frame that it shatters.

Tinted Windshields

It is sometimes said that tinted windshields restrict vision, but I know an optometrist who insists they are a good idea and always has them in his car. It is, he says, a choice between losing a small amount of general visibility or being blinded when someone comes at you with high beams blazing. He reminded me that ordinary "clear" windshields restrict vision to some extent, and there is not much more loss with tinted glass.

Cleaning the Car's Windows

Although impaired vision is responsible for many accidents, sometimes the only attention given to the car's glass is the cleaning of the windshield and rear window, which is usually done by the service-station attendant when we buy gas. While this free service helps, it must be remembered that to maintain maximum visibility, much more cleaning is required. For instance, cleanliness of the inside of the glass is vitally important, especially if you smoke. When deposits of smoke are not cleaned off with a proper detergent, night time vision can be impaired. A casual rub with a cloth or paper towel may make the glass seem clean during the day, but when dark, the streaks you couldn't see earlier may blind you every time a pair of headlights approaches.

In damp weather, the muck sprayed onto the glass from the rear wheels of the cars ahead contains oil drippings, exhaust gases and carbon, rubber particles from tires, plus industrial impurities. Even on a clear day, various types of fallout coat the glass with an almost invisible oily slick. The most important thing is to keep the glass chemically clean, and plain water is almost useless in removing this grime. Use a recommended glass cleaner, or even mild household soap and warm water.

Windshield Wipers

The windshield-wiper mechanism, which may be either vacuum or electrically operated, is reasonably trouble-free. However, the rubber on the wiper blades perishes after a period of exposure to sun, wind, snow, and greasy road film. Dead rubber leads to streaking on the windshield, which makes it hard for even the sharpest-eyed driver to see clearly.

The rubber on the blade is very thin to allow adequate flexing as the blade reverses direction with each sweep across the window. If the wipers are turned on when they are frozen to the glass, or when there are bits of rough, sharp ice on the windshield, the fine rubber edge can be mutilated sufficiently to lose its ability to squeegee the glass dry. The wiper mechanism can also be damaged by doing this.

On occasion, a wiper blade can become so worn that the bare metal of the assembly rubs against the glass. This can lead to a badly scored windshield, for which the only cure is replacement.

High-speed driving and curved windshields cause considerable "wind lift." This must be offset by adequate pressure on the wiper arms. The tension of the arms should be checked periodically to determine that the pressure meets the recommendations of the manufacturer.

The wiper arm is mounted on a shaft which provides the oscillating action. When the wiper blades strike the windshield molding because the arms are not centered properly, it is an easy matter to remove the arm assembly and rotate it so that it cleans the greatest area of glass without hitting the moldings or interfering with the action of the other blade.

Windshield Washers

As with the windshield wipers, the windshield washer mechanism is usually vacuum or electrically operated. Windshield washers are now standard equipment on all vehicles sold in North America. These units are an essential safety feature, and just a little common-sense care is all it takes to keep them functioning efficiently. The most common cause of washer failure is dirt that enters the reservoir when it is being filled, as just a few particles of foreign matter can plug the whole system. Most reservoirs can be removed, cleaned, and reinstalled in minutes.

In warm weather, many motorists forget to fill the windshield washers or just add water. Even in midsummer, it's not good policy to use water alone. Washer additives serve a dual purpose: They prevent ice formation in winter, and their detergent action helps to clean the windshield regardless of outside temperature.

Turning on the wipers when rain first starts can completely obscure vision if the windshield is chemically coated, unless the washers are first used to spray on detergent. To turn on the wipers, especially at night, and expect only the rain to clean chemical slick from the windshield is like attempting to wash greasy hands without soap.

Convertible Tops

If your car has a soft top—the kind that folds away for summer fun and sunshine—you have one more component that requires care and respect. With ever-changing temperatures in the spring and fall, the top and electric-hydraulic mechanisms in convertibles are frequently in operation. If proper maintenance is added to a little care when the top is raised or lowered, costly repairs can be avoided.

When lowering the top, it is unwise just to release the locking handles and let it wind down unheeded; the top material or the pads underneath may become pinched in the steel support arms. Make sure, too, that there are no bottles or other obstructions in the top storage well, and *never* lower the top while the car is in motion.

I know of a man who learned this the hard way. He loaned his convertible to his nineteen-year-old son, who wanted to impress his girl friend. His method of "impressing" her was to lower the top when he was traveling at 30 mph. Wind pressure ripped the top off, and the hydraulic mechanism mangled. Cost: $250.

On recent models, it's not usually necessary to unzip the rear window before lowering the top, but, to be sure, refer to the manual or ask your dealer. It is usually good policy, however, to lower the top slightly before unzipping. This relieves the tension on the zipper, making it easier to operate and prolonging its life. Don't force the zipper, and lubricate it occasionally with a solid, nonstaining grease stick, wiping off excess lubricant right away.

Plastic rear windows should be cleaned with great care. Never use an oily rag or solvents such as gasoline or alcohol, and avoid harsh detergents. These attack the surface and decrease visibility. A moist, spotless cotton cloth should be used—never a dry cloth. Use cold or tepid water—not hot. If a cleaner is necessary, use mild, neutral soap-suds.

Never use a scraper on the plastic window—it could be the end of the window. Remove snow or ice with cold water. If the window is coated with sand, flush it off with water before cleaning with a damp rag. Sand is the prime enemy of plastic windows.

The tempered-glass rear windows now used in most convertibles are much better than plastic. They give better visibility and will not scratch or discolor like plastic. However, they can break if the top is lowered onto an obstruction in the well.

It is not advisable to operate convertible tops in cold weather. The manufacturers spell out the lowest allowable temperature; I have found that this varies from 40 to about 50 degrees.

Check the fluid level in the hydraulic-top mechanism periodically. Shortage of fluid may cause severe damage to both the hydraulic and electrical systems. Adjustments can be made to keep the top dead in line and reduce strain on the folding mechanism.

The Interior

The interior appointments vary according to make and model of car. Instructions for their care and maintenance are provided by the owner's manual. But here are some general tips.

Be careful how you clean the brightwork. Some of those silvery chrome pieces may be made of plastic. If they are cleaned with anything other than mild soap and water on a soft cloth, the plating will soon vanish.

If your dashboard has a dull antiglare finish, it should not be cleaned with auto polish. Use of anything other than the cleaner recommended by the manufacturer can put a shine on the finish and cause unwanted reflections.

Car upholstery should be kept dust-free with periodic vacuumings and given an occasional shampoo. Beware of spot removers on vinyls and other synthetic upholstery materials. Some solvents will melt them. Your owner's manual tells you what kind of cleaner to use.

If the car's carpets are left wet for any length of time, mildew and rot will cause rapid deterioration. Should they ever become thoroughly soaked, it is a good idea to remove and dry them. This is a bit difficult to do, since it is usually necessary to unscrew the sill moldings under the doors. However, a dry carpet will last a lot longer and will not impart a musty odor to the interior.

If the carpets are only slightly damp, leave the windows partly open until they have had a chance to dry out. Rubber mats used to protect the carpets should be removed occasionally to check for dampness underneath.

Waxing and Polishing

Waxing the family car used to be a tradition. But today, few cars ever see a coat of wax between the showroom and the wrecker's. Some of the modern finishes are said to not need waxing or polishing, but in my book a coat of wax never hurt any car. It is a particularly good idea on cars sprayed with a standard enamel, as it removes dead pigment and provides protection against industrial fallout and the sun.

Rust and corrosion will eventually take their toll on both the paint and the metal, but it has been my experience that a little common-sense care will prolong their life for many years.

Accessories

Countless fortunes have been made in the manufacture and sale of cars, and almost as many have been made selling accessories for them. There is an endless variety of accessories, but I will discuss only the two extremes: those I feel are particularly useful, and those I feel are both a waste of money and dangerous.

Many accessories serve a useful purpose and add to the motorist's enjoyment of his car. Others are purely gimmicks and, in my opinion, are sometimes dangerous. I don't mean merely the baubles, bangles, beads, and baby shoes dangling over windshields. These are bad enough, but there is a type of driver who likes to boast of his visits to the Snake Ranch, Gypsy Caverns, and World's Fairs with stickers. If he would just use them on the bumpers, it would be all right, but he bedecks his car windows, too. We fight for every square inch of glass in body design in cars so that drivers can see where they are going, but there are always people who fight just as hard to cover it up.

Mind you, I *have* seen the odd sticker which was perfectly at home on the car it decorated. The best example was one I saw on an old jalopy carrying a tribe of teen-agers down the highway. "Flyin' Fink," it proclaimed in big, bold type, and I couldn't have agreed more, since the car had bald tires, no fenders, and shock absorbers obviously in service since the earliest days of the "horseless carriage."

Safety Belts

The safety harness minimizes accidents by holding the driver in his seat and thereby in control of the car during violent evasive maneuvers, and protects the driver from the danger of going through or into the windshield and steering wheel during sudden stops.

In recent years, various safety agencies have spent millions on safety-belt testing and research. It has now been proven beyond a doubt that to ignore the use of the safety harness built into our modern vehicles is courting disaster. At the Detroit proving grounds I saw cars being crashed into a cement abutment. During these tests the effectiveness of safety harnesses is evaluated by strapping electronically equipped dummies in various seating positions. High-speed cameras are used to record every detail. After each crash, the dummies and vehicles are examined in the laboratories, the high-speed film is shown in slow motion, and the results are carefully tabulated. Few motorists, if given the opportunity to view these tests, would question the value of a safety harness.

One engineer told me that all the safety devices used in modern cars are installed on the assumption that the safety harness will be worn at all times by the driver and passengers. The effect of all other safety features is all but lost if we refuse to buckle up. In a front-end collision, the windshield is one of the major causes of death and disfigurement, and there is no way of padding glass. The safety harness, especially the shoulder type, minimizes the possibility of bodily contact with the windshield. Think about this the next time you find yourself sitting on your safety harness.

After an exhaustive fifteen-year research program on the study of safety-belt use and how belts affect injury patterns in auto accidents, the Cornell University Aeronautical Laboratory has concluded that the chances of serious injury are something like 50 percent greater when safety belts are ignored. And the incidence of death due to not using belts has been estimated at 30 percent higher—maybe more, since the research-program data considers an injury to be fatal only if death occurs within twenty-four hours of the accident.

Upon checking the six most recent casualties recorded in my own accident-investigation files, I found that while all the vehicles involved were equipped with safety harness, not one of the victims was using it at the time of the accident. I am firmly convinced that had they been buckled in, at least four would be alive today.

Even if you personally are a confirmed fatalist, it's hardly fair to insist that others, especially children, should share your beliefs. A fast stop even at very low speeds can send youngsters crashing forward, sometimes resulting in permanent injury or death. Assorted types of special safety harness are available for tiny tots. Make certain at all times that very small children are securely strapped down, and under no circumstances allow them to stand up on the seat when the car is moving.

One of the prime functions of safety belts is to hold the occupants in the car during collision. While some people believe that you're safer when thrown clear of a car in collision, research indicates that the chances of serious injury or death are considerably greater when the occupant is ejected.

A common concern of motorists who won't use safety harness is the fear of being trapped should their car catch fire or become submerged in water. Fire and water figure in less than 1 percent of all accidents. In fact, if a car is submerged as the result of an accident, a belt may save the driver's life—without it, he might be knocked unconscious. With the seat belt fastened, he is more likely to be still in control of his senses and thereby able to escape.

Even in severe collision, it is doubtful whether a seat belt would completely trap the driver. The buckles are designed to release easily despite excessive damage, and I have heard of no instance where a belt buckle has refused to release.

Another advantage is that the seat belt can reduce the possibility of the "second collision"—when the car stops and the occupants don't. When a car jerks to a sudden halt, the driver and passengers can keep right on going and collide with the steering wheel, dashboard, windshield, and roof, or collide with each other, sustaining serious injuries.

Some motorists fear that seat belts may cause serious abdominal injury. Research shows that this is not so in the vast majority of cases. Cornell statistics prove that less than one half of 1 percent of belted car occupants in serious collisions sustain bone fractures or injury to internal organs due to the use of seat belts.

Strangely enough, while many motorists cannot be bothered to fasten their seat belts on the drive to the airport, the stewardess has little trouble getting them to buckle up before takeoff. Yet the chances of crashing in a commercial aircraft are far fewer than in automobiles.

The reasons given by some people for not wearing their belts are almost unbelievable. Once an eighteen-year-old lad drove into my garage in a brand-new car. I noticed he was sitting on his seat belt, and when I asked him why he wasn't using it, he shrugged and muttered, "The guys would think I'm chicken."

Many motorists just can't remember to fasten their safety belts. This I can understand. I overcame this forgetful habit by making a point of fastening the belt before putting the key in the ignition, and after a few weeks I found myself buckling up almost without thinking.

Other drivers say they use their belts when on highway trips, but don't bother in the city. They are often shocked when I point out that my automobile-accident research shows that three out of four traffic deaths occur within twenty-five miles of home at speeds below 40 mph.

Extensive research on various types of safety harness continues. For instance, the major reason for not buckling up—especially the shoulder type of harness—is the difficulty of putting the harness on and the restriction of movement while wearing it. In Detroit I saw a demonstration of a type of shoulder harness which is suspended from a housing in the inner roof of the car. It slips on readily and allows the wearer to move about with ease while a slip-clutch device locks up and holds him firmly in the seat the instant he starts to move suddenly as in a panic stop, sudden swerve, or collision.

A type of air bag which inflates instantly at a given stress point during collision, forming an air cushion in front of the passengers, is being considered as another possible approach to minimizing injury. Undoubtedly, simpler methods of avoiding injury during collision are on the way, but in the meantime, let's take full advantage of those now built into our cars by buckling up.

Safety harness is now installed on the assembly line in the front and rear seats of all cars. If your car is not so equipped, belts may be obtained at auto-accessory stores.

When installing seat belts in an older car which has not been so equipped by the manufacturer, make sure the floor is not too rusty. The belts should be solidly anchored and reinforced by thick steel backing plates. On some cars it may be necessary to attach the belts to the frame.

Head Restraints

Head restraints are now standard equipment on all new cars sold in North America. For cars not so equipped, these restraints are available in automobile-accessory stores. Since "whiplash" and spinal-column injury can occur even in low-speed accidents—as low as 5 mph—and since inability to work after one of these injuries can sometimes last for months, properly designed head restraints are a most important safety accessory. Anyone who has suffered whiplash can testify to the all-round inconvenience of such an injury, and women especially find the neck-supporting "horse collar" most awkward to wear during convalescence.

EMERGENCY ACCESSORIES

Fire Extinguishers

A fire extinguisher is an essential emergency accessory. While fire is rarely a factor in collision, it can still cause a lot of damage. My files reveal that we spend about $25 million annually in North America on repairs to automobiles as a result of fire damage caused by unextinguished cigarette butts.

A cigarette carelessly thrown from the car can be drawn back inside by air turbulence which builds up around the windows, or it can enter another car.

I once returned to my car on a parking lot to find a red glow in the front seat where someone had obviously thrown a lighted cigarette through the open window. I doused the burning area with a pail of water, drove home confident the fire was out, and left my car in the driveway.

The next morning I found the whole inside of the car gutted— the fire had smoldered unchecked all night. It takes a thorough dousing to put out a fire that is embedded deep in the upholstery.

Short-circuiting of the car's electrical wiring can also cause a fire, as can flooded carburetors, gasoline escaping from a ruptured fuel line, or a faulty fuel pump.

I never fail to carry a fire extinguisher in my car. Various types are available, but I recommend the dry-chemical type for gasoline fires.

Keep in mind that most fire extinguishers can become inoperable; they require periodic servicing.

Winter Emergency Accessories

When the weather is wintry, there is no substitute for a good ice scraper and snow brush for car windows.

If your car is not equipped with windshield washers, I can think of few better accessories to buy. Whether in winter or summer, washers allow clear vision and are a major aid to safe driving.

In northern areas, it's a good idea to have at least one blanket in the car at all times. A man I know was driving north with his wife and children when a sudden blizzard blew up. His car slued off the highway and was literally entombed in several feet of snow in a very short time. The temperature dropped to zero, and it would have been extremely hazardous to leave the car and go for help.

Fortunately, the gas tank was full, and he was able to keep his family from freezing by running the engine for five-minute intervals. But he was afraid to run his engine too long at a time in case snow blocked off the tailpipe and carbon monoxide should seep into the car. He wrapped the children in what little extra clothing they had (he carried no blankets) and waited, praying they would not be run over by a giant snowplow.

Fourteen grueling hours later, help arrived in the form of a police cruiser and a snowplow. My friend said he would never again leave on a winter trip without taking along several blankets—and checking the weather report.

A thirty-foot tow rope can be handy when you are stuck—in mud or snow. I say rope rather than chain. A stout rope offers a certain amount of stretch and will do an adequate job of towing without damaging the car. I have seen cases where overzealous use of a tow chain has practically ripped off the bumpers, whereas a rope would have snapped first.

SPARE TIRES

For driving at any time of year, a good spare tire is a must. It is also a good idea to keep a tire-pressure gauge in the glove box. It costs only a dollar or two and enables you to check the pressure of all your tires easily, especially the spare.

While riding back in a friend's car after a skiing trip one cold, blustery Sunday night, we became aware of a bumping sensation. We got out and found the tread of one of his recently recapped snow tires separating from the carcass. The nearest service station was miles away, so we were stuck with the job of changing it.

As we opened the trunk and began stacking the luggage on the shoulder to get at the spare, a highway emergency truck pulled up.

We congratulated ourselves on our good luck as we dug out the spare and the driver of the truck jacked up the car and bolted it on.

But as our rescuer dropped the car down from the jack, we were shocked to see that the newly mounted spare tire was half flat.

Always make sure a spare tire is pumped up and in good working order. And remember, after you have a flat you have no other spare, so have the flat tire repaired as soon as possible.

Jacks

Like the fire extinguisher, the jack frequently lies idle for long periods, but when required, it is usually needed urgently.

Because jacks are so seldom used, they are often neglected and inoperative. A customer once told me of being out in the country about twenty miles from nowhere when a tire blew. When he opened his trunk to get the jack, he found the base plate missing.

To improvise, he placed a piece of plywood under the jack and proceeded to raise the car. The jack mechanism was badly rusted, and it was all he could do to make it work. After he finally got the wheel off the ground, he took his rim wrench and tried to loosen the wheel nuts, but they were seized and would not budge.

In desperation, he gave a hefty tug, the plywood split, and the shaft of the jack buried itself in the soft gravel. On his second attempt he loosened all the nuts while the wheel was still on the ground and jacked up the car again. As he was at the point of removing the wheel from the drum, the car rolled backwards, crashed off the jack, and almost tore off his finger. A passing motorist took him to a doctor, and a service truck was called to finish the job of changing the tire.

Ask your service-station attendant to check the jack's operation periodically and to lubricate it. Never use a jack if the base plate is missing. This plate helps to hold the shaft of the jack in an upright position, preventing the car from rolling backward or forward. Never jack up the car unless the front and rear of one wheel are firmly blocked with bricks, rocks, or blocks of wood. Loosen the wheel nuts slightly before jacking up the car.

If the wheels have not been removed for some time, have your service-station mechanic check the wheel nuts for possible seizure. Alternately loosen and tighten each bolt to free it.

There is a tripod (three-legged) type of accessory jack available at most accessory stores. It is not expensive, and it is more stable than the regular jack; I strongly recommend it for lady drivers. But make sure this type of jack is suited to the bumper design of your car.

First-aid Accessories

First aid for the car can be provided by a simple little tool kit which can be assembled for about $12. The kit should include a set of screwdrivers with flat, square, and "Phillips" blades, a can of general-purpose oil, a pair of pliers, vice grips, an adjustable wrench, hammer, side cutters, and a set of open-ended wrenches. Although for $12 the quality of these tools will not be top notch, they will be adequate for the occasional repair job of the average driver.

Remember, these same tools are handy around the house or cottage —but keep them in the car when not in use.

"Safety red triangles" can be set up behind a stranded car in a matter of seconds. These low-cost triangles will reflect the headlights of oncoming traffic for a distance of up to 500 yards. Flashing lights powered by batteries or the car's electrical system are also available.

Always carry a medical first-aid kit as well. Whether you have to change a tire or not, there is always the possibility of minor accidents such as insect bites or a cut foot at the beach or picnic. First-aid kits are available at reasonable cost and are invaluable in road emergencies.

Cash

The handiest emergency accessory I can think of is ready cash— or traveler's checks—especially on long trips. Personal checks will probably not be accepted in most places any distance from home, and if you have a breakdown you may not be able to charge the cost of repairs and, when necessary, overnight accommodation on a credit card.

INTERIOR ACCESSORIES

Air Conditioning

As well as adding to the comfort of the car's occupants, air conditioning keeps the driver alert by maintaining an even, dry temperature. It eliminates the distraction of road noises by allowing the windows to be kept tightly closed—also keeping the car free of dust, dirt, and flying insects.

Flying insects are no joke. They can lead to costly as well as dangerous complications. I remember a customer in my shop who groaned that he had just cracked up his car to the tune of $800 because he panicked when a hornet flew into the car while he was driving. He escaped with minor injuries.

Over the years, I have seen or heard of dozens of accidents, ranging from minor to fatal, caused by stinging insects entering the vehicle.

Aerosol Bombs

In the summer you might carry a spray insecticide bomb in your car to deal with aggressive insects. One direct blast from the bomb usually does away with any insect's desire to sting. But a spray bomb should not be used if it will interfere with driving.

There are quite a number of handy car accessories in pressurized cans. These range from waxes to plastic coatings to protect chromium plating and other bright trim parts.

There are also sprays for use on ignition wiring to keep out moisture and to allow better starting in cold, damp weather. But before using these sprays on the ignition, make sure every trace of salt, grease, and grime has been cleaned away from wires, coil, and distributor cap. This can sometimes be accomplished by yet another spray—an engine cleaner.

A spray designed for cold weather is a compound which is sprayed directly into the throat of the carburetor to aid starting and is harmless to the engine.

Protective Interior Accessories

Rubber mats help to protect the carpeting on car floors. They can be bought in a wide range of colors at low cost. To prevent mildew or staining of the carpet, it's wise to remove them when water gets underneath.

Rubber heel protectors are also available to save wear and tear on the carpeting—especially from high heels—and to stop the heel from slipping away from the gas pedal.

On some cars the interior rear-vision mirror is quite small. Accessory mirrors can be bought which clamp over the original mirror to give a more panoramic view of the rear. Some have a switch for night or day driving; the night position reduces the unwelcome glare from a car behind that has its high beams turned up.

Clocks

I consider the clock a protective accessory because it does away with the distraction of peering at a wrist watch while driving, particularly at night. I recall seeing a friend driving with one hand and trying to see his watch with the aid of the headlights of the car behind us—at 60 mph.

If your car does not have a timepiece, you can sometimes buy one from your dealer for installation after removal of a simple blanking plate. Otherwise, accessory clocks are available from parts houses, but they may not be designed for custom fitting in your car and will have to be mounted on the dashboard.

Radios

Car radios are listed under protective accessories because of their value in giving reports of weather and road conditions. Radios for cars range from small transistor units with manual tuning through pushbutton station-selecting models.

I recommend a pushbutton model because, with it, changing stations doesn't take too much of the driver's attention. Radios that can be tuned to hi-fi FM stations are on the market, and these can give superb sound.

(Other musical entertainment for the car is provided by stereo tape players, which sometimes sound as good as home stereo consoles. Their cost varies according to quality, but most are worth the investment if the car owner is a music lover.)

Compasses, Gauges, Altimeters

For drivers who spend much time in out-of-the-way areas such as state or provincial parks, investment in a car compass can prove worthwhile. A friend of mine, who is an ardent ice fisherman, wouldn't be without a compass to guide him. When a sudden snowstorm comes up in the middle of a lake, it it invaluable, since there are no landmarks or signposts. There are several models of compasses that can be mounted on the car dashboard.

I don't know whether accessory suppliers are catering to motorists who like to think they are piloting an airplane or to mountain-climbing dreamers, but they now offer altimeters for installation in cars.

In addition to compasses and altimeters, many supply companies sell instrument clusters comprised of an ammeter, a water-temperature gauge, and an oil-pressure gauge. Individual gauges can also be purchased.

Personally, I prefer gauges to warning lights, or, as they are sometimes called, "idiot lights." Progressive deterioration of a system or its components can be measured by gauges, and remedial steps can be taken before the condition becomes critical. Sometimes the damage has already been done before the motorist gets the idiot light's telltale message.

If you like to know your exact oil pressure, how your generator or alternator is behaving, or whether your cooling system is doing its job, accessory gauges can tell you the story. The only drawback I see to their installation is finding a way to mount them in the car without their looking like an afterthought.

Handy Accessories

One of the cheapest and handiest of accessories for the car is the magnetic keyholder. All of us at some time lose our keys or lock them in the car. But with a spare key hidden in the magnetic box, the problem is reduced to a minor annoyance. The magnetic keyholder should be mounted under the hood, but be careful where and how it is mounted. Be sure it is placed against bare, unrusted metal for maximum hold, or, even better, in a corner where its weight does not pull straight down against the magnet.

A frequently overlooked, but most important, accessory to carry in the car is a set of spare fuses. Most electrical devices in the car are protected by a fuse or circuit breaker. The circuit breaker looks after itself, but when a fuse blows, the component it has been protecting is inoperative.

Protective Exterior Accessories

Outside mirrors have been standard equipment on cars for a number of years, but some older cars may not have them. It is also possible for original-equipment mirrors to be broken off. In either case, it is an excellent idea to install an accessory mirror. There are blind spots in any car, and the use of an outside mirror, or even two, can show the driver what is coming up behind.

Fog Lights

There are mixed opinions as to the efficiency of fog lights. I have found that we cannot expect too much from them in the way of increased visibility. In addition, there is not much room to mount them on modern cars so that they are out of harm's way.

One good tip for driving in foggy conditions is to drive with only low headlight beams. High beams do not help you to see any better; in fact, they can actually blind you as the flare is reflected back through the windshield by the shining droplets of moisture in the fog.

When fog closes in, the logical thing to do is to stop driving until it clears.

Spot Lights

The glare from approaching vehicles on our crowded highways, especially during inclement weather, is one of the worst hazards of night driving.

High-intensity spot lights are available, which can aid visibility under adverse driving conditions. One of the most effective of these accessory lights can be hooked up to turn on with the headlights' low beam. This unit supplements the low-beam lighting and provides an intense light aimed well up ahead at the right shoulder of the highway.

This spot light is especially advantageous to drivers whose night vision is below normal.

But, as with fog lights, it may be difficult to find a suitable spot to mount them on your car. Also, it would be wise to check for state and local regulations governing the use of spot lights before investing in accessory lighting.

Gasoline Accessories

Carrying a spare can of gasoline can be dangerous, but if you must carry extra gas in your car, use only an approved container made expressly for this purpose.

A locking gas-tank cap can be a valuable investment. A customer once brought his car into my garage for a tune-up, and after the work was done it ran like a clock. But the next day the customer was back complaining of intermittent stalling. We checked the car thoroughly, but could find nothing wrong. A day or two later, he came in again with the same complaint.

Completely baffled, we carried out the entire procedure all over again and took the car out for a long road test—still it wouldn't stall for us.

A few days later the customer came back to tell us the cause of the trouble. Some children in his apartment building thought it would be fun to remove the gas caps from parked cars and pour in leaves and bits of paper. One of the car owners caught the children at work, and their parents agreed to pay for the removal and cleaning of the gas tanks.

Foreign matter can float around inside a gas tank for days without affecting the flow of fuel to the carburetor. Then a piece of paper or a leaf will be drawn over the pickup pipe in the tank by the suction of the fuel pump.

After the car stalls, the piece of foreign matter drops away from the pipe, and the car operates normally until it is drawn back again. This sort of thing may not happen very often, but it can be avoided by the installation of a locking gas cap. These units, which are inexpensive, can also prevent the cap itself from being stolen.

Bumper Guards and Static Eliminators

Another good protective device is the bumper guard. Available for most cars, these metal units are bolted onto the bumper to cushion the knocks from other cars as they maneuver into a parking position. Some models have rubber insets which add to their shock-absorbing capabilities and preserve their appearance.

If you have ever had a tingling shock upon touching some part of your car, you are familiar with static electricity—that mysterious charge that builds up because of friction between your clothing and car seats or from friction between moving parts of the car.

Static eliminators, made from rubber or steel chain, are attached to the rear bumper of the car so that one end drags on the road. In theory, they are supposed to drain off the static charge into the ground. Admittedly, the chain doesn't add much to the appearance of your car, but some people claim that static causes car sickness. Some parents swear by them for warding off nausea in their children. I also know a veterinary surgeon who says that many of his clients insist that their dogs are unhappy if they ride in a car not equipped with a static eliminator. But electrical engineers seem reluctant to comment on the effectiveness of these dragging chains.

Starting Aids

Winter, at least in the more frigid zones, is the season when a car works hardest and is most likely to let you down. Unless you have a heated garage to protect your car from the elements, you may have difficulty starting your car when the temperature drops. There are a number of accessories that will help to keep the engine warm during the night.

Probably the most effective is the block heater, which operates on house current with a plug extending just outside the grille. It comes in several forms, depending on the type of engine, but usually a frost plug is removed from the lower section of the block and a heater element is installed there. Other models are installed in the lower radiator hose to keep the coolant warm.

You can buy electric heaters that hang down over the top of the engine, and I have heard of high-wattage light bulbs being placed under the hood. While these may retard moisture formation on the ignition, most of the heat must be lost to the atmosphere.

Another approach to the problem is to replace the oil dipstick with an electrically heated wand which heats the oil in the crankcase. This type of warmer is not as efficient as the immersion units, but it is still a help.

For some air-cooled engines, heaters are made to fit on the bottom of the oil pan. Also, there is an electric battery warmer which maintains normal battery temperature on cold nights. These units make a lot of sense when you consider that the efficiency of a fully charged battery is cut almost in half at zero degrees.

I recommend the use of a low-amperage, trickle-type battery charger in cold weather. Plugged in and attached to the battery overnight, it keeps the battery fully charged and ready to start in the morning.

For the driver who wants to take the chill out of himself as well as his car, an interior preheater is the thing. This unit is placed inside the car and plugged into a house-current outlet. The latest equipment comes complete with automatic off-and-on timer.

Traction Assists

People who drive in areas where there is only an occasional winter snowstorm often feel that the price of snow tires is not justified by the slim chance of their being stuck. For them there are two low-price alternatives: a set of either steel or plastic traction plates to put under the rear wheels when the car is bogged down in ice or snow, or a supply of sand in the trunk. Incidentally, a convenient way to carry sand is in cardboard milk cartons; it is easy then to grab a carton, open the top, and pour the sand around the rear tires. Automobile-accessory stores usually carry commercial preparations of grit, sand, and salt for pouring under wheels when stuck in ice or snow.

Hardly anyone uses tire chains now. They are hard on the suspension and, if broken or improperly adjusted, can do considerable damage to the insides of the body panels. Temporary strap-on chains might be used for a limited time in emergencies.

I carry a small spade in the trunk of the car at all times—for mud in summer, and snow and ice in winter.

Power Accessories

Accessories such as power windows and power seats are expensive, but for those who can afford them, they offer definite advantages. Power windows are helpful when rolling along the turnpike, since the driver can close them without contorting himself like Houdini and possibly losing control of the car.

The power seat is easily adjusted to the most comfortable position for driving and can be moved at will without any danger of shifting abruptly. Sometimes a driver releases the catch on a standard seat while accelerating or decelerating, and the seat shifts suddenly, endangering his control.

Cartop Carriers

Cartop carriers and ski racks certainly increase the luggage-carrying capacity of the car, but they can also increase the hazards of driving.

A man I know had a close call while driving from Toronto to Cleveland. The top carrier on the car in front of him blew off and narrowly missed going through his windshield.

While helping to put the carrier back on the roof of the other car, my friend was shocked to see that the four supporting straps were frayed, stretched, and torn—one of them ripped right off as he tightened it. He eventually bound the carrier tightly to the roof with a length of strong cord.

If you use a cartop carrier to carry a heavy load, try to avoid the type that is high and square in front. The height of the load should also increase gradually toward the rear of the carrier to induce a deflecting, or slicing, action to the air stream. The same reasoning applies when carrying a boat on top of the car. Face the bow forward to slice the air—the flat stern bucking the headwinds builds up terrific pressure.

Spare-parts Kit

Finally, a spare-parts kit makes a sensible accessory for long-distance drivers. On a continent as vast as this, it is impossible to set up fully equipped service departments in every remote corner.

On long hauls it is a sound idea to carry such things as a spare fan belt, radiator and heater hoses, distributor cap, rotor, points, and condenser. These small items are not expensive and can help avoid many annoying delays if a breakdown occurs hundreds of miles from the nearest parts depot.

"Rube Goldberg" Accessories

So far I have been talking about the accessories I like. Now perhaps I should warn of some of the "accessories" which I regard as a waste of money—and sometimes a downright hazard.

For instance, I am getting more and more weary of hearing about "new," "revolutionary," "atomic," "electronic," and "scientific" gasoline savers for cars. In the first place, there is nothing very new about them; for thirty years I have been regularly plagued by their innovators.

Take, for example, a type of sparkplug that hits the market periodically, accompanied by a blitz advertising campaign offering fantastic economy and "double your money back if not completely satisfied." Customers have come into my garage over the years requesting a tune-up, handed me a box of these plugs, and asked to have them installed.

These "revolutionary" plugs were about twice the price of standard equipment, and often the car wouldn't even function properly with them, let alone use less gas. The worst of it is that a garageman can't convince some customers that they have been swindled on these "Rube Goldberg" inventions. Another trouble is that some distributors of these "gas savers" move their place of business so frequently that their victims can never catch up with them to get their money back.

Almost every week I hear from some inventive "genius" who

boasts of perfecting a device that will boost gasoline mileage by up to 50 percent. Take it from me, it never does!

There are gadgets which, fitted into the distributor cap, are "guaranteed" in cleverly worded advertising blurbs to run your car forever on a tank of gas. This type of gadget only succeeds in burning out various parts of the ignition system. In my garage I have removed hundreds of them from cars after the damage had been done.

Some years ago, a type of carburetor was heavily publicized as a radically new concept in carburetion that would make cars run better on less gas. I know a specialist who designs and modifies carburetors. He researched the "new concept" and assured me that the fantastic claims were entirely unmerited.

A car buff I know once installed three different "gas-saving" devices, but after several tests there was no measurable change in gas mileage or performance. He finally put the car on a dynamometer with the engine running at fixed rpm, and found that connecting and disconnecting the gadgets made no difference at all.

Not all accessories are a waste of money, however. Many do add to the performance and safety of your car. Usually a little common sense is all that is needed to distinguish between the two.

How to Buy a Car

It is generally accepted that the largest single investment in the average person's life is a house—which is usually true as far as one single purchase goes. But the average driver spends many times the price of a house on buying and operating cars in the course of a lifetime.

Owning a car should be fun, but choosing a car properly can be difficult and time-consuming. The range of models and the options available from the manufacturers are enough to make your head spin, your eyes light up, and your pen hand itch to sign on the dotted line. When shopping for a car you may be tempted as you have never been before. You can buy anything from a little compact costing well below $2000 to a luxury import limousine with a price tag of perhaps $28,000.

If you are an average car buyer with an average income, the selection just might pull across the line that marks the difference between pain and pleasure in owning a car. Many people who handle their normal bread-and-butter affairs well and meet all their rent, fuel, insurance, and other payments, will very often go out and buy a car they cannot possibly afford. I have seen cars bought to pacify nagging families, bolster egos, compensate for unhappiness, and impress the neighbors.

When potential buyers have asked my advice about the type of car they should purchase, a good number of them stressed practicality and economy, suggesting perhaps that they were interested in a compact model. Later they would drive up to my shop in a power-everything dreamboat, grinning sheepishly and offering such lame excuses as: "The salesman made me a special deal"; "I did it to please my wife"; "An expensive car needs fewer repairs" (utterly wrong); "What's an extra thousand dollars?"; or "I raised the mortgage on the house to finance it, so it just means a few more payments." Rationalizations apart, they had fallen into the web spun of chromium, plastic, power, and status.

Just a note on the myth that luxury cars cost less to maintain. They use basically the same type of plugs, condensers, and the like that an economy car uses. You will get no more mileage from tires or anything else that wears out just because the car is a luxury model, and when things like power windows and other trimmings need repair, it will cost you big money.

Buying a New Car

When buying a car, leave your heart at home and use your head. I cannot emphasize too strongly the dangers involved when going out to buy a new car or when trading up. A man I know wound up in a mental hospital because he couldn't stand the pressures of the finance companies, bailiffs, and debt collectors. He was trying to keep a $3000 car on an $80-a-week income. While this is an extreme case, it is true that many people do buy (and drive) their cars emotionally. They refuse to face the real costs of depreciation, repairs, or borrowing money. They don't drive their car; it drives them.

Some years ago a friend of mine bought a $3500 car he could not afford. It had to be refinanced three times, was nearly repossessed several times, and wound up costing him around $5000. One fellow I know simply refuses to go to the showroom, because he knows that he wouldn't have enough will power to resist a "slinky seductress" from the current crop of cars.

As to just what is the best make of car to buy, there are so many variables when it comes to selecting the car of your choice that each individual must work out the answer for himself.

So much depends on what you can afford, how much passenger and cargo space you require, the design you prefer: Two or four doors? hardtop or convertible? Specialty sports model? You should also take into account whether it will be used mainly for city or highway driving? Or perhaps both equally? And, finally, you must decide whether to settle for the basic standard model or succumb to all the tempting options offered?

To begin with, I do not place too much emphasis on any one particular make of car. Whether we select a high- or low-priced American-made or imported vehicle, compact or luxury liner, depends mainly on our own individual preference. With car manufacturers competing so desperately among themselves for the lion's share of the market, and since the car we select will be made of much the same materials and assembled in about the same manner as any competitive make in the same price bracket, we can expect about the same quality and performance regardless of maker. Granted, the automobile industry makes its share of mistakes, but consistently to mass-produce an inferior product would surely prove disastrous.

However, for various reasons, most of us are attracted to a certain make of car. Since we can expect the same value regardless of who produces it, don't make the mistake of buying a machine that does not appeal to your individual taste and requirements. Should troubles develop shortly after you have taken delivery, they are far less aggravating with a car you really enjoy.

Choice of colors can be important. It is a well-known fact that certain colors can prove depressing to some people. Remember, you may be keeping the car for several years, so be sure to choose appealing color combinations.

Before making a deal, it is wise to ask yourself: Can I really afford to deal? Would it provide extra pleasure? Or would the financial burden upset the budget to such a degree that it would end up in a round robin of worry and sleepless nights?

After careful consideration, if a new car is decided upon and you are not acquainted with a dealer you know and trust, ask your friends or business associates to recommend a reputable one. If you are not happy with the prices quoted, shop around at other dealers, but beware of "fly by night" operators who run come-on advertisements offering ridiculously low prices just to get you into the showroom.

As with practically any other commodity, car dealerships have their share of shady executives and salesmen who would not pass up the opportunity of making a fast buck. Whether buying a car or a cart horse, if you rush out impulsively without using common sense, you may wind up getting stung. However, I know several conscientious dealers who have been in business for decades, and they are still selling cars to customers who dealt with them in their first year of operation. They would not enjoy this repeat business if the price were not right and the service were below par.

Buying a demonstrator may save you some money, but if you can possibly afford it, buy a brand-new car. This way you know how every mile is put on the car, and if it is properly maintained, the possibility of a major failure is quite remote.

Optional Equipment

Much thought should be given to the tempting "extras" that are available. Remember that most salesmen work on a commission basis, and if you are foolish enough to spend beyond your means, you can't blame him for going along with it. It is up to the individual to decide what he can afford to spend and stick to it.

Whether it is included in the price of the vehicle or offered as optional equipment, I strongly recommend an automatic transmission. Automatic transmissions are now practically foolproof and, if not abused, can last for many years. (See also the *Drive Train* chapter.)

For extensive highway travel, especially when hauling heavy loads such as camping equipment and trailers, a V-8 engine is likely to give longer service, and the extra power can pull you out of a tight spot, should you find time running out when passing other cars. If you expect to do most of your driving in the city, a four- or six-cylinder engine is more suitable to your needs. Smaller engines are usually cheaper to buy and cost less to repair.

For the modest cost involved, optional oversized tires are a good investment. They can withstand more punishment, offer increased tread life, and the general handling characteristics and riding qualities are better.

For maneuvering in and out of tight parking spots in the city, especially in heavier cars, power steering is well worth the extra money. Unless the driver is physically disabled, I do not recommend it on light compacts, as it makes the steering so effortless you may be inclined to oversteer, particularly on the highway in strong cross-winds.

For heavy vehicles I recommend power brakes, but for intermediate-sized cars and compacts under normal driving conditions—no heavy loads or excessive speeds—they are not really necessary. On light compacts I find they are sometimes too sensitive and lock up the wheels on slippery roads, especially at lower speeds.

For large cars with heavy, high-powered engines, particularly where excessive speed and weight are involved, power disk brakes are definitely an advantage.

While many motorists are not aware of it, there is an optional rear-axle assembly that comes with a limited slip differential. This device can make the difference between bogging down or gliding away in mud, snow, or ice.

If you have small children, a two-door model is safer, since it eliminates the back doors and minimizes the possibility of the youngsters falling out.

To protect the car's body and undercarriage from the ravages of rust due to salt, moisture, and industrial fallout, there is no substitute for the internal rustproofing process explained in detail in the *Body* chapter of this book. A new vehicle that is not internally rustproofed can show signs of advanced corrosion within two years or even less. Rusted-out bodies are frequently the reason why otherwise sound vehicles have no trade-in value. Ordinary external undercoating should not be confused with the internal rustproofing process. There is no comparison.

Options such as radio, stereo tape, extra chrome trim, power seats, and power windows are a matter of individual taste. They are fine for those who can afford them, and the list of accessories runs all the way up to built-in bars on some luxury liners.

Whether bar or bathtub, accessories can push the price of a car way up. A car priced at, say $3000 can easily be pumped up to $4000 or more if it is loaded with all the extras.

Try to buy when it is a buyer's market. Spring is usually the worst time to look for a bargain, but it is often the time when people are stricken with trade-in fever. They are possessed with the irresistible urge to make a "deal," an urge which dates back to the days of horse trading.

Another bad time for impulse buying is when the new cars are unveiled. Things are at fever pitch during this period, and with their showrooms full of car hunters, the dealers do not necessarily have to sharpen their pencils. Remember, a suggested list price seldom really applies, and discounts vary according to how anxious dealers are to unload their stock.

After finding the right car at the right price, read over the agreement carefully before signing it, and make sure that the terms and conditions of the contract have been authorized by the sales manager or some other company official. Also, warranties can vary considerably from one make of car to another. To avoid the possibility of voiding the contract, be certain that you fully understand the terms and conditions of the new-car warranty.

When making a deal, it should be remembered that honesty is a two-way street. To some car owners, trading time is a sort of game, and the plan of attack has been carefully worked out over the previous twelve months. "Challenge and outwit the dealer," is their motto.

They have allowed their car to deteriorate; maintenance work ceased long ago. Only bare essentials have been done to keep the old bus breathing. The speedometer (odometer) has been "adjusted" to a more acceptable mileage reading (sometimes wound so far back that the dealer actually has to advance it again to a more realistic figure). The automatic transmission has been dosed up with chemicals to temporarily hide the expensive fluid leak, and the hole in the radiator has been cunningly sealed with stopleak. The front-brake linings have been replaced with the cheapest material (the rears aren't scraping yet), and scored brake drums are left unturned. The major rust holes in the body have been plugged with putty and blown over with paint. All in all, a masterful piece of camouflage has been accomplished. Now to enter the ring and outsmart the dealer!

The match of wits begins by collecting figures from half a dozen dealers. Sometimes weeks are spent analyzing the trade-in allowances offered by various dealers and deciding which appraiser failed to catch the skillful patchwork and which salesman was talked into offering the most "extras" free of charge.

The dealer is allowed only about ten minutes to look over and road-test the car, but the owner has been preparing for the contest for twelve months. In the boxing ring, there are rigid rules and a referee, but when it comes to the sport of car trading, no holds are barred. There is no liability on the part of the customer if, after a deal is made, the dealer discovers a cracked block. The same customer would howl blue murder and brand the dealer a low-class crook if he had been stuck with the cracked block.

However, doctoring up Old Faithful prior to heading for the auction block is usually a waste of time. The appraisers are wise to all the trading tricks and have a sharp eye and ear for camouflage. Some conscientious motorists invest money in first-class repairs before trading, but since a $100 investment in repairs usually nets perhaps $50 more on the trade-in allowance, the repairs are usually not worth the cost.

Don't be misled by an inflated trade-in allowance on the old bus. To be allowed more than your car is worth simply means that there is little or no discount on the price of the new car; you can't gain at both ends of a deal.

If you are undecided as to whether or not you should trade your present vehicle or sell it privately, first talk a no-trade deal to establish exactly how much is being allowed on your old car. After a definite figure has been established and approved by a company official, ask the salesman what would be allowed on your present car should you decide to trade it in. With this approach, as well as knowing every dollar you are being allowed on your old car, you will know exactly how much the new model has been discounted.

Frequently, motorists are shocked at just how little their trade is worth to the dealer. It must be remembered, however, that the dealer takes in the trade at a "wholesale" figure and "retails" it at the going price for that make and model. With the dollar difference between wholesale and retail, a reputable dealer must do necessary repairs, offer a reasonable guarantee, pay overhead, and hope to make a little profit.

Should you decide to sell your car privately, the first step is to establish a fair retail price. This can be done by comparing the average prices on used-car lots, and by studying the car ads in the newspapers for a similar make and year as your own car, but keep in mind that the prices of two vehicles of identical year and model can vary considerably depending on the amount of optional equipment on one or the other. Of course, there are certain aggravations such as answering the telephone, establishing a price acceptable to both buyer and seller, and demonstrating the vehicle.

Also, most private buyers are looking for a "deal," and since they are buying a car on an "as is" basis, they will argue that they should not be expected to pay the same price as they would to a dealer who would probably offer a guarantee. To avoid problems, ask the would-be purchaser to have the vehicle thoroughly examined by his own mechanic. If a lot of work is needed, adjust the selling price accordingly.

When demonstrating the car, make sure the test driver is licensed. In the event of an accident, you may be in trouble with your insurance company if the driver is unlicensed. To avoid the possibility of abuse or even theft, accompany the prospective purchaser during a road test.

When the car is sold, it is the responsibility of both parties to have the ownership registration transferred. If the car is involved in traffic violations or an accident while still in your name, you may find yourself involved in court proceedings. Remember, too, that in certain areas it is mandatory that a vehicle meet certain safety standards before there can be a transfer of ownership.

Upon closing the deal, mention in your receipt that the car is sold on an "as is" basis and there is no guarantee. For your own protection, both you and the purchaser should sign the receipt. Accept only cash or a certified check as payment. After finally making a deal, there is nothing more frustrating than having an uncertified check bounce, or discovering that the purchaser has instructed his bank to stop payment.

Buying a Used Car

When buying a used car, shopping for a good dealer is even more important than shopping for a good car. You can buy from a franchised dealer's used-car lot or from an independent dealer who handles only used cars. You can also buy privately through the newspaper's classified ads. Beware of doing business with a close friend. Regardless of how perfect the vehicle may be, it is still a used piece of machinery that can suddenly fail and require expensive surgery. Many lifelong friendships have terminated abruptly when the "little jewel" that one friend sold to the other turned out to be a big lemon.

No matter where you buy it, you can't expect a used car to be as trouble-free or need as few repairs as a new car. Some people feel that the dealer should rebuild a used car before offering it for sale, but still sell at rock-bottom prices. This is unreasonable, since it is not profitable for the dealer. The buyer pays for the repairs either in the purchase price or later.

A used car is often one that someone else doesn't want, and unless the dealer can give a written guarantee that the car is in good condition, repairs can be expected, since the original owner is probably ridding himself of anticipated trouble. A reputable dealer is quite willing to let you have your own mechanic check a car over, because he realizes that if the car is good, the mechanic will give a favorable report and clinch the sale for him.

If you cannot get an ironclad guarantee, under no circumstances pay any money down or sign forms until the car of your choice has been completely and thoroughly road-tested, both in the city and on the highway, and checked by your mechanic. This is a must. I have found as much as $1000 worth of work needed on cars I have checked over for customers, and many of the cars were not even worth restoring. If the dealer will not go along with such a check, don't buy a car from him.

Ask for the name of the previous owner, phone and diplomatically ask him for the history of the car. Mileage is not the chief criterion. I would prefer a highway-driven car with 40,000 miles on the clock to one with 20,000 miles put on only by short city runs. Even experts can be fooled. A garageman friend of mine once got stuck with a privately purchased taxicab that was one of the finest camouflage jobs I have ever seen.

Whether buying privately or from a dealer, here is what to look for in a used car. Check for marks on the roof and trunk lid, where a cab or police cruiser would have had a sign or an aerial. Also, check the headlining inside. Badly worn draft cords around the doors indicate constant use, possibly that the car was a cab. Look under the dash for holes where a taxi meter might have been mounted. Check the tires for retreading—a line of rubber around the side walls shows this. Look for patchy paintwork, indicating body work or a cover-up on police or taxi insignia, and look carefully at the lines of the car for telltale signs of major collisions.

Consider the condition of the upholstery on the driver's seat, and look for signs of extensive wear on the armrests, pedals, and steering wheel. Lubrication stickers on door jambs are usually removed, or the figures are changed to match the mileage on a turned-back speedometer, but you will sometimes discover one on top of the air cleaner, on the oil filter, or on the top of the radiator tank which may indicate the true mileage.

Remember that in the old game of horse trading, it is the buyer who had better beware; it's well worth the effort to thoroughly check the car you want to buy. Remember, purchase price plus immediate necessary repairs equals the true purchase price. But the line has to be drawn somewhere. I have heard of people taking a knife and scraping the paint on a used car to see if it was a repaint. One could hardly blame a dealer for throwing such an individual off the lot for damaging the car, but apart from such surgery, every effort you make to assess the car properly is well worthwhile.

Besides poor mechanical condition or turned-back speedometers, there are other hazards when buying a used car privately. Possibly the owner has used the car as collateral to buy such things as furniture, and a lien exists. You could get stuck with that lien if the fellow sells you the car and then vanishes. If there is no registry office in your area, there is no definite way of checking for liens, but if there is such an office, don't overlook this important investigation.

When you buy a car privately, there is no onus on the part of the seller. There is no warranty. If some major defect has been camouflaged and the car fails the next day, you are stuck with the repair bill.

When buying privately, even from a friend, don't take the seller's word that the car is in perfect condition. Have your mechanic check it. A well-kept, clean car usually reflects good care, but if the car is beaten up and the upholstery stained, it is likely that the car's mechanical condition has also been neglected.

Many a well-meaning man whose income will not permit the purchase of a new or reconditioned used car will shop around and pick up something for a few hundred dollars, hoping to provide some pleasure for his wife and youngsters. Too often the venture leads to disappointment.

One of my readers became involved in such a deal. He paid $300 for a privately owned car which failed on the first trip out of town. After spending $25 to have it towed back to the city, he had it checked by his local garage. The estimate for repairs was $450, and he was advised to sell the car to the wreckers for $15. Now he's grounded and still owes the finance company the $300 he borrowed plus interest. This man had the best of intentions, but all he did was make even more remote his family's chances of getting away from the city now and then.

We must all face the fact that a car, even under the best of circumstances, is a money-demanding piece of property, and I know of no real shortcuts to make the operation of one any less expensive. The only logical way to avoid disappointment when buying a used car is to wait until you have sufficient down payment to buy a good car that comes with a reasonable warranty.

Renting or Leasing

If buying a car, licensing it, repairing it, and insuring it seems too costly, it is far better to rent a car for an occasional weekend or even for a full two-week holiday.

While many people think renting a car is a luxury and feel they are better off buying their own car, in reality they cannot afford to own a car if the price of renting one for two weeks seems too expensive. In many cases, renting a car is the best bet.

Although rental costs can vary considerably from area to area, from season to season, and by type of vehicle, I know of one company that offers a domestic, six-cylinder, current model equipped with automatic transmission and radio for $35 weekly plus 9¢ per mile. Gasoline is not included. Insurance, including full collision coverage, costs an additional $10 weekly.

The rental companies are responsible for mechanical failure and will provide a replacement car should the rental unit break down. Cars are also available on weekend as well as daily rates.

This is not expensive, and it is far better than inviting misery and financial loss by buying a jalopy. The annual insurance costs on a car are likely to exceed the cost of renting for two weeks.

There has been a growing trend toward leasing cars in the last few years. The idea got started mostly with large commercial fleets, but it soon gained popularity with professional and sales people. Today, many people prefer to lease a car. General advantages include predictable costs, no down payment (although some leasing companies require two or three months' payment in advance as security deposit), and often a top-notch maintenance program.

Some plans allow the lessee to take ownership of the car at the end of the lease period on payment of a "market value" figure which was arrived at—and guaranteed—at the beginning of the contract.

One popular leasing program provides full maintenance and usually insurance. It should be noted, however, that lease plans are tailored to the individual lessees' needs, his credit rating, and his driving record. Monthly leasing costs can vary according to the driver, the length of the lease period, and the geographical location.

No doubt it makes sense for some people to lease a car. Most lease plans do not require any more than a signature on a contract and a series of monthly payments. This frees valuable capital for other investments. At the same time, operating costs, apart from one variable—gasoline—are wholly predictable, as there will be no repairs to pay for, and the leasing company even takes care of routine greasing, oil changing, and adjustments. For high-mileage drivers this is important.

Leasing plans make particular sense for drivers whose vocation makes it possible to write off their lease payments against income or business tax.

For drivers who do not put high mileage on their cars, leasing plans are available which do not provide maintenance or insurance, but do offer a lower payment. This is the kind of plan usually chosen by drivers who want to buy the car at the end of the lease period.

Many dealerships now have leasing departments. I could write another complete book on the pros and cons of leasing, but suffice it to say that leasing should generally be considered only by fleet operators or by individuals, such as salesmen, who drive many miles each year.

To most drivers the automobile is an extension of his own being, and there is something satisfying about owning it, even if it is shared by the finance company.

How Long To Keep a Car

People often ask me how long they should keep a car. There is really no set period or mileage. I have had some customers who had driven 150,000 miles before trading, and others who traded them in after 10,000 miles.

I feel I could buy almost any car and, provided I drove it the way the manufacturer intended it to be driven and maintained it properly, it would be economical to keep it for 100,000 miles or more.

There are "lemons," but lemons today are few and far between. It is usually the driver who makes or breaks a car. If a car is driven with discretion and serviced at proper intervals, with rare exceptions it will give excellent service for several years.

If your finances or requirements run only to a four-cylinder compact, don't drive it as you would a V-8 luxury liner. If you do, it's doomed to a short life, but by and large a car is designed to give much more than a year's service, and the person who like driving the current model, trading in his well-kept, one-year-old car, is going to pay plenty for his driving pleasure.

There is no set answer to the question of depreciation. My auditor tells me that 30 percent depreciation is considered average on each year of a car's life. Thus, if the car costs $3000, the first-year loss is $900. If the car is driven, say, 9000 miles, depreciation works out to 10¢ a mile.

However, this rate is just a rough figure. Some expensive luxury liners and high-performance models have dropped by as much as 50 percent in the first year. Make and model of car, how well it has been maintained, the good or bad deal you made when you bought it, and the price at which you sold it are the major deciding factors. Obviously, depreciation costs are considerably less when amortized over a number of years on a car that is driven average distances and not abused.

One of my customers who kept a car for 100,000 miles found his repair costs (no body or collision work) to be $2000 for the seven years he owned the car. While the body on his car was rusted out and he was only allowed $50 on trade, his transportation costs were still far less than those of a driver who trades every first or second year.

Proper maintenance is the key to prolonged life for a car. Rust is the number-one car killer, and it pays to have a new car internally rustproofed. Lubrication, as outlined in the chapter on that subject, is also vitally important.

Regarding the break-in period of a new car, it seems these days that just about everything is based on speed and hurry. I feel the life of an engine hinges on the care taken during the break-in period. Don't be in a hurry. Don't drive too hard and fast for the first few thousand miles. Highway driving at reasonable speeds is usually preferable during this period.

A Second Car

Nowadays the trend is to owning two and sometimes three family cars, often considered a necessity in the suburbs. Frequently, Dad is talked into buying the second or third car because the family feels it is a downright hardship to take public transportation or walk a few blocks.

Many of us are reluctant to face facts and are inclined to play ostrich when it comes to the true cost of operating just one car, let alone two or three. Let's figure out the approximate cost per year of operating just a small car.

Say we buy a car for $2000. Depreciation could be calculated at 30 percent per annum, or $600 the first year. Insurance costs will vary depending on location and the age and record of the driver, but let us add another $150. If the car travels 5000 miles a year and gives about 23 to 25 miles to the gallon, while the cost of fuel varies depending on area, let's say that gasoline would run to about $100. Then come lubes, oil changes, traffic tickets, running repairs, washing, parking, and the occasional bent fender to repair, all of which could easily amount to $3 weekly, or another $156 annually.

If the car is financed, we must add, say, another $175 depending on interest rate and down payment. So far the expenditures work out to $1181 or about 24¢ a mile for the first 5000 miles.

It is interesting to note that while the number of miles to the gallon is often the foremost thought of the motorist, at $100 for 5000 miles, gasoline is the lowest item on the list of expenses.

I'm all for the convenience of a second car, or third, if finances permit, but think it over. Will the budget stand it? Will it lead to sleepless nights? If so, diplomatically ask your family to take an occasional taxi—and charge it to you. You can pay for a lot of cabs with the money you will save.

Financing

When you have eventually figured out how much you can afford to spend for a car and have selected the car of your choice, you have to decide how to pay for it. If, like most of us, you cannot afford to spend several thousand dollars for a car, or if you would prefer to use the cash in some other way, shop around for the best means of financing.

If you are a member of a credit union, obtaining funds at relatively low cost is simple. Some people still argue that cash is not the cheapest way, because of the money you could be making with the funds and the depreciating value of future dollars. This may be true for an astute real estate or stock market speculator, but we're talking here of the average motorist.

On ordinary savings, such as bank and trust company deposits, the interest is appreciably less than the interest you pay on a loan. It is not wise to draw out your entire savings just to pay for a car. You should always leave a reserve for a rainy day. However, it is just common sense that the greater the down payment, the lower the balance, and therefore the lower the carrying charges for the money borrowed.

It is sometimes said that by paying cash you don't get as good a deal, because the dealer likes to tie you to a finance contract from which he gets a kickback. Since the big three auto makers have their own finance companies and they are in business to make money, it would be silly to argue that they don't prefer the financed deal. However, it is a little far-fetched to believe that a deal would be rigged against someone who wanted to pay cash. In most cases this is quite impossible, since the price of the car is usually established before the method of payment is discussed.

Sometimes people merely ask how much they will have to pay monthly. Naturally, the amount is lower if extended over 36 months rather than 24 months, but obviously you will pay considerably more in interest. With interest rates varying all over the continent from one source of financing to another, and from one moment to the next, it is easier and more effective to be governed by the cost of the loan itself.

Here, just as when you were looking for the car, go to various sources of capital with a constant dollar amount and repayment period in mind. Ask each for the total amount of all payments (including interest, of course). A signed statement or printed pamphlet should be sought. Then, all you have to do is compare this one figure and select the best one, unless someone throws in a little extra, such as life insurance on the loan. Then you will have to weigh the extra dollar amount with what you are getting for it.

At any rate, if you go to one or two banks, an independent loan company, and the dealership itself with this standard question, you should obtain the going market cost for money, and you won't be taken. Remember, there are various ways of interpreting percentage figures, and payments can be made to look ridiculously easy if extended over a long period of time. However, if you compare the cost of the loan from several reputable lending agencies, you can't go wrong.

If for any reason you are unable to make your payments, don't sit glumly waiting for the creditor to come and take your car away. Tell him the problem, and you will usually find that he will wait until you can pick up on your payments.

And don't be like the fellow I know who bought a shiny, but used, car. When I asked him what it cost, he said, "$55 a month for two years, and then I should have enough equity to trade it in." He had no idea what the car was costing him, what it was worth, what the finance charges were, or what allowance he had received for his older car.

Sometimes people add to their house mortgage to buy a car at what they regard as a relatively low interest rate. The annual rate may be low, but if it is a closed mortgage, they may be paying interest for years and years and wind up paying more interest than principal. With an "open" mortgage it is sometimes possible to save on interest by adding the cost of the car, but the savings can be quickly offset by legal fees. Check very carefully with a lawyer before adding to your mortgage.

Whether you buy a new or used car, or lease a car, if you have given the decision sufficient thought, used only your head and dollars-and-cents considerations—and left your heart at home—your car should be a source of pride and pleasure. Enjoy it!

Trouble-shooting Guide

While there are thousands of things that can go wrong in your car, for quick reference I have attempted to list a few of the causes of various conditions here.

Under each problem, there is a list of the possible causes. This list is by no means comprehesive, but it will give you an idea of the type of faults that can cause each difficulty in the car's operation.

BRAKES

Brakes Drag

Improper adjustment; plugged master-cylinder breather; insufficient master-cylinder free pedal adjustment; broken or weak brake springs; worn front- or rear-wheel bearings; sticky wheel-cylinder pistons; sticking parking-brake cables; grease or brake fluid on one or more brake-shoe assemblies.

Brakes Fade

Overheating of linings, drums, or brake fluid during prolonged or frequent high-speed stops; burned or glazed brake linings; inferior brake linings; brake drums worn or machined too thin; fluid bypassing primary cup in master cylinder; slow fluid leak in hydraulic system.

Brakes Fail Suddenly or Intermittently

Brake-fluid leak somewhere in hydraulic system resulting in drained master cylinder; brake-adjusting mechanism dropped away from brake shoes; connecting link between brake shoe and wheel-cylinder piston dropped out of position; parking brake left on in error; excessive brake application or dragging brakes causing the brake fluid to boil and turn into a vapor; defective internal components in the master cylinder; lack of free pedal (clearance) between the brake pedal and master cylinder; contaminated brake fluid; loose brake lining on one or more brake shoes; master cylinder disconnected from brake pedal; brake linings saturated with water.

Brakes Lock Up Wheel

Grease or brake fluid on linings; moisture on linings (usually temporary in damp conditions); linings torn loose from brake shoes; broken brake springs; broken rear leaf spring.

Brake Pedal Height Varies

Low brake-fluid level in master cylinder; faulty components in master cylinder; linings torn loose from brake shoes; improper master-cylinder free pedal adjustment; dragging brakes; plugged breather in master-cylinder cap; overheating from excessive brake application; thin brake drums; air in lines.

Brake Pedal Is Spongy

Air in lines; brake shoes or disk brake pads not seated properly; brake drum worn or machined too thin; improperly adjusted brakes; improper free pedal adjustment; plugged breather hole in master-cylinder cap.

Brake Pedal Requires Excessive Pressure

Vacuum hose from power-brake booster disconnected, leaking, or restricted; vacuum power piston seized; blockage in master cylinder or brake lines; seized pistons in wheel cylinder or calipers; sticking brake-pedal mechanism; condensation frozen in power-booster unit; glazed brake linings; wrong type of lining; improperly installed brake shoes or mechanism; congealed brake fluid; lining on shoe or pad worn too thin.

Brake Pedal Vibrates or Jackrabbits When Brakes Applied

One or more brake drums out of round; sides of brake disk not parallel; drums, disks, or linings badly scored; broken brake spring.

Brakes Pull to One Side

Brake fluid or grease on lining; moisture on lining (usually a temporary condition); brake shoes or pads wrongly installed or badly out of adjustment; mismatched brake linings with different friction characteristics; bent or restricted steel or flexible hydraulic brake lines; sticky or seized wheel-cylinder or disk-caliper pistons; brake drums of different inside diameter; loose front-wheel bearings; broken rear leaf springs; loose steering mechanism, uneven tire inflation or tire tread; air in lines; wheel cylinders of different sizes, linings torn loose from brake shoes; worn brake linings.

Brakes Squeal

Worn brake linings; out-of-round brake drums; scored brake drums or disks; dust or dirt buildup in brake drums; weak or broken brake springs or faulty disk-brake caliper mechanism; loose backing plates; curvature of brake shoes not matching that of brake drums; hard or baked linings; external sound-deadening spring (where drums so equipped) missing from brake drum; loose front- or rear-wheel bearings; defective or missing insulator tips on rear leaf springs; loose U-bolts on rear-axle housing.

Knocking Noise or Roughness When Brake Applied

Loose suspension components; loose front- or rear-wheel bearings; cracked brake drum; spiral groove in drum from improper machining, usually right after brakes have been serviced; loose road wheel.

Groaning Noise from Brakes

Any loose condition in brake or, possibly, steering mechanism; normal to some degree with disk or drum brakes when wheels on hard lock or car almost stopped.

Grinding Noise When Brakes Are Applied

Brake linings worn off shoes or pads and metal contacting drum or disk; broken brake springs; brake shoes rubbing on side of drum; small stones in brake drum.

Parking Brake Inoperative or Won't Release

Broken, seized, or improperly adjusted cables; seized pulleys or control mechanism; seized linkage or broken springs in rear brake-shoe assembly; worn brake linings; improperly installed mechanism; grease or brake fluid on brake lining; in cold weather, cables frozen in the ON position. Sometimes moving the car gently back and forth and applying the parking brake more firmly will release it. In desperation, it is sometimes possible to reach under the rear of the car and pull sharply at the emergency-brake cables until they are free.

Car Won't Move When Clutch Pedal Released

Clutch slipping due to wear; insufficient free pedal in clutch adjustment; broken clutch disk; disconnected, worn, or maladjusted gearshift linkage not selecting gear; clutch saturated in oil; car not in gear; damaged internal-transmission mechanism; broken rear axle, driveshaft, or universal joint.

Clutch Grabs or Chatters When Starting Away in Low or Reverse

Oil on clutch facings (a common cause); clutch worn out; rear flat leaf springs loose on rear-axle housing; broken or loose motor mounts; defective front transmission bearing or rear main-bearing seal resulting in oil-soaked clutch assembly; scored flywheel (especially if a new clutch assembly has been installed and a scored flywheel has not been replaced or machined).

Clutch Squeal or Growl When Clutch Pedal Depressed

Worn clutch-release bearing; worn or dry clutch pilot bearing.

Convertible Top Won't Operate

Low hydraulic-fluid level in system; inoperative electric motor; defective hydraulic cylinders; loose or broken wiring; defective switch on dashboard; seized or damaged top linkage or side rails.

Door Flies Open While Driving

Loose or improperly adjusted striker plates; misaligned or damaged door, lack of lubricant on striker plates; defective door-lock mechanism; stiff hinges; loose weatherstripping jammed in door.

To counter air-pressure buildup inside car, open a window before attempting to close door.

Doors Stiff

Seized, improperly lubricated hinges; bent or poorly lubricated door hold-open mechanism; maladjusted doors.

ENGINE

Engine Backfires

Lean fuel mixture; raw gasoline in exhaust system as a result of flooding due to excessive use of the starter before the engine starts; excessive carbon deposits; late ignition or valve timing; unwanted air leaking into engine; sticking or burned valves; cracked distributor cap; crossed sparkplug wires; loose wires in ignition system; high-tension wires damaged internally, resulting in intermittent delivery of high voltage to one or more sparkplugs.

Engine Keeps Running When Ignition Turned Off

Engine idling too fast (the most common cause); heavy buildup of carbon in combustion chambers; overheated engine; late ignition timing; wrong fuel; lean fuel mixture.

Engine Makes Rattling Noise When Idling

Worn or loose timing gears or chain; loose piston wrist pins; loose flywheel or cracked automatic-transmission drive plate; loose generator or alternator; loose power-steering pump or air-conditioning compressor; broken heat-riser valve; worn water pump; loose carburetor air cleaner; loose front-crankshaft pulley; worn motor mounts; loose exhaust system.

Engine Makes Tapping or Clicking Noise at All Speeds

Faulty hydraulic lifters; low oil level or pressure; plugged or restricted oil passages to valve mechanism; worn valve-stem ends; worn valve guides; worn rocker-arm assemblies and pushrods; excessive valve clearance; loose tappet adjusting screw; broken valve spring; worn lobe on camshaft; excessive carbon in combustion chamber jamming between top of piston and cylinder head; damaged piston hitting top of cylinder head.

Engine Oil Consumption Excessive

Faulty positive crankcase-ventilation valve; worn valve guides or valve-guide seals; plugged oil-return passages in valve mechanism; worn piston rings; defective vacuum diaphragm in double-action fuel pump; wrong type of engine oil; engine oil too light; raw gasoline entering crankcase, diluting oil; excessive high-speed driving; oil pressure too high; engine overheating.

Engine Oil Leak

Faulty gaskets; broken oil lines; seeping oil filter or fuel pump; seeping oil-pressure sending unit; faulty rear main-bearing or timing-cover seals; defective crankcase-ventilation system.

Engine Oil Warning Light Comes on or Oil Gauge Reads Low

Low oil level; oil leak; malfunctioning oil pump; plugged oil-pump screen; oil heavily contaminated; faulty sending unit or wiring; engine overheating; oil too thin; worn crankshaft bearings, worn piston rings; stuck oil-pump bypass valve; cracked oil lines inside engine; engine oil too light.

Engine Overheats

Low coolant level or contaminated coolant; thermostat sticking or installed backwards; plugged or collapsed radiator hoses; plugged radiator; exterior of radiator core plugged with insects or other foreign matter; cardboard of baffle left in front of radiator; inoperative water pump; defective radiator pressure cap; low engine-oil level; extremely high altitudes or temperature; prolonged idling in heavy traffic, especially when automatic transmission is left in gear when car stationary; valve or ignition timing excessively retarded or advanced; loose fan belt; car driven too long in lower-gear ranges when driver does not change gears or automatic transmission does not shift up; blown head gasket; cracked head or block; under-sized radiator core; loose cooling fins on radiator cooling tubes. *Warning:* Wait for overheated engine to cool before removing pressure cap and also before filling the radiator with coolant.

Engine Races on Idle

Idle-adjusting mechanism improperly adjusted; sticky accelerator linkage; faulty choke mechanism resulting in choke fast-idle cam not releasing; broken or weak pull-back spring; sticking pivot on gas pedal; unwanted air entering engine due to such things as worn intake manifold or carburetor gaskets or disconnected vacuum hose.

Engine Rough Idles

Engine idling too slowly; carburetor idle-adjustment screws un-balanced; disconnected vacuum hose; leak at intake manifold; stick-ing positive crankcase ventilation valve; improper carburetor float level; incorrect setting on automatic-choke linkage; sticking heat-riser valve; faulty modulator valve in automatic transmission; poor compression usually due to burned valves or worn piston rings; spark-plugs worn or not properly gapped; ignition points worn or not properly adjusted; defective motor mounts; excessive carbon buildup in combustion chambers resulting in higher-than-normal compression ratio. (High-performance engines tend to idle roughly.)

Engine Stalls After Short Run in Cold Weather

Icing in carburetor; frozen fuel lines; choke opening too soon; defective pump circuit in carburetor; heat-riser valve stuck open; defective thermostat; wrong fuel.

Engine Stalls When Gas Pedal Suddenly Released

Dashpot defective or improperly set; leaking carburetor gaskets; disconnected vacuum hose; leak at intake manifold; engine idling too slowly; poorly tuned engine.

ENGINE STARTING TIPS

Engine Turns Over but Won't Start (Engine Cold)

Driver has omitted the all-important procedure of depressing the gas pedal right down to the floor, which releases the automatic choke and allows it to move into the correct cold-starting position. When extremely cold, it may help to depress the gas pedal two, three, or even four times. *Failure to depress the gas pedal at least once is one of the major causes of starting failure in cold weather.* A sticking or improperly adjusted automatic choke is another likely cause. Ask your mechanic to demonstrate the simple procedure of removing the air cleaner in order to check for a sticking automatic choke. He can also show you how to lock the choke in the open position by using a screwdriver. This knowledge may readily get you started if your engine is thoroughly flooded and you are stuck miles away from a garage.

Frequently in damp weather, moisture on the ignition components will prevent the vitally important high voltage from reaching the sparkplugs; usually it is quite simple to cope with this problem. Even the uninitiated can dry off the moisture on the high-tension wires, sprakplugs, the top of the coil, and the distributor cap with paper tissue. If in doubt, ask your mechanic to show you the location of these ignition parts. *Warning:* Be sure the ignition switch is off before starting this procedure.

Other common causes of starting failure are: Engine oil too heavy; accelerator linkage disconnected or jammed; poor compression due to worn valves or piston rings; poorly tuned engine; malfunctioning caburetor; empty gas tank.

Engine Turns Over but Won't Start (Engine Hot)

A common cause of this type of failure is when the engine is flooded with an excessive quantity of gasoline. This can usually be overcome by waiting a few minutes and then pushing the gas pedal *just once* all the way down to the floor. (Pumping the gas pedal up and down several times only accentuates the flooding condition.) Then, with the gas pedal held down to the floor, engage the starter motor and turn over the engine several times, and usually the engine will start. To avoid engine damage, release the gas pedal the moment the engine starts to rev up.

Occasionally, especially after a long fast run, the engine tightens up to the point where the starter motor cannot turn it over fast enough to start. Under these circumstances, about the only hope of getting going is to wait until the engine cools and try again. A problem of this nature is sometimes difficult to pinpoint and should be diagnosed by an electrical specialist.

Engine Will Not Turn Over When Starter Is Engaged

Dead battery; defective battery cables; corrosion between the cables and the battery posts; faulty automatic-transmission safety switch; automatic transmission not in NEUTRAL or PARK position, or linkage maladjusted showing NEUTRAL or PARK on the selector panel, when in fact transmission is in gear. If so, switching from one gear position to another will sometimes temporarily result in the engine starting.

A common cause of no action when the starter is engaged is corrosion between the battery cables and battery posts. To check for this fault, push the blade of a screwdriver gently down between one of the two battery cables and posts. Then twist the screwdriver and have someone else engage the starter. If there is still no action, do the same thing to the other battery post and cable and try the starter again. If this doesn't work, there is a good chance that the battery is dead. If booster battery cables are available, try getting started by hooking the booster cables to the battery in the car of a helpful motorist. To avoid damage to the electrical system of both cars, be sure to hook the positive battery post of one car to the positive post of the other; likewise, the negative posts of both cars.

Engine Will Not Accelerate Properly After Normal Warm-up Period

Faulty pump circuit in carburetor; throttle valve in carburetor not opening fully; late ignition or valve timing; inadequate fuel supply to carburetor; faulty vacuum or centrifugal advance mechanism in distributor; automatic transmission not shifting down, or appropriate gear not selected in manual transmission; fuel mixture too lean or too rich; sticking choke; defective accelerator linkage; air leak at intake manifold; restricted exhaust system; heat-riser valve stuck open; sticking or burned valves; worn piston rings; engine running too cool due to faulty thermostat; malfunctioning carburetor; worn or improperly adjusted sparkplugs or ignition points; defective high-tension wires, weak ignition coil.

Engine Won't Idle After Sustained High Speed or When Hot

Engine too tight from improper lubricant; engine running too hot; new rings improperly installed; vapor locks; excessive fuel-pump pressure; malfunctioning positive crankcase-ventilation valve; automatic choke stuck on; clogged carburetor air filter; improper idle-speed adjustment.

EXHAUST SYSTEM

Exhaust Gases Leaking into Car

Worn or missing grommets in firewall; holes in floor or firewall, holes in trunk allowing fumes to enter from any leak in system; exhaust-manifold gasket blown or improperly installed; cracked exhaust-manifold; worn heat-riser valve assembly; blown or loose gasket between exhaust manifold and exhaust pipe; hole in muffler, exhaust, or tailpipe.

Exhaust Pipe Breaks at Manifold

Loose or broken motor mounts; pipe mounted too rigidly to frame.

Exhaust Smoking

Black smoke indicates rich fuel mixture from malfunctioning carburetor, sticking choke; excessive fuel-pump pressure; blue smoke is caused by excessive engine-oil consumption; white smoke or steam is caused by condensation (normal for first few minutes in cold weather); leaking head gasket; cracked head or block.

Exhaust System Noisy

Wrong muffler or one of inferior quality; bent muffler or tailpipe; cracked exhaust manifold; leak in any exhaust-system component; loose baffles in muffler; worn heat-riser valve assembly; blown exhaust-manifold gasket; blown gasket between exhaust manifold and exhaust pipe; blown head gasket allowing exhaust gases to escape between head and block.

Muffler or Pipes Fail Frequently

Inferior components; excessive corrosion from chronic slow-speed, short-run operation; severe road-salt conditions; constant battering by flying stones on road; loose motor mounts; improper installation; scraping on rutty roads.

FIRE OR SMOKE IN CAR

Turn off ignition immediately. Short circuit in electrical wiring; exhaust-system components pressing against bottom of car body; carelessly discarded cigarette in interior; gasoline leaking from fuel system; dragging brakes; tire rubbing against body or steering components; underinflated tires.

FUEL CONSUMPTION EXCESSIVE

Short, slow, stop-and-go runs, especially in cold weather; excessive high speeds, strong headwinds; engine operating below normal temperature due to defective thermostat; sticking automatic choke; malfunctioning carburetor; faulty positive crankcase-ventilation valve (PCV); plugged air cleaner; engine idling too fast; improper ignition timing; stuck heat-riser valve; automatic transmission not shifting into high-gear range soon enough; automatic transmission slipping; excessive use of automatic-transmission kickdown or passing switch; driver omitting to shift into high gear at recommended speed with standard transmission; savage acceleration; slipping clutch; engine in generally poor condition; underinflated tires; dragging brakes; external fuel leaks; plugged or undersized exhaust system; fuel being stolen from gas tank; odometer on speedometer not recording correct mileage traveled.

FUEL GAUGE READS INCORRECTLY

Sending unit in gas tank faulty, or wire leading to gauge grounded or broken; gas tank dented or collapsed; faulty gauge in instrument panel.

HEATER PROVIDES LITTLE OR NO WARMTH

Burned-out blower motor; loose or broken wires; blown fuse; bent, broken, or disconnected control cables; vacuum hose to controls bent, broken, or disconnected; plugged heater core; plugged or bent heater hoses; faulty coolant flow-control valve; defective automatic heater-control thermostat; defective cooling-system thermostat; faulty blower switch; warped or loose cylinder head; defective cylinder-head gasket; defective water pump.

HOOD JUMPS OPEN TO SAFETY LATCH OR WIDE OPEN

Sticky locking mechanism or cable; broken springs in mechanism; lack of lubrication; improper adjustment. If at high speed the wind blows hood all the way open, lean down and attempt to see through lower section of windshield and rear of hood. Otherwise, quickly lean head out of window.

HORN INOPERATIVE, INTERMITTENT, JAMMED, OR MUTED

One or both horns inoperative: discharged battery; loose, broken, or shorted wiring controlling one or both horns; faulty horn relay; poor ground; defective horn ring or horn-button contact mechanism.

LIGHTS

Headlights Inoperative

Burned-out sealed beams; defective headlight switch; defective dimmer switch; disconnected wiring; corroded ground-wire connections; flat battery or corroded battery posts and cables; blown fuse on the few vehicles that do not use a circuit breaker to protect the headlight wiring.

Instrument Panel Lights Inoperative

Burned-out bulbs or fuse; disconnected wiring or bulb sockets. Many cars have a rheostat in the headlight switch that controls the volume of light to the instrument panel when the outside lights are in the ON position. The rheostat is operated by turning the headlight switch clockwise and anticlockwise. Be sure that the rheostat is not turned to the OFF position.

Parking Lights or License-plate Light Inoperative

Burned-out bulbs or fuse; defective wiring; poor ground connection; corroded bulb sockets; taillight bulb-and-socket assembly pulled away from light housing in trunk; taillight or license-plate-light wiring-plug connectors disconnected in trunk.

Courtesy or Door Lights Inoperative

Defective switch in door jamb; burned-out bulbs or fuse; faulty wiring; bulb and socket dropped away from support; poor ground connection.

All Other Small Lights

Burned-out bulb or fuse; faulty control switch; defective wiring; poor gound connection.

Stop Lights Inoperative

Burned-out bulbs or fuse; corroded bulb sockets; defective or maladjusted stoplight switch; disconnected wiring plugs in trunk; bulb-and-socket assembly pulled away from light housing in trunk; poor ground connections.

Signals Inoperative—Flash Too Slowly or Burn Steadily

Bulb-and-socket assembly pulled away from signal-light housing in trunk (This can occur when the trunk is heavily loaded and the luggage is forced against the bulb-and-socket assembly.); faulty flasher or flasher too light for number of bulbs in circuit; defective mechanism in selector switch; disconnected wiring-plug connectors in trunk; one or more bulbs burned out; broken wire or poor ground; corroded bulb sockets; defective ignition switch.

Headlights Flash Off and On

Short circuit in wiring, causing circuit breaker to go into operation; broken or loose wire making intermittent contact; corroded connectors; faulty dimmer switch.

Headlights Too Low or Too High

Improper adjustment; minor collision that showed no other apparent damage; when lights do not illuminate road for sufficient distance, rear of vehicle may be too high. If lights glare into oncoming traffic, the rear of vehicle may be too low—possibly due to overloaded trunk or heavy trailer.

Alternator or Generator Warning Light Comes on, or Ammeter Shows Discharge

Defective generator or alternator; loose or broken wires; broken or slipping drive belt; loose or corroded battery cables; engine idling too slowly; voltage regulator inoperative; short circuit.

ROUGH RIDE

Springs too resistant for weight of car; weak shock absorbers; seized shock absorbers or other seized suspension components; over-inflated tires; broken springs; weak springs resulting in bottoming; shock absorbers too severe for weight of car.

Seat Adjuster Inoperative (Power or Standard Seats)

Underseat obstructions such as rags, papers, toys, beverage containers, jamming adjusting mechanism; seized or broken mechanism; mechanism needs cleaning, adjusting, and lubrication.

Power seats: same as above, plus possible inoperative electric motor, loose or broken wiring, faulty control switch.

SPEEDOMETER

Speedometer Fluctuates (Sometimes Accompanied by a Rasping Noise)

No lubricant in speedometer cable; malfunctioning speedometer head; bent or broken speedometer-cable casing.

Speedometer Reads Too High or Too Low

Faulty speedometer head; gear that drives speedometer cable is wrong ratio (too many or not enough teeth); oversized or under-sized tires.

Speedometer Stops Registering

Broken speedometer cable; defective speedometer head; speedometer cable and casing disconnected from transmission-drive gear or from speedometer head under instrument panel; worn or loose driving gear in transmission, or worn gear that drives speedometer cable.

Speedometer Registers Speed but Odometer Does Not Record Mileage Traveled

Faulty mechanism in speedometer head.

STEERING

Power Steering Suddenly Becomes Stiff

Loose or broken power-steering-pump drive belt; underinflated front tires; low fluid level in power-steering reservoir; defective power-steering mechanism; defective steering linkage.

Whining Noise When Turning Steering Wheel (Power Steering)

Low fluid level in power-steering reservoir; air in power-steering fluid; defective power-steering pump.

Shimmy or Vibration in Steering Wheel (Standard and Power Steering)

Unbalanced road-wheel assemblies; caked mud on wheels; loose, maladjusted, or worn steering components; loose front-wheel bearings; improper front-end alignment; broken suspension springs; bent or cracked frame; weak shock absorbers; defective tires.

TIRES

Tires Squeal When Cornering

Cornering too fast, underinflated tires, front end out of alignment, overloading of car.

Slow Leak

Perished rubber-valve assembly, defective valve core, improper seating of tire bead on rim or bent rim, porous wheel rim, minute hole in tire.

TRANSMISSION

Car Won't Move When Put into Gear (Automatic Transmission)

Low fluid level; disconnected, worn, or maladjusted gear-selector linkage; broken rear axle; parking brake not released; seized parking-brake mechanism, causing rear brakes to drag; stripped splines in driveshaft; broken universal joint; defective mechanism inside transmission; gas-pedal linkage disconnected from carburetor; broken torque-converter driveplate.

Car Won't Move When Put into Gear and Clutch Released (Standard Transmission)

Burned-out clutch; clutch slipping due to improper adjustment; disconnected, worn, or maladjusted gear-selector linkage; broken rear axle; parking brake not released; seized parking-brake mechanism causing rear brakes to drag; stripped splines in driveshaft; broken universal joint; defective mechanism inside transmission.

Rough Shifting, or Does Not Shift Up or Down, or Does Not Shift Gears at Proper Time (Automatic Transmission)

Low fluid level; improper carburetor-to-transmission linkage adjustment; defective modulator valve or lack of vacuum-controlling modulator valve; defective electrical controls; maladjusted gear-selector linkage; malfunctioning mechanism inside transmission.

Gearshift Mechanism Jammed in the PARK Position (Automatic Transmission)

Parking mechanism damaged inside transmission; parked on hill with full weight of vehicle resting on internal parking mechanism; maladjusted gearshift-selector mechanism; gearshift-selector mechanism disconnected; loose or broken motor mounts.

Steady Knocking Sound in Low, Second, or Reverse Gear (Standard Transmission)

One or more teeth stripped from a gear in the transmission.

Cars Jumps out of Gear (Standard Transmission)

Loose motor mounts; loose transmission-mounting bolts; flat-leaf rear-suspension spring broken; broken spring in transmission-shift-lever mechanism; worn synchromesh unit; gearshift-selector linkage maladjusted or worn; gearshift handle not being moved the full length of its travel, resulting in the selected gear not being fully engaged; worn synchromesh unit; faulty front-transmission bearing or other defective mechanism inside transmission.

Car Won't Go into Gear, Sticks in Gear, or Gears Clash When Shifting (Standard Transmission)

Clutch not completely disengaged due to improper clutch adjustment; clutch not being depressed right down to the floor; burned-out clutch-release bearing; faulty clutch pilot bearing; oil on clutch facings; worn clutch linkage; defective clutch pressure plate or clutch hub; gearshift-selector linkage worn, maladjusted, or jammed; transmission dry of lubricant; loose transmission-mounting bolts; defective synchromesh unit or other faulty mechanism inside transmission.

Oil Leaking from Standard Transmission

Oil level too high; worn oil seals; defective gaskets; loose drain plug; damaged threads on drain plug; inside diameter of drain-plug gasket too large, preventing proper seal; drain-plug gasket left off; transmission-mounting bolts loose; cracked transmission case; plugged breather; oil leaking at point where speedometer cable is attached to transmission; defective components inside transmission, such as front or rear bearings.

Fluid Leaking from Automatic Transmission

Defective torque converter; defective filler tube O ring; cracked filler tube; loose drain plug; damaged threads on drain plug; inside diameter of drain-plug gasket too large, preventing proper seal; drain-plug gasket left off; defective gaskets or oil seals; fluid level too high; plugged breather; oil leaking at point where speedometer cable is attached to transmission; cracked transmission case or extension housing; malfunctions inside transmission.

Automatic Transmission Frequently Needs Fluid but no Sign of External Leaks

Vacuum line from engine drawing fluid from transmission through defective modulator valve. *A word of advice:* Many makes of cars use a modulator valve. If your car is so equipped, be sure the modulator valve is thoroughly examined for defects before authorizing major transmission overhauls.

TRUNK LID WILL NOT CLOSE OR JUMPS OPEN

Luggage interfering with locking mechanism; trunk overloaded; lack of lubricant on locking mechanism; mechanism improperly adjusted.

UNUSUAL NOISES

Clanging or Clunking Noise When Shifting from Forward to Reverse, or When Accelerating or Decelerating

Worn universal joints; broken or loose motor mounts; broken springs in clutch hub; loose shaft in differential case; broken or worn teeth in rear-end gears; worn pinion or carrier bearings; worn rear-axle splines; loose hub on tapered rear axles; play in rear end; defective automatic transmission; worn driveshaft splines; loose road wheel; parking brake not released; seized parking-brake mechanism causing rear brakes to drag; broken suspension spring.

Grating, Groaning Noise when Maneuvering

Shifting front coil spring; dry suspension bushings; dry ball joints; partially seized shocks.

Hum or Howl—Continually, or When Accelerating or Decelerating

Insufficient or contaminated lubricant in rear-end assembly; worn carrier or pinion bearings; improper adjustment between teeth of crown and pinion gears; loose pinion-gear nut; worn transmission bearing; worn center-hanger bearing; wor clutch-release bearing due to insufficient free pedal; low fluid level in automatic transmission.

Rattles and Squeaks

Loose parking-brake cables striking undercarriage; poorly adjusted door; hood or trunk poorly adjusted; loose shock-absorber bushings; worn insulators on multiple-leaf-spring tips; loose or improperly adjusted window-winding mechanisms; dry steering components due to plugged or damaged grease fittings; squeaking bushings that normally do not need lubrication at regular intervals; worn window-channel felts; worn swaybar bushings; loose radio, loudspeaker, or other accessories or controls in dashboard; loose glovebox lid or odds and ends in glove box; loose tools, jack, wheel wrench, spare tire, or luggage in trunk; rusted and loose body panels; small stones in wheel disks or hubcaps; wheel-disk flexing on road wheel; broken suspension spring; loose exhaust-system components; worn heat-riser valve; loose generator; loose air cleaner; loose air-conditioning compressor; broken battery hold-down mechanism; broken or loose motor mounts; loose drive pulleys; loose bumpers or bumper guards; broken bumper supports; loose seat or worn adjusting mechanism; loose baffles in muffler; loose steering-column support; loose steering box or steering linkage.

Squeal When Pulling Away

Burned-out universal joint; slipping drive belts (i.e. fan, generator, power steering, air conditioning); driven wheels spinning due to excessive acceleration.

Squeal When Turning Steering Wheel Hard Left or Right (Power Steering Only)

Loose or worn power-steering drive belt; steering wheel turned too far left or right.

Vibration When Driving

Unbalanced wheels; new or used tires out of round; high and low worn spots on tires; steering out of alignment; loose or bent road wheel; worn or loose wheel bearings; broken or bent fan blades; bent driveshaft; worn center-hanger bearing supporting driveshaft; broken hanger-bearing support; bent axles; worn universal joints; unbalanced flywheel or clutch assembly.

WHEEL NUTS OR BOLTS DIFFICULT TO REMOVE

Attempt to loosen nuts or studs before jacking up car. If they remain unyielding, tap sharply with hammer and apply penetrating oil. Make sure lefthand-threaded nut or stud is not being turned in wrong direction.

WINDOWS WON'T OPERATE (Power or Manually Operated)

Stripped gear teeth or other malfunctioning parts on window-winder mechanism; stripped splines on window-winder handle; obstruction or glass too tight in window channels; when temperature is below freezing, ice jams window glass to channels; window mechanism requires lubrication; mechanism improperly aligned.

Power windows: same as above, plus possible inoperative electric motors, loose or broken wiring, faulty control switches.

WINDSHIELD WIPERS INOPERATIVE

(Electrically operated type): blown fuse; disconnected wiring; defective electric motor; maladjusted wiper arms; seized or disconnected control linkage; faulty control switch.

(Vacuum-operated type): maladjusted wiper arms; seized or disconnected control linkage; faulty control switch; disconnected, perished, or pinched vacuum hose; no vacuum suction from double-action fuel pump. Occasionally a sluggish vacuum-operated wiper motor can be temporarily brought to life by squirting light oil up the vacuum hose into the wiper motor, and at the same time carefully moving the wiper arms back and forth.

Index

Accelerator, 10
Additives, 34
Aerosol bombs, 264
Air cleaners, 59–60, *ill.* 59
Air conditioning, 263–64
Air-cooled engines, 113–14
Air pollution, 129–31
Alternator, 74
　warning light, 300
Altimeter, 266
Ammeter, 80
　shows discharge, 300
Antifreeze, 91–93
Aquaplaning, 191–92
Automatic transmission, 141–46
　car won't move in gear, 301
　cooler, 110–11, *ill.* 110
　desirability of, 276
　fluid, 148–49, 232
　　excessive amounts used, 303
　　leaks, 303
　jamming in PARK, 302
　lubrication, 235–36
　maintenance, 146–50
　push starting, 149–50
　shifting failure, 302
　towing, 149
Axle, 153–54, *ill.* 153
　breather, 156
　lubrication, 155–58
　shafts, 157–58

Backfires, 291
Back pressure, excessive, 121
Back seat, packing of, 168
Ball joints, 173, *ill.* 171
Batteries, 67–73, *ill.* 68
　chargers, 269
　checking, 72–73
　correct handling of, 73
　failure of, 69, 71–72
　filling, 70–71
　ratings of, 69–70
　replacement of, 70

Bearings
　insert, 27–28, *ill.* 28
　main, 29
　wheel, 179–80
Belts, 109–10
Blankets, 261
Block, 21–24
　cracking of, 100–1
　heater for, 269
Body plastic, 243–44
Body repairs, 242–48
Boiling over, 114–15
Brackets, exhaust system, 123–24
Brakes
　bleeding, 203
　disk, 215–16, 276, *ill.* 215
　drag, 288
　drums, 210–12, *ill.* 211
　dual master cylinders, 205–6, *ill.* 206
　emergency, 216–17
　　sticking of, 290
　erratic, reasons for, 218–20, 288–89
　fade, 209, 288
　failures, reasons for, 14, 203–5, 207, 209, 210, 218, 219
　fluid, 201–3
　grabbing, 219
　grease seals, 217–18
　grinding noise, 290
　groaning noise, 290
　historical development of, 199
　hydraulic system, *ill.* 200
　knocking noise or roughness, 290
　lights, 208–9
　　failure of, 299
　lines and hoses, 207–8
　linings, 209–10, *ill.* 211
　locking, 218, 289
　master cylinder, 203–6, *ill.* 206
　mechanical functioning, described, 11
　overheating, 202
　pedal height varies, 289

pedal requires excessive pressure, 289
pedal spongy, 289
pedal vibrates, 289
power, 214–15, 276, *ill.* 214
primary cup, 204
pulling to one side, 219–20, 289
repair, cost of, 199–201
riding the pedal, 218
self-adjusting, 212–13, *ill.* 212
shoes, 209–10, *ill.* 211
springs, 213–14
squeals, 161, 290
wheel cylinders, 206–7, *ill.* 207
Breaking in, 285
Bug bombs, 264
Bumpers
  guards, 268
  repair of, 244

Camber, 172–73
Camshaft, 31–32, *ill.* 31
Carbon monoxide, 127–29, 242
Carburetor, 50–55, *ill.* 51
Carpets, maintenance of, 255
Cash, need to carry, 263
Caster, 172
Chains, 270
Choke, 53–55, 294, *ill.* 51
Chrome maintenance, 254
Circuit breakers, 75–76
Clanging or clunking noises, 303–4
Clocks, 265
Clutch, 133–35, *ill.* 133
  car fails to move when engaged, 290
  double clutching, 140
  grabs or chatters when pulling away, 291
  squeals or growls when engaged, 291
Coil, 82
Combustion of fuel, *ill.* 64
Compasses, 265–66
Compression stroke, *ill.* 63
Condenser, 85–86
Connecting rod, 27–28, *ill.* 28
Convertible tops, 253–54
  failure of, 291
Cooling system, *ill.* 90
  defined, 10
  leaks, diagnosis of, 104–5
  See also specific entries
Cooling tubes, 101–2
Corrosion and rust, 238–42
  rustproofing, 239–40
Courtesy light failure, 299
Crankcase ventilation, 226–27, *ill.* 226
  Positive (P.C.V.), 227–28, *ill.* 227

Crankshaft, 28
  pulleys, 30–31, *ill.* 30
Crown gear, 53–54
Cylinder head, 24–25, 102–4

Dashboard
  lights, failure of, 298–99
  maintenance of, 254–55
Dash-pot, 55
Diagnostic centers, 15–16
Differential, 154–56
  limited slip, 276
Dimmer switch, 77
Directionals, 77
  failure of, 299
Distributor, 83–85
Door
  flies open, 291
  light failure, 299
  slamming, 248–49
  stiff, 291
Drainage vents, 241–42
Driveshaft, 151–52, *ill.* 152
Drive train, *ill.* 132. *See also* specific entries
Dual exhaust system, 118, 122–23

Electrical accessories, 75
Electrical motors, 78
Electrical system
  defined, 11
  See also specific entries
Engine, *ill.* 22
  backfires, 291
  block heater, 269
  keeps running when turned off, 291
  racing, 293
  rattle when idling, 292
  rough idle, 293
  size, 276
  See also specific parts
Exhaust-emission systems, 129–31
Exhaust manifold, 118–20, *ill.* 117, 118, 119
Exhaust pipes, frequent failure of, 296
Exhaust system, *ill.* 117
  alignment of, 124
  damage, types of, 124–26
  defined, 10
  problems
    leaks into car, 296
    noises, 296
    pipe leaks at manifold, 296
    smoking, 296
  repairing, 126–27
  See also specific entries
Expansion plugs, 102
Extension lights, correct use of, 19

Factory manuals, 18
Fan, 107–8
  belt, 109–10
Financing, 286–87
Fire extinguishers, 260
Fire in car, 297
First-aid accessories, 263
Flat spots in acceleration, 53, 55–56
Float chamber, 51–52
Flooding, 56
Fluid coupling, 143
Flywheel, 38
  overheating of, 134
  scored, 135
Fog lights, 267
Four cycles of internal combustion, 21, *ill.* 23
Frames, 169–70
Frost plugs, 102
Fuel burning process, *ill.* 64
Fuel pump, 48–49, *ill.* 48
Fuel system, *ill.* 42
  defined, 10
  See also Gasoline entries
Fuel tank vapor emission control systems, 46–47
Fuses, 75–76, *ill.* 75
  spare, 266

Gaskets, head, 24–25, 103–4
Gasoline, 39–42
  cans, 267
  caps
    locking, 267–68
    plugged, 45–46
  choice of, 62–65
  filters, 49–50
  gauge, 61–62, 80
    incorrect reading, 297
  lines, 47–48, *ill.* 48
  mileage, 60–62, 297
    boosting gimmicks, 271–72
  tank, 42–43
    plugged cap, 45–46
    vapor emission control systems, 46–47
    water in, 43–45
Gauges, 61–62, 79–82, 266
Gears, 136–41, *ill.* 138
  synchromesh, 139–40
Generator, 73–74
  warning light, 80–81, 300
Glass, 250–51. *See also* Windows
Grating, groaning noises, 304
Greasing points, 232–37

Head gaskets, 24–25, 103–4
Headlights, 76–77
  failure of, 298

flash on and off, 299
  improper adjustment, 299
Headrests, 259–60
Heater, 99–100, 111–13
  control cables, lubrication of, 236
  failure of, 297–98
Heat-riser valve, 118–20, *ill.* 119
Heavy loads, 116, 167–68
Hesitations in acceleration, 53, 55–56
High-speed circuit, 52–53
High-tension cables, 87–88
Hood jumps open, 298
Horn, 79
  breakdowns, 298
Hoses, 99–100
Hums and howls, 135, 304
Hydraulic valve lifters, 33–35, *ill.* 33

Ice scraper, 260
Icing of carburetor, 56–57
Idle
  racing, 293
  rough, 293
  stops when engine is hot, 296
Idle circuit, 52
Ignition, 82–88, *ill.* 83, 84
  cleaning, 88
  switch, 86–87
  system, defined, 10
Independent suspension, 162–63, *ill.* 163
Insecticides, 264
Insert bearings, 27–28, *ill.* 28
Intake manifold, 58–59
Interior
  lights, 77–78
  maintenance of, 254–55
  preheater for, 269
Internal combustion, four cycles of, 21, *ill.* 23

Jacking, correct technique for, 19
Jacks, 262–63

Kingpins, 173, *ill.* 171
Knock, 64

Leasing of cars, 282–84
Lighting failure, 298–300
Loading a car, 116, 167–68
Locks, lubrication of, 236–37
Lubrication
  importance of, 221–22
  system, *ill.* 222
    defined, 10–11
  See also Oil
Luxury cars, maintenance cost of, 274

Magnetic keyholders, 266
Main bearings, 29
Maintenance
  importance of, 15, 17–18
  See also specific entries
Manual transmission. *See* Standard
  transmission
Master manuals, 18
Mechanics, 12–14
Motor mounts, 35–36
Motors, small electric, 78
Muffler, 120–22, *ill.* 120
  explosion of, 125
  frequent failure of, 296

Needle valve, 51–52
New car, purchase of, 276–80
  extras, 276–77
Noises, 19, 179. *See also* specific noises;
  specific parts

Odometer, stops registering, 300
Oil
  burning, 292
  changing, 222–26
  classification of, 229–30
  crankcase ventilation and, 226–28,
    ill. 226, 227
  detergent, 225–26, 230
  excessive consumption of, 292
  filters, 228–29
  gauge, 79
    reads low, 292
  gear lubricants, 231–32
  leaks, 292
  ML, MM, and MS, 229–30
  pan, 36–37
  pump, 37
  SAE grades, 230–31
  viscosity, 230–31
  warning light comes on, 292
  water in, 223–24
  weight, 230–31
Outside mirrors, 266
Overdrive, 141
Overhead camshaft, 31
Overheating, 114–15, 292–93
Overloading, 116
Owner's manual, 12

Paint, 244–48
Parking light failure, 299
Passing gear, 147
P.C.V. (Positive Crankcase Ventila-
  tion), 227–28, *ill.* 227
"Ping," 64
Pinion gear, 153–54
Pins, 27, *ill.* 25
Pistons, 25–27, *ill.* 25

Points, 83–85
Post-ignition, 291
Power, transmission of, 11
Power delivery, 153–54, *ill.* 153
Power steering. *See* Steering
Power windows and seats, 270
  failure of, 300
Pre-warmers for engine block, 269
Push starting, 149–50

Racks, 270–71
Radiator, 93–97
  cap, 96–97
  care of, 91
  hoses, 99–100
Radios, 265
Rattles, 249–50, 304
Rear-axle assembly, 153–54, *ill.* 153
  breather, 156
  limited slip differential, 276
  lubrication, 155–58
Rear-view mirror, 264–65
Red warning lights, 81
Renting cars, 282–84
Repairmen. *See* Mechanics
Repairs
  do-it-yourself, 18–19
  estimates, 15
  timing of, 16
  when far from home, 17
Resistor, 86
Resonator, 118, 123
Rings, 25–27, *ill.* 25
Rough ride, reasons for, 300
Rubber mats and heel protectors, 264
Run-on, 291
Rust, 238–42
Rustproofing, 239-40, 277

Safety belts, 256–59
Salt, 238–41
Sand, 270
Scraping noises, 213
Seals, 29
Seat adjuster, failure of, 300
Seat belts, 256–59
Second car, 285–86
Selling a car, 279–80
Shock absorbers, 163–65
  function of, 12
  replacing, 165–67
Shovel, need for, 270
Skidding, 191–92
Sloshing noise, 241–42
Smoke in car, 297
Snow brush, 260
Spare parts kit, 271
Sparkplugs, 87
  gas savers, 271

Speedometers, 79
  fluctuation of, 300
  lubrication of, 236
  rasping noise from, 300
  stops registering, 300
Spot lights, 267
Springs, 160–62
  function of, 12
  rubber bushings, 161–62
Squeaks, 304
Squeals, 161
  of belts, 109–10
  of brakes, 161, 290
  of power steering, 304–5
  of tires, 301
  when pulling away, 304
Stabilizer bars, 168–69
Stalling
  after short run in cold, 293
  when engine is hot, 296
  when gas pedal is suddenly released,
    293
  when starter is disengaged, 293–94
Standard transmissions, 136–41, *ill.*
    138
  car won't move in gear, 302
  gear grinding, 302
  jumps out of gear, 302
  lubricants, 231–32
  oil leaks, 303
  steady knocking in lower gears, 302
  sticks in gear, 302
  won't shift, 302
Starter motor, 81–82
Starter solenoid, 82
Starting
  jump, 150
  mechanical description of, 10
  problems
    acceleration difficulty after
      warmup, 295
    engine won't turn over, 295
    starting procedure, 54
    when engine is cold, 294
    when engine is hot, 294–95
Static eliminators, 268
Steering, 11
  alignment, 170–71
  bolts, 174
  box, 174–75
    lubrication of, 235
  failure, reasons for, 233
  linkage, 173–74
  lubrication of, 233
  mechanism, *ill.* 171
  power, 175–77
    belts, 176–77
    desirability of, 276
    squeal, 304–5

  stiffness, 301
  whining noise from, 301
  shimmy, 301
  vibration in, 301
Stickers, 256
Stick shift, 145–46
Stop-leaks, 115–16
Suspension system, *ill.* 159
  functioning of, 160
  See also specific entries
Switches, 78
Synchromesh gears, 139–40

Tailpipe, 123
Temperature of engine, 105–7
  gauge, 79
Thermostat, 105–7, *ill.* 105
Tie rods, 173, *ill.* 171
Timing gears and chains, 29–30
Timing marks, *ill.* 30
Tinted windshields, 251
Tires
  air pressure, 188, 198
  aquaplaning, 191–92
  balancing, 190–91
  bald, 191–92
  bead, 182
  bias-belted, 185
  construction of, 181–88, *ill.* 182,
    186, 187
  fiber glass, 181–82
  flats, 196–97
  inflation, 188, 198
  leaks, 196–97
  maintenance of, 188–89
  nylon cord, 181
  odd-sized, 157
  out-of-round, 190
  overheating of, 188, 189
  oversized, 276
  plies, 182
  ply ratings, 189
  polyester cord, 181
  profile, 186, *ill.* 187
  radial ply, 187–88
  rayon cord, 181
  reliability of, 183–85
  replacement of, 188–89
  retreads, 197
  rim size, 196
  rotation, 195–96
  sidewall markings, meaning of, 185–
    87, *ill.* 186
  sizes, 186
  slow leak, 301
  snow tires, 192–93
  spare, 261–62
  squeal, 301

studs, 193–95
  tread, 183, 188–89, 191–92, 196
  used, 195, 197
Toe-in, 173
Torque, defined, 143
Torque converter, 143–44
Torsion bars, 160–62
Towing, 149
Tow rope, 261
Track bars, 162
Traction plates, 270
Trading in, 277–79
  when to do it, 284–85
Trailing links, 162
Transmissions. *See* Automatic transmission; Gears; Standard transmission
Trunk lid failures, 303
Turn signals, 77

Universal joints, 151–52, *ill.* 152
  lubrication of, 232
Upholstery maintenance, 255
Used car, purchase of, 280–82

Valve lifters, 33–35, *ill.* 33
Valve train, 32–33, *ill.* 32
Vapor locks, 57–58

Vibrations, 191, 305
Voltage regulator, 74

Warning lights, 266, 300
Washing parts, 19
Water, 91
Water pump, 97–99, *ill.* 98
  lubrication of, 232
Waxing and polishing, 255
Wheels, 177–79
  alignment, 171–73, *ill.* 172, 173
  balancing, 190–91
  bearings, 179–80
    lubrication of, 233–35
  hubs, 179–80
  nuts or bolts stuck, 305
  threading of bolts, 177–78
Whines, 135
Windows
  cleaning, 251–52, 254
  plastic, 254
  stuck, 305
Windshields, tinted, 251
Windshield washers, 253, 260–61
Windshield wipers, 252–53
  failure of, 305–6
  lubrication of, 236
Wrist pins, 27, *ill.* 25

15.50